50 Years
of
Rock Music

Other titles in
Chambers Compact Reference

To be published in 1993

50 Years
of
Rock Music

Philippe Paraire

Chambers

EDINBURGH   NEW YORK   TORONTO

Published 1992 by W & R Chambers Ltd
43–45 Annandale Street, Edinburgh EH7 4AZ
95 Madison Avenue, New York N.Y. 10016

First published in France as *50 Ans de Musique Rock*
© Bordas, Paris, 1990
© English text edition W & R Chambers 1992

Library of Congress Cataloging-in-Publication Data applied for

ISBN 0 550 17011 1

Cover design   Blue Peach Design Consultants Ltd
Typeset by Hewer Text Composition Services, Edinburgh
Printed in England by Clays Ltd, St Ives, plc

Acknowledgements

Translated from the French by Sara Newbery

Adapted for the English edition by Trevor Pake

Entries provided for the English edition by Trevor Pake:

Phil Collins
Sam Cooke
Diana Ross

Chambers Compact Reference Series Editor   Min Lee

Illustration credits

Contents

Introduction

Rock, or the aesthetics of opposition

There is no doubt that rock is the dominant cultural phenomenon in the world today. With both literature and the cinema having lost their former supremacy, rock music is the most accessible, and therefore the commonest, mode of individual expression available to man today; rock, which one could have been excused for thinking was a purely American or English music form, has taken on board new languages and cultures: Johnny Clegg and Savuka sing in Zulu, Alpha Blondy from the Ivory Coast in Dioula, and Cheb Khaled, pioneer of North African *rai*, in Arabic. Elsewhere, it is pulling down the last bastions of censorship; in Eastern bloc countries, the political spring and rock music have burgeoned at the same time: perestroika has allowed for the growth of punk, heavy metal and new wave groups. The Soviet Union now permits concerts in which European and American bands take part. Whether official or otherwise, these concerts are the manifestation of a dissidence that has long been held in check, expressed today by the voice of Russian rock. Where there is a touch of hard-earned freedom, or the seeds of revolt, it would appear that there is also bound to be rock, like a banner made of rhythms and sounds.

Like a unique battle-cry, the three or four notes that accompany the polyglot lyrics of adolescent rebellion transcend any geographical frontier. The memory of the race-riots in Soweto, South Africa, and in Notting Hill, London, and of the street fights in Kingston, Jamaica is beginning to fade, but no one has forgotten that all three began with a carnival and a concert. It is as if rock, instead of bridging the generation gap, pushes the youth of today into a direct confrontation with the establishment. As if rock was not just a music form.

Male supremacy in the rock world was soon challenged by women who in turn expressed their vision and perception of things. The violence, particularly violence of a physical nature, which comes so naturally to men was unattractive to women, the eternal spectators of their male counterparts' fights. Nevertheless, they were quick to adopt the black leather jackets and boots, the Indian cotton, the safety-pins through the cheeks, the mohican haircuts, the spiky, dyed hair, and the heroin and LSD drug habits that were part of the male way of life. Rock insidiously contributed to the Women's Liberation movement by giving them the chance to demonstrate their equality to men. Rock pressed for sexual freedom, advocated the contraceptive pill and took part in the controversies surrounding abortion. Rock broke up families, turned good little children into leather-wearing rockers, beatniks, hippies and punks. Parents did not deserve this, nor husbands or bosses, whether it be at home, at work or even in the corridors of power themselves. Rock divides, shocks and disturbs. Rock is dangerous. It has become the mainstay of the demands of youth.

Rock music and its image: contradiction and ambiguity

Describing the history of rock is not without pitfalls: in fact, there is not one rock form par excellence followed by other lesser forms; from 1955 to the present day, each successive generation has had a completely different, distinctive way of expressing itself in terms of musical style, subject matter and clothing (in short, culture). Someone active in Presley's heyday will naturally confuse rock with rock 'n' roll. Anyone who liked the Rolling Stones might have difficulty identifying with the Sex Pistols. For your average punk in 1977, any rocker with long hair was a hippy. Rasta audiences at reggae concerts would find little interest in the metaphors of Jim Morrison or Bob Dylan. While heavy metal fans sew badges that look as if they were bought in a joke shop onto their denim jackets, Bowie or Roxy Music fans take great care with their suits and silk scarves. And while many adolescents brought up on new wave back-comb their hair à la Cure and dress completely in black, others stick to their long hair and their jeans, which were long since internationally accepted as standard youth dress.

In many respects, rock seems to lack definition: between the different looks and behavioural patterns that are part of every rock sub-category there are what seem to be

1

insurmountable distances and oppositions that occasionally verge on open hostility. Rock culture lacks the formal unity, the conceptual uniformity normally associated with a lasting cultural phenomenon. And yet, in the 50 years of its existence, rock has continually headed the list of the cultural phenomena specific to young people, despite the disparate times, places and styles, and the gravity of the crises it has survived.

The secret of rock culture's success is to be found in its protean core; elusive, it can be adapted to almost any situation; it can be white, black, creole, coloured or even yellow (Japanese teddy-boys have been spotted in the streets of Tokyo, complete with winkle-pickers, black jacket and Brylcream), the one constant being that, through dance, rhythm, melody, vocals and instruments, it brings people together. Today, rock the world over is governed by the same party spirit, the same joy at being part of a rowdy crowd. The solidarity of protestors from all eras unites all rock sects and schools. The great pagan rock festivals are a tribute to the god of legitimate protests. And very often we are talking about peaceful protest, like those who, marching behind Martin Luther King, began to sing James Brown songs when they were encircled by the police; like the well-meaning crowds at some of the charity concerts in the 1980s (Live Aid, the Anti-Apartheid concert at Wembley, etc). The criticism expressed in rock is not always savage nor is it mere criticism for criticism's sake; it voices a feeling of general unease, tells a tale of inner conflict; it can be shocking, but this is usually by the most anodyne aspects such as dress or behaviour. The perfect example is Woodstock: 500 000 young people gathered together in difficult conditions constituted a population at risk, but there was not a single fatality. A few reported cases of theft, some fist-fights and three births. In the final analysis, rock is less dangerous than certain tragically memorable football matches.

Parallel development

Changes in subject matter, fashions, venues and musical structure and instruments are inevitable and tend to follow the same patterns as general changes in society; thus the changes in Western ideology account for the thematic changes which have occurred in white rock between 1955 and 1990; by the same token, the changes in the

Third World and, above all, the dawning realization of the nature of the power relationship between the West and the Third World, gave birth to the rebellious songs of reggae. At the end of the 1950s, the increasing impoverishment of the black American population and the civil rights movement went hand in hand with the rapid expansion of soul music; the nihilist despair of punks, with their deliberately ugly, provocative look, flew in the face of a complacent Britain. At the same time, technical developments in the music world were responsible for many stylistic changes in rock: the more powerful electric guitar supplanted the piano. The electric guitar was in turn ousted by the highly versatile synthesizer: could rock 'n' roll, psychedelic rock and new wave have existed without the instruments which gave them their instantly recognizable sounds?

Thus, there is both logic and coherence in rock history, a history which must necessarily be examined as a separate culture, made up of attitudes and recurring themes and characterized by techniques which define the different schools and styles. The aim of this book is to demonstrate this coherence.

Themes and attitudes

From the very beginning, lyrical subject matter has quite naturally been divided between simple love songs and harsh criticism of organized society; then, more recently, of injustice on an international level, as well as the dangers facing our environment today.

Initially, there was a tendency in both the rural blues and rock 'n' roll towards light-hearted songs or ditties: up-tempo or slow ballads intended for dance halls went no further than to evoke the white teenage experience or the heartaches of lovesick black Americans. In this case, the inevitable exception that makes the rule comes in the form of Woodie Guthrie, one of the fathers of rock, who wrote and sang a number of texts in support of the unions during the 1930s depression. The blues often drew attention to social ills such as tuberculosis (Josh White's 'TB Blues'), the severity of prison warders (Leadbelly's 'Midnight Special') or lynching (Billie Holiday's 'Strange Fruit').

During the 1960s a sort of cultural revolution swept over Europe. It seemed natural that rock music should become its main vehicle, carrying to the rest of the world the themes of the new American culture: sexual freedom, drug taking, pacifism and anti-racism.

In the 1970s the emerging theme seemed to be satanism (the Rolling Stones, hard rock, decadent rock), for some people delighted in calling up the powers of evil, revelled in lust and invoked the devil's aid, in the tradition of *Rosemary's Baby* (Roman Polanski, 1968) and *The Exorcist* (William Friedkin, 1972). Punk rock got rid of all these trends by putting them into practice in real life as well as on stage. The punks' truly nihilist attitude, expressed by the famous phrase 'No future', went much deeper than the immoral front presented by decadent rock.

Yet while this radical trend developed along parallel lines, the neutralist tradition continued to dominate rock music: throughout the Fifties, Sixties and Seventies, in terms of subject matter, most of the songs produced still dealt with traditional love theme: separation, despair, joy, jealousy, meetings, beauty, money, sex and fast cars. And finally, while it is true that the music written as a protest upset the old balance between neutral songs and politically engaged texts, this could never be termed a revolution. The 1960s brought about profound changes in rock, particularly in terms of melody, sound, and rhythm. The true revolution, then, was much more formal, and certainly more lasting and efficient. This can also be applied to punk and new wave: the revolution was in the style of play and dress on stage. Rock, as Andy Warhol was quick to point out, is an attitude. For him, to define the essence of rock, music, clothes and lifestyle should not be separated.

The 1980s saw the militant entry of the Third World into rock: the reggae pioneers (Desmond Dekker, Jimmy Cliff, Bob Marley) brought the question of poverty to the attention of the public and allowed African rock musicans (Alpha Blondy, Fela) and their often stringent demands to become known. Made aware of the Third World problems, white rock musicians took matters into their own hands by organizing massive charity concerts in aid of famine relief in Ethiopia or the victims of apartheid, thereby giving rock music the moral respectability and humanitarian values it had been chasing for 50 years.

Each generation therefore has associated some sort of attitude with 'its' rock music. Despite the obvious differences, certain constant trends stand out in rock

attitudes: first of all there is *adolescent rebellion* (1955–1958, 1964–1969, 1977–1980), which in whatever form it might take, attacks the moral and social institutions erected by preceding generations. Secondly, there is the *eccentric dress* associated with each rock generation: black leather jackets and slicked-back hair, then long hair and flowery shirts, followed by shaved heads, vinyl trousers, and ripped T-shirts, and finally the rastas with their dreadlocks. The third category is *the use of stimulants*: alcohol for the blues, rock 'n' roll and hard rock; marijuana and LSD for the Sixties' generation; harder and harder drugs including heroin, crack and amphetamines for the 1970s. Today, cocaine is the fashion.

Rock Media

The diversification in rock music is also linked to the development of its media which have changed dramatically: due to the pressure of events, the leisure industry has been transformed and this in turn has brought about major upheavals in music. It goes without saying that rock was first brought to the ears of the world by the audio medium. Initially, the rural blues 'race records' spread black music throught the Afro-American community. The sound was not very good, but it was sufficient to organize dances using gramophone horns. Then the long-playing record (seven-inch, 45 and 33rpm; then 12-inch, 33rpm), which appeared after World War II, gave a better sound as well as demanding more musical precision. The compact disc, which came on the market in 1980, has compounded the financial success of the rock industry.

Radio played an important role in the 1950s and 1960s. With an extended listening audience, the first thematic American radio stations played new music forms and ensured their popularity. With its pirate radio stations on boats and anchored outwith French and English territorial waters, the following decade showed just how efficient a vehicle radio could be for rock. During the 1980s, the mushrooming of FM stations the world over has attracted a new rock following. Its continuing growth is due to the almost blind faith of the younger public. Numerous programmes provide information on new groups, concerts and releases; others are more academic, attempting to give a balanced view of rock music

3

by broadcasting the biography of a particular group or genre. There is a general movement towards wanting to learn and understand. The FM rock stations therefore play an important role in the amplification of rock 'culture'.

Video was first used only for televised shows. Then, in the 1960s, the first real rock magazines started to appear on TV channels all over the world; these programmes are still extremely popular with young people today. From the start of the 1980s, a new mode of rock diffusion began in the shape of video recorders and pre-recorded tapes: films of concerts and montages of clips contributed to the popularity of rock. At the same time, the first TV channels totally dedicated to rock emerged. MTV, the American rock channel, increased the rock audience tenfold by bringing it into every home: nevertheless, the clips, filmed concerts and programmes centred on one particular subject, and all came under the watchful eye of the censor, for it would not be possible to show the frequent excesses endemic in rock concerts to the general public. The inevitable toning-down gave birth to another musical genre known as FM rock. FM is a milder, acceptable version of hard rock, new wave and funk minus some of their more eccentric traits. With the original rocky centre taken out, FM is really nothing more than a flat and commercial background music, close to easy listening.

Radio and television have doubtlessly increased the rock listening audience in a 40-year period, but in return their technical development and advances have exerted a profound influence over changing rock styles: the invention of stereo sound, for example, put new pressures on rock musicians. The exceptionally fine sound quality of compact discs precludes cruder styles and favours sophisticated sound. The original rural blues performers were not noted for their skills in terms of sound mix. Today, simplicity in this field no longer exists.

The cinema has also played an important role in the popularization of rock: without the use of his classic trademark 'Rock Around the Clock' in Richard Book's *The Blackboard Jungle*, Bill Haley would never have become so famous. This record was already one year old when, in 1955, the film brought it into the limelight, launching a movement that was soon to become the major musical impulse of the century. Since that time, many films have starred rock musicans, from Presley to the Beatles. Prince has followed in their footsteps, while other films use rock music to create a certain ambience. The cinema woos many rock musicians both as composers and as actors.

The two principal rock media, audio (vinyl records, compact discs, cassettes, FM stations) and visual (music TV channels, video tapes, films of concerts) are totally inter-dependent.

In addition to the above, the influence of rock magazines, which are the written part of rock culture, must be added: initially rock critics were disc-jockeys. Today they are true experts, capable of tracking down the stars, getting interviews, and producing learned analyses of records and films. They play a substantial role in that their personal preferences can influence buyers and thus make or break an artist. The case of one of America's most important contemporary singer/songwriters is the perfect illustration: it was after an article written by John Landau, the United States's best known critic, that Bruce Springsteen was discovered by the general public.

Rock instruments

Rock was only able to diversify into its different schools, movements and genres thanks to the development of the musical instruments which gave each era and style its distinctive sound: on the whole, all the basic rock music instruments have undergone a technological transformation which has completely modified their original sound.

The acoustic piano was used by the first rockers in the 1950s, but was supplanted by the electric organ in the following decade. At the start of the 1970s, the invention of the synthesizer revolutionized the whole sound of rock, to the extent that in the 1980s, there seemed to be a direct relationship between synthesized sound and commercial success.

The guitar was also subject to profound changes: made electric in the 1940s then synthesized in the 1980s, with its range of effects pedals, the guitar is the main protagonist and emblem of rock history. The double bass, which became the electric bass guitar in the 1950s, is now complemented by the bass synthesizer; now that the classic double bass with its huge sound box used by jazz orchestras has been abandoned in favour of the smaller, easier-

4

to-play electric version, bass players have become more versatile. In modern rock, the rhythmic and melodic element provided by the bass is of the utmost importance.

At first, the continuing survival of the brass section seemed questionable, but its return to the forefront of the current music scene is now a certainty. Although it is frequently associated purely with jazz, properly amplified, and sometimes replaced by a synthesized equivalent (saxaphone, clarinet and flute) the brass sound is still very much a part of rock music.

The sound and tone of the acoustic drum kit has changed according to technological innovations. Today the trend runs towards the sharp dry sound provided by a drum synthesizer, which drummers try to emulate on stage and in the recording studio.

The technological evolution of rock instruments has had a long-lasting effect on certain periods of its stylistic history. At present, electronic gadgets are well on their way to replacing the more traditional acoustic and electric instruments; moreover, wind and stringed instruments are being rendered obsolete by the keyboard. Contemporary rock has become something of an exact science, whose technological complexity can be easily monitored by a visit to a concert or recording studio.

What can be properly termed 'rock music'?

The question which has caused so much ink to flow is: How exactly can one separate rock music from jazz and easy listening, which are its two closest neighbours, even though numerous groups have borrowed symphonic structure and the suite of themes and movements from classical music, while still others claim to have composed 'rock operas'?

Firstly: it is not possible to limit the content of the word 'rock' to that of the expression 'rock 'n' roll'. Since 1955, rock music has expanded to such an extent and has diversified into so many genres, subgenres, schools and movements that only sectarianism and sheer ignorance could exclude styles like jazz-rock, afro-rock, funk, soul music and the rural blues from belonging to it.

Rock is not Presley. Not, in any case, just Presley. What the Beatles produced may sound like light-hearted ditties, but their work does indeed come under the category of rock. To distinguish them from the

Rolling Stones, they used to be classed under the 'pop music' heading. But in Britain, 'popular music' is an umbrella term covering *all* the varieties of light music, including rock . . . In the United States, the term 'rock music' is applied to all types of rock: from what the Americans call 'rock 'n' roll' and 'country music' to Michael Jackson's electro-funk, taking in the Chicago blues and British pop on the way. The American conception is by far the most efficient and the least open to dispute.

The African presence

In terms of melody and rhythm, rock music is closely linked to Africa. Its very roots have been transplated from African soil, as is demonstrated by the pentatonic scale used by the rural bluesmen, then by all rock musicians, the throbbing rhythm of the tom-toms, the fluid, lazy beat of reggae and the walking basses of boogie piano.

Black music from all over the world has been the source and inspiration for the major changes in the course or rock music: the only two striking, genuinely white, stylistic changes are British pop and punk rock. All the other important creative work was accomplished by black artists, whose innovations were swiftly, and often unscrupulously, exploited and popularized by the white rock industry. In a sense, from the cotton-pickers of the rural blues to the afro-rock of the Guinean savannah, rock has never stopped interjecting the original drive of the black continent into white culture.

Rock music: the major phases

In 1990 therefore, we can talk of 50 years of rock music: rock was not born at the same time as rock 'n' roll; with the emergence of the very first blues music, all the basic ingredients for its creation were already there.

In fact, Robert Johnson's rural blues and then Chicago blues laid down the guidelines for rock music between 1935 and 1955, in terms of melody, rhythm and structure. The original rock tempo was first provided by the songs of former slaves. It was only then that the music scene was irreversibly changed by the appearance of rock 'n' roll which, from 1954 to 1962, managed a musical and cultural synthesis between black music and white adolescent rebellion. The 1960s saw the United States lose her status as music's world leader to

Britain, but the student protests in the United States relaunched the national rock movement. This was the most productive period in rock history: the American counter-culture joined forces with British sound, while California became rock's second home. Until 1977, the 1970s were dreary, stagnating in a combination of stylistic exhaustion, commercial exploitation, isolation of the major stars and the appearance of a 'rock establishment'. Rock was suffocating under the weight of all the dollars it produced. The white revolution that was punk rock made the complacent stars look to their laurels and overturned established rock philosophies and fashions. With its massive, ill-placed release of energy, punk soon burned itself out, to be replaced by the more temperate new wave groups. The 1980s were ruled by the inheritors of punk, much to the distress of those nostalgic for 'old rock'.

In the same way, black music from 1960 experienced independent developments and invaded white rock through those doors half-opened by the early black performers: from 1954 with the black rock of Ray Charles, Chuck Berry, and Little Richard, in 1965 with the soul music of James Brown and Otis Redding, again 10 years later thanks to rastas from the Jamaican ghettos like Jimmy Cliff and Bob Marley, and finally in the 1980s with Michael Jackson and Prince, whose electro-funk style links rock back to its African roots. Simultaneously, African rock musicians such as Johnny Clegg and Savuka, Fela, Mory Kanté, and Alpha Blondy injected fresh rhythms and songs typical of Black Africa into rock, nurturing the regeneration of dance music.

A guide and critical anthology

Without being a history book, the aim of this brief guide is to shed light on the evolution of the most widespread music form of the 20th century. The intention is to put it into perspective by studying the major periods, styles and schools from the musician's and music-lover's point of view. Without any particular bias, this guide is in the form of an anthology of the most important creative spirits who, between 1940 and 1990, have contributed towards making rock the rich and popular music form it is today. Two hundred entries in a book which covers a 50-year period may seem an insignificant number. But it is a first step towards a better understanding of the music we listen to and like. It can only intensify the pleasure, without a doubt.

The original rock tempo
The blues (1935–1955)

The blues musical revolution

On close inspection, rock appears to be a purely African addition to the Western musical institution. A hybrid music form and the result of an uneasy synthesis between the traditions of two civilizations and two continents, rock would never have been assimilated but for the blues.

For rock dominates all other contemporary music forms: it has eclipsed American folk music, wiped out the albeit long-standing French, British and German traditions, is well on its way to supplanting Spanish folk, and perhaps one day even the folk songs that make up the USSR's national musical heritage will lose the battle against imported American music. Until 30 or 35 years ago in France, people still rushed to the popular dances where performers sang in French accompanied by standard instruments such as the accordion. During the 1960s, French language singers of quality composed in a distinctly European musical style (Brel, Brassins, Ferrat, Ferré, Montand, etc). Today, no performer can hope to make a name for himself without complying to the rules of rock, even if only in a watered-down or re-worked form. So what happened?

Western European musical habits have altered considerably and, where they have been more or less upheld, have lost credibility, particularly in the eyes of the young. In many respects, this cultural colonization of Western music by Africa is blackly ironic: after a gradual contamination, white culture has been swamped by what the colonials first considered a sub-culture, the music of 'monkeys' or 'niggers', the meaningless, amusing mumblings of uneducated and despised slaves.

A new musical culture

While classical music is performed in privileged venues (opera houses, music-halls, theatres, universities and churches) which are either purpose-built or specially adapted to be worthy of 'real music', the original blues, like contemporary rock, were performed in rough-and-ready conditions on stages that were easy to dismantle. The penniless travelling musician from the Mississippi Delta has perhaps very little in common with the

world tours of Pink Floyd or the Rolling Stones, but all three lack what Offenbach and Mozart always had: a hall, a temple of music. Today's rock stars are like a luxury travelling circus, and to reaffirm their ties with the blues of the travelling musician, they make use of a specific vocabulary: going on tour becomes 'being on the road' . . .

Classical music demands intimate knowledge of the rules of harmony and a highly developed musical technique. Rock musicians, like the poverty-stricken rural bluesmen before them, have only the most basic of musical educations. One of the biggest names in the rural blues, Big Joe Williams, knows no more than 50 guitar chords; the Seventies' punk rockers deliberately used their musical ignorance to differentiate themselves from commercial rock which worshipped the high technicality of such 'guitar heroes' as Clapton, Gilmour, Beck and McLaughlin. The self-taught character of the first blues is still very much admired in the rock world.

Non-conformist attitudes

Classical music is most often symphonic, disciplined and written. It should be played steadily and audibly. Classical music is supposed to be actively listened to; it is music for thought and for concerts. Following in the footsteps of the blues, rock is not composed along symphonic lines; the instruments are often heard one after the other, swopping solos to a regular, rhythmic background bass beat. Just as in the original blues, rock prizes improvisation over any fixed, written version of the melody, which can only be musically transcribed in an artificial fashion – classical notation cannot express even the simplest of blues or rock solos; in fact, on stage, blues singers and guitarists and rock groups are free to do whatever they like with their more flexible scales. Blues and rock concerts often give an impression of musical chaos rarely found in classical concerts.

The acoustic qualities of the Paris Opera or the Pleyel concert hall allow performers total control over their volume level. The audiences are quiet, attentive, and seated. At a country dance in Southern Mississippi, or in a Chicago nightclub or a Harlem theatre, in a New Orleans or Memphis brothel, a bluesman could scarcely hope to be heard, let alone listened to. Here we enter a realm of habits and problems common to both acoustic and electric blues and rock: members of the audience stand, talk, dance and drink, shout, clap and sometimes even fight among themselves. In the early blues, there was a total lack of respect for the artist, who often could not even hear himself play: to overcome this problem, contemporary rock groups have made use of an increasingly loud volume: 5000 watts for the Rolling Stones in 1965, 8000 for Pink Floyd in 1970, 30 000 for AC/DC in 1979 and 50 000 for the mammoth concerts in the 1980s. We have indeed come a long way from the small 50-watt amplifiers used by Chicago club guitarists in the 1950s, but the main concern remains the same: whether as background music or dance music, the blues and now rock have to fight to be heard.

Linked throughout recent history to the European powers-that-be, despite a gradual and undeniable democratization, classical music is still associated with the leisure hours of the upper classes and is conformist both in presentation and content.

The blues could scarcely be more different: they were created by the sons of slaves, by poor sharecroppers and sometimes by jailbirds and other unstable, dissolute characters, at least 10 of whom died poisoned or stabbed by mistresses or rivals, not to mention all those who were eventually killed by drinks or drugs. From the very start, blues lyrics were crammed with slang and everyday language, pornographic allusions and salacious double entendres. As an important aside, the blues must never be confused with that other black American art known as gospel, which, in terms of subject matter, has absolutely no connection whatsoever with the blues, the devil's art, the art of the 'blue devils'.

Rock borrowed the love theme from the blues, first in a watered-down version, then more explicitly. Drugs also supplied rock with a great deal of subject matter (J J Cale's 'Cocaine', the Beatles' 'Lucy in the Sky with Diamonds' signfying 'LSD') and replaced the whisky and beer common in the first blues to become popular during Prohibition (Tommy Johnson's 'Canned Heat', Robert Johnson's 'Malted Milk', and Jimmy Rogers's 'Sloppy Drunk').

Another trait, again inherited from the blues, which sets rock apart from Western tradition is the relationship between musicians and business: in general, blues and rock musicians are quite simply business-orientated. The more cultured, aesthetically motivated, classical musican dreams of creating a work of art. Blues players and rock musicians dream of women and money. This difference also applies to the kinds of audience these two genres attract: the classical aficionado appreciates quietly with the aim of becoming more cultured. The original blues audience, like that of rock today, participated existentially in the show.

The African roots of the blues and rock

The overall contribution of the blues, and therefore Africa, to rock far exceeds what we have described above; in fact, while it is true that the rural blues left rock a new attitude composed of nonconformism and adaptability, but also simplicity and naivety due to its popular roots, it is much more important to measure the influence of the African music preserved by black slaves on rock's musical idiom.

The blues have left their mark on all the possible areas of study in white rock: these two completely interwoven forms of musical expression have rhythm, harmony, subject matter and sense of show in common.

Harmony

Where in some instances rock has merely inherited traits from the blues, their harmonic structures are identical: all musicians know that Chicago blues scales are interchangeable with Presley's early songs, and an amateur guitarist starting to play in the 1980s always begins with the 'little blues' to get used to the 'three chords' and the 'rock feeling'.

What exactly are these?

Without becoming too technical, the fact that the blues in general (and not jazz, which is a totally different genre) always uses the same five-note harmonic scale must be underlined; this scale, termed pentatonic, is difficult to superpose on the eight-note (do, ray, me, etc) diatonic scale. The former is African, and simple and incomplete (no sharps or flats), the latter is European, complex and complete. All blues and rock musicians use the five-note scale. As they have to make certain concessions to the European style, blues and rock musicians flatten a series of notes (known as 'blues notes') by bending the strings or using vibrato. In fact, in both the elementary blues and rock, the five notes are enough to play any solo in any song. Could anything be more simple? Not, of course, if one subscribes to a European conception of harmony. But, surprisingly enough, there is an even greater degree of simplicity: all the blues and rock numbers composed in the classical period were designed to be played using three major chords; later, more complex works have the same basic schematic form, reworked and enriched without any fundamental changes.

The three-chord theory taught in Californian universities (where rock is studied as a musical genre in its own right) was actually empirically worked out by black musicians whose ignorance of the rudiments of music was balanced by their perfect knowledge and use of the pentatonic scale passed down to them by their African ancestors. The religious nature of African music proper explains the repetition of the first sung line in both the blues and rock. Initially, this line is sung on the first degree of the Western diatonic scale, for example on the chord C. Then, when the singer repeats the line, he moves up three degrees on the scale to an F, then goes back to C and, quickly uses the third chord (a G, fifth degree on the Western scale) then comes back to the second chord in the middle of the last verse, which he finishes, playing the same note with which he started. Five notes for the solo and three chords for the accompaniment. This astonishing harmonic simplicity, so far from traditional Western music, is the principal reason for the worldwide success of the blues and rock.

Rhythm

Like the blues, rock music is a music of percussion. The rhythm is basically very simple and repetitive; despite the syncopation and improvisation of the drummer, it runs steadily throughout the song, providing a dance beat. In general, the blues have left rock a structure of rhythm verses composed of three four-bar phrases. Occasionally there are 16- and even 32-bar phrases, but on the whole the rhythm of the blues and rock is almost hypnotically regular. The rhythms of African folk music testify to the origins of the steady blues/rock beat.

On the plantations where they eked out their miserable existence, slaves were forbidden to use the drums in any form as well as any of the other percussion instruments so central to African music. The planters' main fear was that their slaves would use them as a method of communication to spread a message of revolt. This ban, so cruel for a people whose attachment to rhythmic music was much more than superficial, was to push black Americans to transpose the regular rhythm, which they were not allowed to express freely using the correct instruments, on to the melody. Thus the hammering walking basses of the first boogie guitarists and pianists are reminiscent of the African drum beat. Players such as John Lee Hooker, Muddy Waters or Big Joe Williams use repeated riffs whose insistent, throbbing intensity recreates the forbidden tones of the tom-toms.

The close relationship which links the blues and rock with their African roots in no way impinges on their flexibility: off-beat rhythms are common and line length varies in both the modern forms. Verses are interrupted by spoken lines, like in Africa. The 'Oh, yes Lord' of the early blues gave birth to the frequent 'Oh, yeah' which has become a trademark of rock.

As soon as they were freed, the black slaves literally threw themselves into music and invented a rhythmic, jumpy musical genre, ideal for dance. A selection of brass, percussion, classical (violins, clarinet) and home-made (jug, washboard, kazoo) instruments mixed together to give early jazz its rich variety. Born in the country, poorer and less educated, the blues only kept the bare essentials: guitar, drums and vocals. Modern rock is still run along those lines, despite recent modifications due in particular to the synthesizer.

Composition

The mark of the African blues on white music is obvious in this area too. The relationship between guitar and voice is identical: conceived as a sort of question and answer session, the guitar solo answers the singer's questions, sometimes even by imitating the notes of the vocal line. By popularizing this technique, rock opened the way for an even greater understanding between the guitarist and his instrument, known as 'skating'. A result of the early blues and especially bebop, this style encourages the singer to sing along with a particular instrument, using the same notes and timing. The mixture of voice and instrument sound is arresting. Otherwise, in terms of strict verse composition, it is worthwhile noting that in rock, rhyme is approximate and the lyrical vocabulary is slangy, humorous and often erotic. And finally, like all oral-tradition music from Homer's *Iliad* to the present day, there is a frequent use of all-purpose phrases, clichés, and rhetorical devices which allow the author to 'pad out' his lines. In the blues, the author's main concern is to create an atmosphere, not a coherent narrative. Rock musicians rarely diverge from this policy.

The instruments

The early rural blues left rock with the range of instruments still in use today as well as an open-minded attitude towards technical innovations.

The six-string guitar, first acoustic and then electric, was principally designed for blues and jazz players. The electric bass guitar met the needs expressed by Chicago bassists long before their white contemporaries. The drum-kit, used by jazz groups in the 19th century, then by the blues in the 1920, is a must for every rock group. Perhaps the two most interesting gifts left to rock by the blues are the unceasing creativity and the openness of spirit. To make themselves heard, the Mississippi Delta blues players immediately adopted the Hawaiian-style metal-stringed guitar and the 'bottleneck' to obtain a loud, sliding effect. Others used the equally resonant 12-string guitar; as soon as the electric guitar appeared on the music scene, they snapped it up, despite the fact that before coming to the town they were unaware of the very existence of electricity! In the blues, as they say, anything goes: some, like Big Joe Williams or Little Son Jackson, played simplified open chords; others used individual picks on one or more fingers to boost sound; still others, including Broonzy, Albert King and Hooker, used their fingers directly on the strings, while the King himself, B B King, uses a plectrum. The same variety is found in rock: Mark Knopfler (Dire Straits) uses his fingers, Clapton, a plectrum and George Thorogood, two individual picks (index and thumb). Each blues and rock performer disposes of a certain amount of technical freedom; there is no one school, tradition, or obligation; like their African musical forefathers, they simply do their best . . .

The themes

The blues were born in one of the most troubled periods in black American history, characterized by an upsurge in the frequency of lynchings, the cotton crisis, the industrialization of Southern agriculture, a mass rural exodus, the creation of black ghettos, virtual slave labour and non-existent civil rights. The 1920s and 1930s imbued early blues lyrics with the despair of an entire people obsessed by hunger, unemployment and disease. However, it would be untrue to state categorically that the blues were an attempt at social criticism; anger is only just perceptible between the lines of such classics as Leadbelly's 'Midnight Special' and 'On a Monday', which are about prisons, or Josh White's 'TB Blues', on tuberculosis. Lots of texts on unemploy-ment and homelessness, and on the hostility of big towns, but almost nothing on lynchings or slavery. The blues prefer to dwell on love, pleasure, alcohol, the separation of lovers and the loneliness of the travelling man.

Rock is less influenced by the misfortunes of a whole people than the blues: for whites, the lyrics started out as light-hearted ditties, went on to take a short-lived political stance, and then returned to generally anodyne subject matter. Of course there was Bob Dylan, and today we have Sting and U2, but on the whole, rock artists tend to avoid delicate subjects and see themselves as simple entertainers. In this respect, bluesmen and rock musicians share the same sense of show:

loud clothes, provocative stage play, ad-libbing, shouting and squealing, and a whole unrestrained stage management aimed at hypnotizing the audience contribute towards making the blues and rock music for pleasure and dance, music which disguises the harsh realities of life rather than highlighting its more desperate aspects. Happiness, through the fleeting oblivion of the party, was the original aim of the early blues and is carried on by rock today.

The massive contemporary rock concerts have broken with all aspects of classical tradition. In the heart of Western cities, despite the huge increases in both decibels and attendance figures, it is almost as if the Mississippi dances and the music of ancient African kingdoms were still alive. Blacks have finally exacted their revenge: the whole white world dances to the music of slaves. Through rock, the blues have propelled Africa to the very heart of the conqueror's country, leaving the musical fingerprint of a tortured continent and her people.

The blues modestly relate the extent of black misfortune. And it is here that music retrieves its magical properties: just like in Africa, it becomes a method of collective exorcism.

The contribution of blues to rock, region by region

In fact, it is possible to give a precise description of each region's contribution to rock, for the cultural, geographical and social isolation of the communities of freed slaves produced in each area with a substantial black population characteristic musical styles which are easily definable, at least until the emergence of rock 'n' roll in 1950.

The Chicago 'Delta'

Let us first set the record straight: the expression 'Mississippi Delta', which is generally considered to be the cradle of the blues, does not describe a river delta, but a delta-shaped region situated between Vicksburg and Memphis. This is actually the cotton 'triangle', a rich alluvial plain which is still densely populated today, despite the mass exodus of the descendants of slaves to the North.

In this triangle, which also covers part of Arkansas to the west, Tennessee to the north and Louisiana to the east, the black population was kept in a state of total isolation and illiteracy that was unmatched by any of the Southern states. Terrorized by the very real threat of lynchings (there were 1900 between 1900 and 1920),

crushed by debts and interest rates that averaged out at 47.5%, uneducated (40% still could neither read nor write in 1930), shattered by natural disasters (in 1927, the Mississippi flooded, causing 142 000 deaths), forced into hard labour (all vagrants were thrown into jail then 'hired' out to private companies by the state of Mississippi) and stripped of all civil rights, the Delta blacks were well acquainted with misfortune.

Gathered together into small villages or living in cabins spread out over their tiny farms, the Delta blacks had virtually no contact with whites and developed an especially lively musical culture, which was stylistically very different from white music but close to its African roots. The Delta gave birth to a great number of performers who made a name for themselves in their home towns or later, after they had moved to Chicago. These include Charley Patton, Son House (who taught Robert Johnson to play), Bukka White (B B King's cousin), Albert King, Big Bill Broonzy, John Lee Hooker, Muddy Waters, Howlin' Wolf, Skip James, Jim Jackson, Big Joe Williams, J B Lenoir and Elmore James. They all took part in the creation of a typically black musical idiom which is at the same time the driving force behind white rock: the Delta and Chicago (favourite destination of artists moving North) passed on the use of the bottleneck (used by Clapton, The Allman Brothers, The Rolling Stones, The Animals, ZZ Top, Dire Straits, John Mayall, Jimi Hendrix, Mick Taylor, Stevie Ray Vaughan to name but a few), the catchy rhythms with a slow or fast tempo (Robert Johnson's 'Love in Vain' taken up by the Stones, John Lee Williamson II's 'Good Morning Little Schoolgirl', later recorded by Johnny Winter, John Lee Hooker's distinctive riff in 'Boogie Chillen', which ZZ Top used in 'La Grange', and Elmore James's 'The Sky is Cryin'', taken up by Thorogood). The group Cream played Bo Carter's 'Sittin' on Top of the World' and Robert Johnson's 'Crossroads', Hendrix played Broonzy's 'Rock Me Baby', Clapton played Jazz

> **Chess Records**
> In 1947, Chicago club owners Leonard and Phil Chess decided to found a record company. Convinced that there was a great future in the electric blues that Southern artists were now playing in their town, they signed almost all those who were later to make the style famous; shrewd businessmen, the Chess brothers rocketed the best Chicago bluesmen, including Muddy Waters, Bo Diddley, Little Walter, Sonny Boy Williamson and John Lee Hooker, to fame and brought them a much wider listening audience. The Chess brothers also gave a young hairdresser from Memphis called Chuck Berry his break. Both the blues and rock owe much to this talent-spotting team.

Gillum's 'Key to the Highway' and Albert King's 'Crosscut Saw' etc. By welcoming black performers to its South Side clubs, the city of Chicago produced the modern rock group form; Chicago also brought discipline to the Delta blues, standardized style through recordings and laid down the ground rules for the formation of all rock groups: vocalist, one or two guitars, bass, drums and perhaps a harmonica or brass section (trumpet and saxophone).

Texas and the Southern cities

In Texas, the huge state neighbouring the 'blues country', blacks were in a minority and tended to work either on the oil-rigs or in the great train workshops (the famous Texas Pacific line). Their higher salaries and more frequent contact with the white world did not mean that Texas in the Twenties and Thirties was a black paradise, but it is certainly true that the Texan blacks' quality of life was a good deal higher than in neighbouring states. Illiteracy and lynching were less common than in the Delta, and black Texan music demonstrates these different conditions: the melodies are more sophisticated and the guitarists more 'technical'. Blind Lemon Jefferson, Texas Alexander and Leadbelly were all 'trained' in the Texan school. Lightin' Hopkins popularized the boogie guitar accompaniment, with the result that the 'walking basses', inherited from the piano, pervade rock: they are instantly recognizable in all of the early rock classics such as Bill Haley's 'Rock Around the Clock' and Elvis's 'Jailhouse Rock'. Gene Vincent, Eddie Cochran and all the English rock musicians adopted the walking basses after the Texan bluesman and their black Southern counterparts (Fats Domino and Little Richard in New Orleans, Joe Turner in Kansas City and Chuck Berry in Saint Louis).

Blacks escaping the Delta gathered in the squalid ghettos of the Old South's biggest cities, and it was there that they began to assimilate white techniques. The most eloquent examples of this phenomenon are Atlanta and Jacksonville in Georgia, Jackson in Mississippi, Helena and Memphis in Tennessee and Saint Louis in Missouri. The dispossessed from all over the country met in the ghetto clubs, or more frequently in white quarter brothels, where they were supposed to provide musical entertainment, thus perpetuating against their will the traditional scenario in which the slave plays his violin so that his master might dance. New Orleans probably invented 'piano rolls', otherwise known as boogie, in 1920. In Memphis, wind instruments, including the sax, trumpet and especially the harmonica, were the most successful (this is where Sonny Williamson I became famous). In Saint Louis, the next step closer to Chicago after Memphis, jazz chords were integrated into the early blues without difficulty. One of the first blues guitarists to 'go' electric was Lonnie Johnson, who spent many years performing in Saint Louis. This title is · disputed by T-Bone Walker, a Texan guitarist who gave the blues and rock the chance to use a more sophisticated series of chords and scales. The East coast (Georgia, Florida, Virginia and the Carolinas) contributed some great guitar masters to the blues: Blind Blake is considered to be a master of 'rag', a genre initially confined to the piano, Blind Boy Fuller and Blind Willie MacTell influenced another east coast guitar great, Brownie MacGhee who, with his partner, harmonica player Sonny Terry, popularized the traditional blues with New York audiences in the 1960s.

The cities, south west, and south east therefore gave the blues something that the Delta by definition could not provide: a characteristic urban sophistication in terms of both melody and instruments. Rock owes much to the Southern cities: the greatest rock composers were black and had been profoundly influenced by the Forties' blues. Little Richard, Fats Domino and Bo Diddley drew up the rules for the new genre. Ripped off by white business, called 'rhythm 'n' blues' artists and classed in special hit-parades, it was only with great difficulty that they won the right to call

---

Compilations

There are several high quality rural blues compilations: **Mississippi Blues** (1927–1941) (Yazoo), **Blues Roots/Mississippi** (Folkways), **The Roots of Robert Johnson** (Yazoo) as well as **The Great Bluesmen** (Vanguard). Many collections have also been made of the Chicago blues: **Best of Chicago Blues** (Vanguard) is excellent, as is the recently re-edited Fontana series **American Folk Blues Festival** (especially the years 1963 to 1969), and **Living Chicago Blues** (vols 1 to 6, Sonet).

John Lee Hooker

Big Bill Broonzy

through the efforts of English musicians who openly acknowledged the extent of the debt owed to these men: where would these last bluesmen from the black ghettos be had not the Rolling Stones, Eric Clapton, Jeff Beck and Jimmy Page extolled their virtues?

Justice must done to all those who created a new art, whether it was in the forgotten corners of the Delta, the poor rural areas of the cotton country or in the slums of Southern cities and Chicago. It is rock history's duty to attempt to make amends for all these lives of injustice and misery; while white rock musicians strutted in the hallways of five-star hotels earning money from music that was not really of their own making, the true composers were neither recognized nor recompensed. At the very latest, rock history should begin in the 1930s, with a study of the rural blues and not with Bill Haley's 'Rock Around the Clock'.

Whatever happened to the blues?

The true blues

Today, the ethnic and creative musical genre that was the blues is only a memory: on the one hand, it has ceased to be the exclusive province of black musicians and is even less attractive to the younger black generation, who associate it with the dark days of slavery and early emancipation, and on the other, no new blues are being composed; the true blues written and performed by the first pioneers have, of course, disappeared from the music scene. Until the end of the 1970s, artists such as Robert Lockwood or Son House and Johnny Shines, both of whom once played with the legendary Robert Johnson, were still performing live. Today there are no more acoustic blues concerts; Sonny Terry and Lightin' Hopkins died recently, and old age prevents the few remaining survivors from going on tour. Even the more recent, outwardly hardy, Chicago blues have suffered, with the deaths of Freddie King in 1976 and Muddy Waters in 1983 and the increasingly hackneyed live performances given by John Lee Hooker and B B King, despite the fact that the latter managed to appear on stage as U2's special guest (*Rattle and Hum*, 1988)

The youngest Chicago bluesmen are all over 50. Worn out by personal and professional difficulties, they tend to give unworthy performances: Luther Allison is drifting closer and closer to hard rock; Buddy Guy seems ill-at-ease with his obviously enfeebled partner, Junior Wells, and Johnny Copeland, Albert Collins and Albert King spend more time playing in Europe than in their home country.

According to the American magazine *Frets* (January 1989), there are still some black musicians in the Old South who are carrying on the true blues tradition, by giving small concerts and recording a number of albums; some are relatively well known (Homesick James, Larry Johnson, Yank Rachell and Taj Mahal), others should be (James 'Son' Thomas, Precious Bryant and Johnny Weston).

But on the whole, the future of the true blues looks rather gloomy: much of today's diminishing audience is made up of those same, principally white, fans who were attracted during the blues boom period of the 1960s.

The blues today

In a somewhat diluted form, the blues still survive in rock and easy listening. However, having been deprived of its original historic, ethnic and stylistic content, the word is basically hollow and meaningless.

Some of the biggest names in white blues still play music similar to that of the first bluesmen, despite the audible influence of rock on their style: Eric Clapton ('Just One Night', 1981), Stevie Ray Vaughan ('Texas Flood', 1984) and Johnny Winter ('Nothing But The Blues', 1977, 'Serious Business', 1986) are all active in the blues concert scene, as well as John Mayall, George Thorogood, Ry Cooder and J J Cale, although the latter two appear to have been more strongly influenced by white music than the others. Only two names stand out amongst the up-and-coming black bluesmen: Robert Cray, a guitar genius whose fondness for rhythm 'n' blues pervades his work, and Melvyn Taylor with his essentially funky style.

The blues have left an indelible mark on the face of rock music; while most of today's younger audiences are unaware of it, most rock musicians are not, and some have the grace and honesty to refer openly to the debt owed by the new to the old: the Rolling Stones, Eric Clapton, Angus Young from AC/DC, Eddie Van Halen and Edge from U2. This is why the black creators of the genre listed in the following pages should never be forgotten.

Luther Allison

1939–   Singer and guitarist (Chicago blues)

Leader of the second generation of the blues

Although he arrived in Chicago in 1952, it was only during the blues revival of the 1960s that his highly personal style became popular.

In the wake of the gods

Born in 1939, Luther came from his native Arkansas to Chicago at a time when B B King, Freddie King and Otis Rush were already making a name for themselves in the South Side clubs. He nevertheless managed to find work in some of the legendary shrines of Chicago blues, in particular the 708 Club, where he played rhythm guitar for Freddie King and his bassist, 'Big Mojo' Elem. But Luther soon grew weary of being a second-class citizen in the blues capital of the world and decided to try his luck with Big Mojo and 'Shakey' Jake in California, where the current atmosphere seemed to be more open to his rocky style. There he met some of the living legends of the rural blues, including Johnny Shines, with whom he played and recorded.

Honesty

'It's the same every night, I have to give myself completely, whether I'm playing for 30 people or thousands. I don't want people to be able to say that Luther Allison was slipping, that he didn't give everything he'd got. Me, I never hold anything back. I have to give my all at every concert! (*Le Guitariste* magazine, June 1981).

From the blues to rock

From 1969 onwards, Luther was a star performer at the festivals organized by white students at Ann Arbor, Berkeley and Miami; with his youth and irresistible energy he brought a largely white following to existing Chicago blues audiences. At the start of the 1980s, when punk was sweeping over Europe, Luther was playing to audiences of 3000 to 5000 in halls which rock groups rarely managed to fill to capacity!

One of Luther's greatest assets has been the ability to move with the times. Not only did he help lay down the foundations of a new, much harder, blues sound with Magic Sam and Freddie King, but he was later to take this experiment further by changing his guitar. From that time on, with his Stratocaster and his Marshall amp (the same equipment Hendrix used), he could compete with hard rock groups without any difficulty. After an unsuccessful, brief flirtation with soul and funk (*Time*, 1983) he has now come back to a more classic repertoire, performed in the rock style that has become his trademark.

Love Me Mama (Delmark, 1969) is his first album. Several standards ('Dust My Broom', 'Five Long Years') rub shoulders with his own daring and creative compositions.

Live In Paris (Paris album, 1980) provides an overview of Luther Allison's extraordinary talents. This album is representative of modern Chicago blues.

Life Is A Bitch (Encore!, 1984) is an extremely dynamic compilation, containing a mixture of tight rock numbers ('Backtrack', 'Parking Lot') and blues mixed with soul and funk ('Life Is A Bitch', 'Serious').

Albert Ammons and Pete Johnson

1907–49; 1904–67   Boogie pianists

The kings of boogie-woogie

Following in the footsteps of 'Pinetop' Smith and Jimmy Yancey, this virtuoso duet helped define the basic rhythm drive of what was later to become rock.

Albert Ammons, a pianist noted for his solid and regular style, teamed up with Pete Johnson who, like Count Basie, came from Kansas City, to form a piano duet. Taxi-drivers by day, they also shared a little apartment with another boogie master, Meade 'Lux' Lewis (who recorded 'Honky-Tonk Train Blues') and played in clubs at night. Pete Johnson was a more sophisticated player than Ammons; he had been profoundly influenced by Jimmy Yancey's laid-back technique, mixing both the Saint-Louis (Roosevelt Sykes) and Kansas City (Big Joe Turner) styles with a jazzy phrasing reminiscent of Earl Hines or Art Tatum when they played boogie. He is best remembered for 'Death-Ray Boogie' and 'Basement Boogie'.

Rock tempo

Continuing the work of the Thirties' piano players, Ammons, Johnson and Lewis popularized walking basses (more commonly associated with the early rural blues guitarists) on the piano, to which they added right-handed solos. Due to its acoustic powers, the piano soon became the most popular instrument in the barrel-houses, honky-tonks and speak-easies of the pre-war period. Whether as dance music or simply as background music, boogie was the perfect combination of swing and the marvellous capacity of the blues genre, with its 12 bars and minor keys, to express both joy and sorrow. The piano (Ammons-Johnson) and piano-guitar (Carr-Blackwell, Big Bill Broonzy-Memphis Slim) duets were never as famous as the big white swing bands (Glen Miller, Henry James), but their contribution to what was later to become known as rock is undeniable. One only has to listen to the early recordings of Fats Domino, Little Richard, Ray Charles, Bill Haley, Elvis Presley and Jerry Lee Lewis to realize just how much primitive rock 'n' roll owes to the boogie-woogie pianists who, in the smoke-filled bars of the black quarter, worked out the basic rhythm of a new kind of music.

King of Blues And Boogie-Woogie, **Masters of Blues and Boogie-Woogie** are compilations of the best of Ammons and Johnson. Unfortunately, the American distributor (Oldie Burns) has sold out.

> **French boogie**
> The jazz pianist Claude Bolling, whose fame has spread overseas, recently recorded an album, *Original Boogie-Woogie* (Philips, 1970), as a tribute to the early boogie masters.

19

'Big Bill' Broonzy

1893–1958   Singer and guitarist (acoustic)

Acoustic guitar genius

Although Broonzy was famous during the 1930s in Chicago, he disappeared from the music scene and was only resdiscovered through his much later European tours.

William Lee Conley Broonzy made his first guitar out of an old cigar-box when he was 11 years old, and played at picnics in the Little Rock area of Arkansas. Then, after his National Service, he went 'up' to Chicago, where he worked on his technique under the supervision of Papa Charlie Jackson.

He then went into partnership with Tampa Red and, thanks to his powerful voice and flowing style, formed a series of duets and trios with Jazz Gillum and the pianists Black Bob Alexander then

---

Compact disc

Big Bill Blues (CD Vogue, 1984) groups together the original recordings (1951 to 1954) of Broonzy's top hits. The sound remix on the compact disc is of an excellent quality.

Experienced

On the compilation **Hollering And Crying The Blues**, recently edited by Vogue, Big Bill sings with such emotional intensity that at the end of one number he breaks down in tears. In **See, See Rider – Sixteen Tons** (Musidisc), a coughing fit, due to the illness that later killed him, brutally interrupts one song.

Memphis Slim. These groups were extremely popular in Chicago's South Side bars and nightclubs.

At the root of rock

Big Bill Broonzy then began to appear on stage as a solo vocalist and guitarist; picking out his melodies with a plectrum on an electric jazz guitar, he gradually emerged as Lonnie Johnson's one serious rival. His small band thus took part in the definition of what was later to become rock 'n' roll's rhythm section: drums, plus one other instrument (bass or piano) intended to highlight the guitarist's playing.

Too reminiscent of the traditional rural blues and too crude to be musically assimilated to jazz, this form of the blues slowly went out of fashion, leaving the way clear for the rise of swing, performed by bigger and louder bands.

1951: Europe

Broonzy was the first Chicago bluesman to tour Europe. He gave up his usual stage presentation, in favour of an acoustic guitar. His incredible finger-work, the regular bass notes coupled with a flowing lead solo on the higher strings, stunned first Parisian then European audiences, who saw in him the incarnation of the original true blues; in fact, Broonzy had been profoundly affected by his Chicago years and, even on an acoustic guitar, his style was never to lose that aura of urban sophistication lent by the combined influences of jazz, ragtime and boogie-woogie.

His gravelly and expressive voice transformed traditional rural blues melodies and his own, rare compositions. His instrumental pieces, performed at extraordinary speed, owe much to the rag of the 1930s. He is still regarded as an idol by many contemporary rock musicians.

Arthur 'Big Boy' Crudup

1905–74   Singer and guitarist (electric)

Great, unrecognized composer

Although he wrote such classics as 'That's All Right Mama', which later made Presley famous and launched rock 'n' roll, Big Boy died poverty-stricken.

His roots

Born in Mississippi in 1905, Arthur Big Boy Crudup experienced the prejudices and difficulties common to all blacks living in the South at the time. Forced to leave by the Depression and racial harassment, he moved to Chicago where, from 1941, he began to make a name for himself with his first recordings. At the same time, he played in many of the South Side bars, and was instantly recognizable for his rough-and-ready, rhythmic style, a legacy from the country blues, which he was perhaps the first to adapt for the electric guitar. In 1942, he recorded 'Mean Old Frisco', one of the first blues numbers to be performed on an electric guitar, which became an all-time classic and was adopted by many other black artists. Famous in Chicago and respected by his fellow-musicians, he is part of the group of bluesplayers who unwittingly laid down the foundations of rock 'n' roll.

Innovator

A prolific recording artist, Big Boy Crudup's trademarks are his high, shrill voice, slap-bass, discreet drumming, brief solos inspired by the blues and a guitar accompaniment that owes much to boogie-woogie. This jumpy style soon gained widespread acceptance. Down on his luck, Big Boy unthinkingly sold the rights to his songs for a few thousand dollars. The best known of these, 'That's All Right' appeared on the A-side of Elvis's first single for the Sun label. Elvis later had a second hit with another Big Boy number 'My Baby Left Me' without having to pay a cent in author's rights. Had Big Boy fought back, as Chuck Berry and Little Richard were later to do, could he have overcome the cynicism of Elvis's managers and won back what was rightfully his? Who knows?

Despite a comeback to the European stage and an impressive body of recordings (roughly 30 albums), Big Boy died alone and forgotten in 1974. This is probably one of the most serious cases of injustice in the history of rock: while the author lies dying in poverty, the thieves dine out on the stolen fruits of his labour. Big Boy, whose story should be kept in mind as a lesson to us all, was regrettably neither the first nor the last of these cases.

Star Bootlegger (Krazy Kat, G B, 1982) is the only album easy to find in Europe. It includes his best known songs. A must, to demonstrate just how much rock owes to a little-known but worthy performer.

> **Iniquitous**
> Because he had sold the rights to his music, Crudup could only play his own songs if he paid a certain amount of money to the new owners or if he changed the lyrics; thus, for example 'That's All Right' became 'I Want My Lovin'', 'Star Bootlegger' or 'Gonna Be Some Changes Made' and 'Mean Old Frisco' was changed to 'Mean Old Santa Fe'.

The Gibson Guitar Company

Guitar manufacturers

The father of the electric guitar

Founded in 1902 by Orville Gibson, a guitar-maker from New York, the tradename Gibson has become synonymous with quality and daring design.

The first jazz guitars

Although Orville Gibson had been trained in traditional guitar-making, he was quick to understand that acoustic guitars would soon have to be amplified. He began by producing a guitar with a larger body, then replaced the traditional sound-hole with the distinctive 'f' hole copied from the violin. The Thirties' jazz guitarists immediately fell in love with the full and rounded sound of these instruments which allowed them to play solos in jazz ensembles. However, to be heard above the brass section in bigger bands, the new guitars had to be amplified. The Gibson firm then decided to add a pickup –

The 'vintage'

Gibson guitars are much sought-after collectors items. According to their 'vintage' and condition, they can be bought and sold for quite extraordinary prices: an L 5 with a Charlie Christian pickup or an early Fifties' Les Paul 'Gold Top' can fetch up to £2000 at auction. On average, a Sixties' 335 with a cut-away body is worth over £1000. At the present time, the Gibson sound is still so desirable that even a simple SG costs in the region of £1000 new.

---

composed of a magnet with a fine casing of copper – to their guitars.

Thus, the legendary Gibson L 5 was born. The jazz guitarist Charlie Christian gave it his blessing. Bluesmen immediately started buying them. But these were still only amplified acoustic guitars which did not have any great sound capacity. Under pressure from the Chicago guitarists, Gibson innovated the cut-away body and put two pickups on his new creation, the '335'.

The 'Les Paul' period

Thanks to the use of several, almost simultaneous inventions including the violin-breasted guitar and the 'humbucker' pickup, from the start of the 1950s, the Gibson firm produced a range of silent and powerful guitars, masterminded by an inventor called Lester Polfus, who was to give his name to a new instrument, the Gibson 'Les Paul'. Virtually unchanged since its very first appearance on the music scene, the 'Les Paul' has been a firm favourite with successive generations of rock musicians, from Duane Allman in the 1960s to Led Zeppelin in the 1970s. The firm went on to develop the 'SG', its greatest money-spinner, designed to meet the same sort of demands as the 'Les Paul'. Used by Frank Zappa, Angus Young from AC/DC and even Mick Jagger, it was the lightest and least cumbersome quality electric guitar.

Japanese competition

With its instruments copied a hundredfold, the production-line at Kalamazoo, Michigan is now threatened with closure: for a third of the American price, the Japanese are offering passable equivalents which undermine the future existence of one of the greatest names in modern guitar-making.

Stefan Grossman

1945– Acoustic guitarist

White intellectual blues player

Grossman was so fascinated by the techniques of the forgotten early blues players, that he set out to find them and bring them back into the public eye.

Born in 1945, from the end of the 1950s onward, his passionate interest in the black pre-war guitarists led him to collect their 78rpm albums. Supported by his friends and fellow blues players, he headed an investigation whose aim was to hunt down and find those once mighty rural blues masters, now forgotten and living in squalor: they tracked down Son House, then found Skip James lying in a Mississippi hospital, followed by Bukka White,

Mississippi John Hurt and 'Reverend' Gary Davis. Through prolonged contact with these technically superb players, he became a master in his own right. Following the publication of his first instructional book *How to Play Blues Guitar*, he travelled to England, where he met Eric Clapton. He then began producing his own records in association with the English folk stars Bert Jansch and John Renbourn.

Teaching methods

Grossman invented a special tablature designed specifically to teach blues-guitar to people with no formal musical training. His methods can be found in *How to Play Blues Guitar* (Transatlantic, 1971), *Finger Picking Techniques* (Transatlantic) and *Country Blues Guitar* (Sonet, 1977).

Buddy Guy

1936– Singer and guitarist (Chicago blues)

Off the beaten path

Once he had shrugged off the influence of his mentors, Magic Sam and B B King, Guy seemed to gravitate naturally towards a funkier style.

Born in 1936 in the South, he moved up to Chicago and found work in the South Side bars. His first recordings are obviously influenced by Magic Sam (he played a Stratocaster, distinctive for its clear, ringing tone) and B B King (flowing style, pure velvety sound and jazzy phrasing). During the 1960s, he became involved in the rock scene, and even supported the Rolling

Stones in France on the first leg of their European tour. His subsequent partnership with the harmonica-player Junior Wells revived his flagging career. In the 1980s, he became attracted to funk, and interspersed more traditional blues with modern rhythms and sounds.

The Blues Giant (Isabel, 1982). Modern Chicago blues.

Seemingly for fun, Buddy Guy and his acolyte Junior Wells recorded a totally acoustic album in France, which they ironically entitled *Going Back*. The record is remarkable for its high technical standards and authentic blues sound.

John Lee Hooker

1917–   Singer and and guitarist (electric)

Instantly recognizable insistent rhythms

Influenced by his country roots, his syncopated riffs and rough style (which he was able to adapt for the electric guitar) set him apart from the Chicago blues mainstream.

He was born in 1917 in Mississippi, and is still touring today both in Europe, where he is considered as a living legend, and in the United States. His musical career is astonishing on more than one count: in fact, it is based on the impact of two revolutionary but stylistically similar records, one of which, the 1948 'Boogie Chillen', (his first real recording) was an instant hit with all the black radio stations. Hooker was quick to adapt his Southern bluesman's technique to the new possibilities offered by amplified sound, transposing the hynotically repeated riffs of the Delta blues onto the electric guitar; his deep voice, catchy rhythms and provocative, slangy lyrics sung with a Southern accent did the rest. The success of 'Boogie Chillen' was an inspiration to other players who had also recently arrived in Chicago.

Despite his rather simplistic style, Hooker is considered to be one of the founders of the Chicago blues. This initial celebrity was not enough. In 1962, he took part in the first wave of Chicago performers to hit European, and particularly British, stages. His influence was perhaps strongest on the generation of future British rock stars which included the Stones, the Irish band Them, and the Animals, who came to see him perform. In the eyes of the British public, Hooker was the embodiment of the true blues.

Second career

Secure in his fame and defending his primitive style against the onslaughts of the many other Chicago blues forms, Hooker brought off the last great coup of his career: he managed to get an hypnotic blues number, 'Shake It Baby' into the white rock charts. Going straight into gold, the single, which had another similar blues tune 'Let's Make It Baby' on the B-side, was a worldwide hit with white audiences. From then on, Hooker has cashed in on his living legend status. Although his mere presence on stage is enough to make his concerts a success, musically speaking his performances have become a little run-of-the-mill.

House Of The Blues (Chess, 1967) and **The Real Folk Blues** (Chess, 1968) are strikingly authentic.

Shake It Baby (45rpm Polydor, 1968) is a classic. We could also list the innumerable compilations of Hooker's work.

> **Adventures**
>
> An orphan from early childhood, at the age of 12 he began to earn his living playing at picnics and dances in the Clarksdale area of Mississippi; shortly afterwards, he ran away to Memphis and was reduced to begging in Cincinnati then in Detroit. Travelling from town to town, he experienced the misery that affected all the black farm-workers during the Depression. John Lee Hooker seemed set to share the same dismal future of unemployment and unskilled labour as thousands of others. This kind of life forms a major part of recent black-American history, whose joys and pains the blues celebrate.

Sam 'Lightnin'' Hopkins

1912–85   Texan singer and guitarist

His speed earned him the nickname 'Lightning'

Trained in the Texan blues school, he was able to bridge the gap between blues and rock without compromising his traditional style.

Two careers

Like many rural blues guitarists, he disappeared without a trace from the music scene in the 1950s; throughout the first part of his career, he worked incessantly on his style, adding phrasing which owed much to the swing bands, to the teaching of Blind Lemon Jefferson. By the end of the 1940s, he was something of a local celebrity and, despite his unwillingness to part with his acoustic guitar, was still in demand as a performer in Houston clubs and at outdoor parties in the region. However, the emergence of the black ensembles using the electric sound made famous in Chicago coupled with the sudden rise of rock 'n' roll (to which he was close in terms of melody and rhythm) consigned him to oblivion.

Rediscovery

At the start of the 1960s, the feeling was running high among blues specialists like Sam Charters that forgotten legends such as Lightin' Hopkins should at all cost be found and reinstated. Convinced that Lightin' was still alive, Charters began to make enquiries in the black quarters of Texan towns and eventually uncovered some trace of the great guitarist. He spent several weeks looking for him in the Houston ghetto, found him, then convinced him to start working again. For a handful of dollars, Charters and Hopkins rented a guitar from a specialist shop and shut themselves away in a hotel room for an afternoon, during which time Lightin' began to play; he showed that he had lost none of his legendary speed. Recorded in extraordinary circumstances, the resultant double-album highlights his deep, powerful voice and fast-flowing style. The mixture of humorous lyrics, tragic narratives, spirited ballads, and up-tempo swing numbers, laced with sudden breaks and fast but controlled solos, showed that at least one old and forgotten performer had lost none of his skill. At the age of 52 he finally stepped back on stage, playing for white, mainly student, audiences and heading for the glory he so richly deserved. His recent death was announced with great respect in the worldwide rock press.

Early Recordings (Arhoolie, 1963) is, in the words of Stefan Grossman, one of his best recordings.

The Roots of Lightnin' Hopkins (Folkways, 1968) groups together his most impressive performances.

Blues In My Bottle (Blues Legacy) in a recent re-edition is very easy to find.

Festivals

Lightnin' Hopkins's second career began with a bang. In the year following his rediscovery by Sam Charters, he recorded nine albums. He also went on a number of European tours with other bluesmen of his generation and attended several festivals in the United States. Until he died, he was to remain faithful to his new followers, who had rescued him from the bitterness of the long dark days of his musical exile.

Little Son Jackson

1916–76   Texan singer and guitarist (accoustic)

Modest and underrated early blues player

More of a dilettante than a professional musician, he was one of the first to use the expression 'rock and roll'.

Born into a poor family, Jackson combined his work as a farm labourer with playing at local picnics, before leaving the country for the city; he then gave up music for a career as a mechanic, eventually owning his own garage. Pressed on by his friends to return to the music scene, he accepted weekend spots in local nightclubs. The changeover from acoustic to electric guiter left his rough style virtually the same. Little Son carried on playing in the old Texan way (regular bass, steady rhythms, rapid runs) while his voice relayed a dark, underlying sadness.

Paradoxically, the 1951 hit 'Rockin' and Rollin'' which rocketed him to fame, was a blues number with a vibrant, repeated guitar riff. Between 1950 and 1954, he recorded more than 50 numbers, then went back to his cars for good.

'Rockin' and Rollin'' (Charly, 1978) is very representative of his style. Unpretentious, straightforward blues.

> **Royalties**
> 'Rockin' and Rollin'' directly inspired (note for note) 'Rock Me Baby', the number which made B B King famous. Little Son never formally denied giving birth to the theme or the form. Without realising it, he gave a name to a whole musical genre. He was more interested in his cars.

Elmore James

1910–63   Singer and guitarist (electric)

Architect of the Chicago blues

His version of 'Dust My Broom' turned the 'bottleneck' into one of the most astonishing tools in rock music.

Born on a Mississippi plantation, he took to the road as a wandering musician. His meeting with Robert Johnson was a determining factor in his musical development. He discovered the bottleneck style, the application of a glass bottleneck to the guitar strings to obtain a slide (*glissando*) effect. Then, travelling from town to town, he moved back towards the city. In 1951, he used a bottleneck on an electric guitar with a thick, distorted sound to record his

hit 'Dust My Broom', which later became his theme song. The Chicago blues were born. English rockers adopted his style and it became one of their distinctive techniques. Elmore James, with his forceful riffs and falsetto voice, is one of the closest relatives of Sixties' rock.

One Way Out (Charly, 1980) contains all his major hits.

> **Royalties**
> Elmore James owes his fame to a song for which he didn't pay a cent in royalties: as the composer had died, the song had fallen outwith copyright legislation. 'Dust My Broom' was later taken up by a wide range of rock musicians.

Robert Johnson

1911–38   Mississippi singer and guitarist (acoustic)

Great early rural blues composer

*With his blues standards like
'Sweet Home Chicago' and 'Dust
My Broom', he is one of the
fathers of rock music.*

Unsettled childhood

From early childhood, he suffered the injustices of being born black in the racist South: his mother only narrowly escaped being lynched; poverty and squalor were to be Robert Johnson's lot in life. As his mother's series of lovers virtually ignored him, his school attendance was erratic and it was only through chance meetings that he learned how to play the harmonica, then the guitar, by watching Son House and Charley Patton play. He also listened to Skip James, and teamed up with Elmore James and Johnny Shines, who made good use of his songs after his dramatic and untimely demise: he is said to have been poisoned by a jealous husband.

Anonymous
There are no extant photographs of the most influential musician in rural blues history. He only recorded 32 songs and did not receive one cent in royalties. He is reported to have been so shy that at times he played with his back to the audience. The precise location of his grave remains a mystery.

Original guitar style

He is remembered for his ability to pick almost any guitar style: picking is the use of all the fingers on the right hand to play a steady accompaniment on the bass strings and a lead solo at the same time. He also often played with a bottleneck on the little finger of his left hand, which gave the distinctive metallic, *glissando* effect often heard in Hawaiian music. These effects of 'slide' and bottleneck have since been adopted by many other artists such as Emore James, and then Sixties' white rock musicians including Eric Clapton, Mick Taylor, Duane Allman and Ry Cooder.

Rock roots

The Robert Johnson lyrics are simple and colloquial, highlighting the usual themes of the daily life of Southern blacks; fleeting love, a longing to be elsewhere or for home, the sadness of parting. As an artist, he was relatively disciplined and skilled: he composed real lines, often equal in length, thus moving away from the traditional oral improvisation common to plantation music, and defined a strict order in the way in which a song should develop, which is used almost without change in rock music: an instrumental introduction, several verses or instrumental solo, last verse and end.

King of the Delta Blues Singers, vols 1 and 2 (CBS, 1961 and 1985). Some of the most famous rural blues airs: 'Crossroads' (taken up by Clapton), 'Sweet Home Chicago', 'Dust My Broom', 'Ramblin' On My Mind' and 'Love in Vain' (also recorded by the Rolling Stones, Clapton, John Mayall and the Blues Brothers).

Albert King

1923– Singer and guitarist (Chicago Blues)

The giant with the velvet voice

Although he was a limited guitarist, his sober and unpretentious style influenced many rock musicians.

Born in Indianola, Mississippi in 1923, he and his family moved to Osceola, Arkansas, near Memphis, where he began to play in nightclubs, working his way up through the ranks of Jimmy Reed's band, firstly as his drummer then as his rhythm guitarist, until he was promoted to a more frontline position.

The birth of a master

Albert King perhaps used the fact that he shared the same name as the great B B King to his professional advantage, but he had neither the strong voice nor the sophisticated style of his idol. A self-taught, left-handed player, he turns the guitar the other way round, without inversing the order of the strings: because of this, the bass strings are at the bottom, and the high strings at the top!

Albert King's slower style with its shorter riffs is a direct result of this handicap. His solos all sound rather alike. But what might be a weakness in someone else, is actually his strength: not only did this self-effacing giant of a man have a more 'rural' style, close to future rock, but his voice was, and still is, soft and husky. Some of his hits such as 'Born Under a Bad Sign', 'Laundromat Blues' and his version of 'Kansas City' and 'Crosscut Saw' would later be performed by all the principal English and American rock musicians, including Eric Clapton and

Cream. For many years Albert King has played a peculiarly shaped guitar, the Gibson 'Flying V', of which he owns one of the very rare originals. The V-shaped, symmetrical body is ideal for his style. It was as a tribute to this master of the Chicago blues that Jimi Hendrix, another left-handed guitarist, often used the same instrument.

Albert King: Masterworks (Atlantic, 1982) contains all King's greatest hits: 18 unforgettable numbers.

Albert King: Live Wire/Blues Power (Stax, 1980), recorded live; the version of 'Please Love Me' shows his skill in the up-tempo areas while 'Blues Power' is a slow, lazy ballad, in King's typical style.

Blues for Elvis (Stax) is an original idea: a black musician recording cover versions of Elvis's greatest hits ('All Shook Up', 'Hound Dog', 'Jailhouse Rock', 'Love Me Tender' etc). This album is unmistakeably an Albert King production. Short breaks, a few brief solos and always that velvety voice pouring out melodies punched out by others.

Rudimentary?
A K is one of the few guitarists to play without using fingerpicks or a plectrum. He strums or picks the strings directly with his fingers like the rural blues acoustic guitarists, which results in a slightly muffled sound and precludes hard play. Albert King's technique is also used by Mark Knopfler, vocalist and lead guitarist with the English rock group Dire Straits, although the latter combines it with his own, incredibly fast style. The secret of the 'Dire Straits sound' lies in this synthesis.

B B King

1925–   Singer and guitarist (Chicago blues)

Even his name predestined him to be the 'King of the blues'

An unparalleled guitarist and showman, King's highly original style was a blend of rural blues, jazz and rock which soon attracted a devoted following.

Little Riley King learnt to play the guitar at the tender age of nine. During the week, he worked in the cotton fields and on Sundays, he sang in the gospel choir. Then he met Robert Lockwood Jr, the legendary Robert Johnson's adopted son, and played with Sonny Boy Williamson. His first appearances drew largely on the early blues tempo and clearly demonstrate his strong attachment to the music of the South.

However, when he was 20, Riley King moved from the country to Indianola, Mississippi, where he worked as a disc-jockey for a black radio station; by 1947 he had moved on to Memphis and was combining his radio work with a budding career as a singer-guitarist. He was an instant hit on the Southern black club circuit; his tours in Tennessee, Arkansas and Mississippi were met with enthusiasm by black audiences who were already familiar with his style from the radio. He became 'Blues Boy' King, B B King, the King of the Blues.

Creative spirit

His first recordings were to establish a style that is still copied and re-copied today. In fact, two out of three blues guitarists play like him.

B B King's guitar playing is certainly the most developed of all the Chicago blues players, and therein lies the secret of his success. He retained the traditional rural blues rhythms, but integrated points borrowed from jazz into his phrasing; King's major influences have been the guitarist Charlie Christian, T-Bone Walker and Lonnie Johnson, from whom he got his long and flowing torrents of notes.

B B King started to play the electric guitar in the early 1960s, and has used it to 'swamp' his sound. Not as much as Elmore James, but enough all the same to distance him from the Southern acoustic blues mainstream and also from urban jazz. Moreover, he popularized controlled effects including vibrato and dazzling, swift breaks. These techniques are balanced by his dramatic singing voice, matchless understanding of the star-system and showmanship. Even today, B B King's all-round musical *savoir-faire* is staggering.

Live At The Regal (ABC 1971) is played in every rock and blues club; a combination of 'shuffles' (fast, rocky numbers such as 'Please Love Me') and superb ballads ('Sweet Little Angel', 'It's My Own Fault'). Quite simply, great.

Warning
If you are going to buy a B B King album, be sure to check the date at which the recording was made. His best recording work was done between 1950 and 1965. In more recent times, he seems to have felt obliged to open up to the influence of disco (in the 1970s) and funk (in the 1980s). Some of the recordings made between 1965 and 1975 have an overwhelming brass section on which King relies a little too much. Apart from the classic album mentioned here, we can only stress that prospective buyers should listen to the records before committing themselves. This would allow individuals to make a choice based on taste and, perhaps, age.

Freddie King

1934–76   Singer and guitarist (Chicago Blues)

He inspired the greatest rock guitarists

Attracted to hard and saturated sound, he prepared the ground for the English Sixties' blues revival.

Born in Texas, he settled in Chicago in 1945. A metal-worker by day, Freddie compelled recognition as much for his physical size as for his contrasting delicate style and intense vocals. Initially influenced by B B King, he played with bands which performed every night in the South Side clubs. However, by 1960 he was playing in his own individual style, with its high-speed instrumental solos and hard, rocky sound: 'Hideaway', 'The Stumble' and 'Have You Ever Loved a Woman?' (of which Clapton brought out a cover version) were his top hits in the 1960s. After a brief detour via R & B with the saxophonist King Curtis, he

was back playing the blues from 1970, and before his untimely death in 1976, managed to bridge the gap between his blues and rock audiences.

Hideaway (Bellaphon 1976) is a collection of some of his hits.

Freddie King (1934–1976) (Polydor–RSO, 1977) is a live album recorded shortly before his death and gives an excellent overview of his style. Now available on CD.

Gratitude

'He taught me everything I needed to know', states Clapton on the sleeve of *Freddie King (1934–1976)*. The last number on the album is centred on a breathtaking duel between the two guitars, during which Freddie gives a friendly lesson to his pupil.

Leadbelly

1889–1949   Singer and guitarist from Louisiana (acoustic)

First to play the blues for whites

With his 12-string guitar and folk ballads, he immortalized the daily life of the Old South in his songs.

He first played in meeting-houses then, before the First World War, he partnered Blind Lemon Jefferson. In 1917, he killed a rival in a brawl and was sentenced to 30 years' imprisonment. Discovered in prison by the folklorist A Lomax in 1925, his sentence was reduced and he began recording his repertoire of black American folk songs, then went on to narrate the lives of the poor whites with Pete Seeger and Cisco Houston. In 1939, he received a further prison sentence for assault. A few

years later he was in New York with Sonny Terry and Brownie McGhee. He died shortly afterwards.

Leadbelly Sings Folksongs (Folkways, 1968) and **Leadbelly Last Session** (Folkways, 1953) introduce us to an original guitarist and songster, representative of nascent blues.

The 12-string guitar

This instrument was rarely used by any other blues players apart from Robert Lockwood and Big Joe Williams (who only played on nine of the 12 strings). Leadbelly used it because its sound capacity was greater than the standard six-string instrument.

J B Lenoir

1929−67   Singer and guitarist (acoustic and electric)

The only politically engagé blues author

His two careers are totally different.

Born near Monticello, Mississippi, he left at a tender age for Chicago where he took on all kinds of odd jobs as well as playing lead (electric) guitar with his club band composed of drums, piano and saxophone. With the boogie-mad drummer's fast-moving tempo, and J B Lenoir's lead vocals, the band soon had a first hit with 'Mamma Talk To Your Daughter' (1955). After years of being one of the most popular artists in Chicago, Lenoir disappeared from the music scene. He re-emerged, singing about racial segregation and Vietnam, appearing alone on stage with his acoustic guitar.

J B Lenoir (Chess-Vogue, 1969) is a double album representative of his 'Chicago' period.

Alabamba Blues and **Down In Mississippi** (Bellaphon L+R, 1980) contain several of his unique and unusual blues numbers.

> **Censored**
> Initially, J B Lenoir's (his name is pronounced 'Lenore' as in his native South) two acoustic albums were only on sale in Europe, because the songs were considered to be too critical of the American political regime.

Mance Lipscomb

1895−1976   Texan singer and guitarist (acoustic)

One of the blues revival's greatest discoveries

He became famous at the age of 60.

Born into a musical family, he was forced to become a farm labourer in order to earn his living, but was still able to play at local dances. He was to lead this double life for 40 years; influenced by Blind Lemon Jefferson and Mississippi John Hurt, Mance Lipscomb was to guard the original Texan rural blues jealously against all outside influence. A master of the picking technique, and at his best in the fast passages, he played a sometimes steady, sometimes intermittent bass line, while his other fingers followed the actual melody. His deep voice and thick accent seduced white guitarists in the 1960s.

Texas Sharecropper and Songster (Arhoolie, 1960) is his first album. Authentic sound and style.

> **Festivals**
> It was not until the age of 60 that Lipscomb left his native Texas on a voyage of discovery that was to bring him into contact with the stars of the professional music world. From then until his death, he took part in almost all the major music festivals (Monterey, Berkeley, Newport, Ann Arbor . . .).

Christian Frederick Martin
1796–1873 Guitar maker

Inventor of the modern acoustic guitar

By placing an X-shaped block under the sounding board, he created a resonant guitar which could take metal strings.

A German guitar maker who emigrated to the United States, C F Martin adapted the traditional guitar to meet the needs created by 19th-century American folk music. His children carried on the family business and, one century later, the Martin firm had become leading guitar manufacturors in the United States. This make of guitar still has the flat sounding board, like its classical counterpart, but the neck has been slimmed down and given extra length, while the body is bigger. From the 1930s onwards, by preference, all white folk artists used the Martin guitar. Then, once they had 'made it', (these guitars are still relatively expensive) blues players were also to use them to advantage. At the present time, the Martin D-28 is the most frequently copied acoustic guitar in the world. It is famed for its appearance and its deep resonance. Acoustic guitarists the world over dream of possessing a Martin, whose ample and even sound has become extremely sought-after.

> **List**
> It would be impossible to list all the blues and rock guitarists who made the Martin famous: Big Bill Broonzy, Brownie McGhee, Eric Clapton, John Lennon, Johnny Winter, Duane Allman, Doc Watson and Bob Dylan are but the tip of the iceberg.

Jimmy Reed
1925–76   Singer, guitarist and harmonica player (Chicago blues)

Songwriter whose works were taken up again and again by rock musicians

With his enchanting and simple style, he added walking basses to the Chicago blues.

Born on a Mississippi cotton plantation, he went to Chicago to make his fortune. A metal-worker by day, he played in the South Side clubs at night. Very popular with the rootless and nostalgic black audiences, he performed with a strong Southern accent and drawling voice. He mainly played ballads or shuffles, punctuated by distinctive walking basses, very much in the rural blues and boogie piano styles. His greatest hits ('Baby, What You Want Me To Do?', 'Bright Lights, Big City', 'Honest I Do' and 'Big Boss Man') became part of many rock musicians' repertoires, from Presley to the Rolling Stones. Jimmy Reed nevertheless died a penniless alcoholic.

Upside Your Head (Charly, 1980) is probably his best work.

> **Idea**
> Jimmy Reed used a special tool to hold his harmonica up to his mouth, so that he could play the guitar at the same time. Bob Dylan noticed this innovation in a photograph of Jimmy Reed, adopted it and made it popular.

Sonny Terry and Brownie McGhee

Acoustic harmonica-guitar duet with vocals

Their musical partnership has inspired many rock musicians

From 1950 onwards, they became known to white audiences as the last true blues duet.

In contrast to the majority of the legendary blues songwriters, Terry and McGhee were not born in the Deep South, but in the south east of the United States. The former is a Georgian, the latter a native of Tennessee. They represent a branch of the blues that, on the one hand, was influenced by white folk, and on the other, by urban music, as most of their respective musical careers were spent in New York.

An original combination

Terry and McGhee, who met in 1939 and began recording together under the supevision of Blind Boy Fuller, were quick to realize the advantages to be gained by joining a wind instrument (harmonica) with a stringed instrument (acoustic guitar). Playing cover versions of the great rural blues standards in a modern swing style first for black audiences in Harlem, then for white students in the 'Village', Sonny Terry and Brownie McGhee are not creators in the strict sense of the term, but their absolute mastery of their respective instruments and the precision exacted in their arrangements helped popularize a genre. They both use rock structure to the full (two instruments, alternating solos, up-tempo beat) to which they add gospel-style vocals (they frequently sing either together or one after the other on the same song) and rural blues-influenced lyrics (the themes of travel, separation and brief love-affairs can all be found in their works). Populated by fickle women, goods trains and bottles of whisky, their songs are characteristic of a style that does not lack humour.

Back Country Blues (Vogue, 1968) is very often poignant. Highly technical. A work of art.

Brownie McGhee and Sonny Terry (Storyville Musidisc, 1970) gives a more 'white' repertoire performed by two genuine blues players. An interesting combination.

Brownie and Sonny's Blues (Blues Legacy, 1958) is very hard to find. A challenge for the patient collector, with the satisfying promise of the original blues sound as a reward.

Cinema
Sonny Terry appeared in Spielberg's *The Color Purple* (1986) and Brownie McGhee in Alan Parker's *Angel Heart*. Both, of course, played themselves.

Hit
A European tour with the Sixties' Folk Blues Festival coupled with the commercial success of their one and only hit, 'Walk On' (*Folk Blues Party*, Fontana, 1967) finally brought them well-deserved fame. This number encapsulates the duet's acoustic style with its voice duets, alternating solos, harmonica effects, drawn out notes on the guitar, 'boogie' basses, and the typical question–answer structure between vocals and harmonica, and guitar and harmonica. In short, a work of art.

T-Bone Walker
1910–75   Singer and guitarist (electric)

The first blues musician to use an electrically amplified guitar

Author of the famous 'Stormy Monday Blues', he had a far-reaching influence on all jazz, rock and blues guitarists.

In his youth, he was linked with some of the legendary figures of the blues (Ida Cox, Ma Rainey) and jazz (Charlie Christian), and took part in the creation of the electric blues with Lonnie Johnson. Profoundly influenced by jazz phrasing but attracted to the rural blues musical idiom (he claimed to have played with Blind Lemon Jefferson), T-Bone attracted an astonishing number of devoted followers: B B King integrated several aspects of T-Bone's style into his own guitar-playing and even Chuck Berry

declares him to be one of his mentors. 'Stormy Monday' became a Chicago blues hit, and has since been taken up by a wide range of rock musicians. The cover version recorded by The Allman Brothers is extraordinary.
Stormy Monday Blues (Charly, 1978) brilliantly sums up the expertise of one of the greatest guitarists of the century.

> **Improvisation**
> When T-Bone plays numbers from one album or another, it often sounds as if he were playing a different piece altogether. We recommend the following albums: *T-Bone Jumps Again, Plain Ole Blues, The Natural Blues* (Charly), *Sings the Blues, Singin' the Blues* (Imperial).

Little Walter
1930–68   Singer and harmonica player (Chicago blues)

In his hands, the harmonica became an instrument to be reckoned with

His technique was so advanced that even jazz saxophonists came to watch him play.

Born in Louisiana, he moved to Chicago in 1947 in search of fame and fortune. After a brief partnership with Muddy Waters, he formed his own band. Probably the most accomplished harmonica player in the history of blues, Walter poured out floods of cascading notes. His style was later adopted by all British and American rock harmonica players. He was also a skilled singer and liked to intersperse his greatest vocal ('My Babe', 'Blues With a Feeling' and 'Last Night') or instrumental ('Juke'

and 'Back Track') hits with fast-moving breaks or long cascades of notes on his amplified harmonica.
Little Walter (1952–1960) (Chess-Vogue). This double album contains all the distinctive sounds of the Sixties' British blues boom and of rock of the same period. A veritable diamond mine, now available on compact disc (1986).

> **The Maestro**
> Little Walter drew such a wide range of sounds from the harmonica that is became known as the 'poor man's saxophone'. His mastery earned him the nickname 'Mississippi Saxophone'.

34

Muddy Waters

1915–83   Singer and guitarist (Chicago blues)

Between the rural blues and rock 'n' roll

Acclaimed as one of the fathers of Chicago blues, Waters was also one of the architects of Sixties' rock.

Delta blues

Although Muddy Waters is best known for having written and performed the most frequently borrowed number in Chicago blues 'I'm a Man', he actually came from the dark Mississippi Delta, where he learnt to play by backing Son House. It was House who passed on the use of the 'bottleneck', so characteristic of the Deep South Blues.

Although he popularized the group format for future rock 'n' roll (rhythm guitar, vocals, bass, drums, harmonica and lead guitar), Muddy Waters, whose name evokes the great Mississippi river, plays repetitive riffs and throbbing rhythms in an accentuated, rough style; his voice is distinctively guttural and resonant. He was an all-round artist, equally at home with up-tempo boogie numbers, moving ballads, simple narratives and happy or tragic love songs: his restrained guitar-playing, backed by a selection of hand-picked musicians, and the emotion expressed by his deep, powerful voice herald the astonishing link between black and white music that resulted in the Sixties' rock-blues.

The blues boom

Like John Lee Hooker, Jimmy Reed, Elmore James and B B King, in the eyes of young British rock fans and musicians, Muddy Waters soon became the incarnation of the true blues, the very soul of real rock. He immediately played the festival-university circuit. Future stars of white rock were seduced by his professionalism, both on stage and in the studio: one of his numbers was to provide the Rolling Stones

with their name. Was there any Sixties' rock group that did not produce a cover version of 'I'm a Man', 'Baby, Please Don't Go', 'Honey Bee' or 'Got My Mojo Working'? That all the major rock guitarists, including Eric Clapton, Johnny Winter, Rory Gallagher, Eddy Van Halen and Jimi Hendrix, respect and admire his work is obvious from their interviews.

Newport 1960 (Chess, 1960) is the recording of one of his first appearances at a white festival.

The Real Folk Blues (Chess, 1966) includes the famous number 'I'm a Man'.

More Real Folk Blues (Chess-Vogue, 1967) is a collection of all his best hits.

Muddy Waters Sings Big Bill Broonzy (Chess, 1966) is a panorama of the traditional blues, played Chicago-style. Interesting and original.

Muddy Waters: Rollin' Stones (Chess, 1988) is a worthwhile compilation on compact disc (23 of his best known numbers).

Refusal

During his lifetime, Muddy Waters categorically refused permission for 'I'm a Man' to be used as the soundtrack for a 'Levi Strauss' jeans ad. What happened after his death is another story . . .

Paternity

Until his death, Muddy was not above appearing briefly at his 'disciples'' concerts: his version of 'I'm a Man' on the Band's *The Last Waltz* (Warner) and his recordings with Johnny Winter round off his double album *Fathers and Sons* for the Chess label, an album on which he is backed by a bevy of big names including Otis Spann, Mike Bloomfield, Paul Butterfield and Donald Dunn. The news of his death was reported with respect and emotion by the international rock press.

Muddy Waters

Big Joe Williams

1903–82   Singer and guitarist (Delta blues)

Live from Mississippi

His harsh voice, primitive 'slide' guitar-playing and a few personal compositions contributed to his success.

Born in Crawford in the very heart of the Delta, he worked in the cotton fields, and learned to play the guitar at dances and picnics. He used a bottleneck to produce his distinctive sliding, plaintive sound, while his thumb would steadily hit the bass strings à la Robert Johnson. Big Joe's style is monotonous almost to the point of being hypnotic, his guitar-playing under-stated and simple. His use of an open tuning on the guitar meant that only a limited number of chords were possible and precluded fast breaks. He wrote 'Baby Please Don't Go' and made 'Rollin' and Tumblin'' and 'Special Rider' famous.

Classic Delta Blues (Milestone, 1986) is a collection of his 'slide' style numbers.

Mississippi's Big Joe Williams (Folkways, 1962) is made up of the slow ballads typical of the Delta.

> **Original**
> Unlike Leadbelly and Robert Lockwood, who played 12-string guitars, Big Joe played a nine-stringed instrument. As a result, his bass lines are clearer, which gives a distinctive overall tone to his music.

Sonny Boy Williamson

1986–65   Singer and harmonica player (Chicago blues)

Forerunner

A prolific songwriter and unmatched technical musician, he loved to be backed on stage by the future stars of British rock.

After collaborating with Elmore James on 'Dust My Broom' in 1951, Sonny boy went solo and was one of the first to hop on the British blues boom bandwagon. Supported by the Yardbirds, he also went on tour with the Animals and at the same time cashed in on his almost legendary status, with the result that a number of his songs became blues boom hits: 'Help Me', 'Don't Start Me Talking' and 'Nine Below Zero' were to be added on to the repertoires of many a spellbound rock group.

Sonny Boy Williamson (Chess-Vogue). This double album contains all his most successful numbers.

Sonny Boy Williamson and The Yardbirds (Bellaphon L&R, 1980). Listen closely and, behind Sonny Boy, you will hear the first fluid and light notes of a very young Eric Clapton.

> **Namesake**
> There was another Sonny Boy Williamson who was also a harmonica player. With a harsher sound, Johnny Winter immortalized his one hit 'Good Morning Little Schoolgirl' (Edsel Records) on his first album.

The rise and fall
of early rock'n'roll
(1954–1962)

1954–1958:
adolescent rebellion

There is no question that the first wave of rock'n'roll shook the musical traditions of white America and Europe to their foundations. However, the musical continent discovered by Chuck Berry and Elvis Presley was of a magnitude unimaginable to a simple explorer such as Bill Haley.

A short, sharp shock

The advent of rock'n'roll was more of a sharp shock than a musical revolution. It was the death rattle of traditional American society which had taken the full force of the blow represented by the first multiracial concerts, Elvis Presley's pelvic grind, and the shame of the black incursion in to white music. At the same time, the puritanical system set in force by the 18th-century pioneers unthinkably began to crumble.

The rock'n'roll revolution was crushed by its inherent doubts and ambiguity: immediately perceived as a black intrusion into a white world, officially denounced as 'nigger music' and banned in certain States, it was unable to gain recognition as a deliberate synthesis of the black blues and traditional Southern white music, the two main musical cultures in post-war America. Although they borrowed wholesale from blues performers' repertoires and stage-acts, including their ways of dressing, playing and singing, Elvis Presley, Jerry Lee Lewis and Bill Haley never fully admitted the extent of their debt to black music. Chuck Berry and Little Richard, two of the biggest black rock'n'roll stars, 'whitened' the content of their songs and orchestration in order to reach a white audience which they must have felt to be outwith their sphere of influence, but which they were nevertheless able to captivate. Thus, early rock'n'roll was smothered by an unmoveable shroud of ambiguity: a crossbreed music form and ashamed of its roots, early rock quickly succumbed to the repeated onslaughts of its enemies.

Contradictions and weaknesses

The emergence of rock'n'roll should be considered as an image of the triple conflict within American society. As a racial conflict, it was the battleground for the showdown between two cultures whose differences were so extreme that they could be called enemies. Initially a black music form, rock'n'roll was absorbed and usurped by the same white establishment that was to rob or marginalize black songwriters. Thus Arthur Big Boy Crudup, who wrote Elvis's first hit 'That's All Right' died poverty-stricken simply because he had not taken adequate care with his author's rights. Chuck Berry wrote both the lyrics and the music for 'Maybellene', but Alan Freed, the famous white disc-jockey, and the music publisher falsely declared themselves to be co-authors, and for years they raked in two-thirds of any royalties the song earned. Little Richard received one penny (one cent) per single sold, and Big Joe Turner heard on the radio that his hit 'Shake, Rattle and Roll' had been recorded by a white singer called Bill Haley!

As a *moral* conflict, rock'n'roll emerged as a vehicle for the demands of a younger generation whose aim was to assert itself to the adult world; against a background created by the generation gap, the number of 'teenage idols' grew: movie stars Marlon Brando and James Dean, and musicians Elvis Presley, Eddie Cochran, Jerry Lee Lewis and Gene Vincent led the attack on sexual puritanism and accepted dress codes. During the three years between 1955 and 1958, America's traditional social mores were directly challenged by angry adolescents who claimed to want only the right to enjoy themselves. But in a very short space of time, social and moral order regained control and rock'n'roll was struck by a series of tragic deaths (see below). By 1960, rock'n'roll no longer existed. It had only lasted five years.

Finally, there was a *commercial* conflict, inasmuch as the very first rock was something of a Southern cottage industry, a product of the studios of Memphis (home of black music) and Nashville (home of traditional white music). The great North–South, town–country and rich–poor divides were soon turned to the advantage of the massive eastern and Californian companies: after accidentally launching Bill Haley's career and the whole rock'n'roll movement (Richard Brooks's *The Blackboard Jungle*, 1955, Frank Tashlin's *The Blond and Me*, 1956) Hollywood immediately snapped up Presley, giving him an excessively restricting contract that was nevertheless supposed to be mutually beneficial. RCA, Capitol and Mercury gradually began to edge out the smaller independent Southern studios. By 1960, all the big names in rock'n'roll were contracted to studios in New York and Los Angeles. Rock'n'roll brought about extraordinary increases in sales and revenues; the microgroove emerged. The whole profession switched to output levels that, in comparison to pre-1955 levels, appeared astronomical. Television used the new music mercilessly, creating more and more shows, making or breaking reputations through shock interviews and trumped-up scandal charges. Rock'n'roll and its stars were swamped by unimagined success.

The conflict between art and business, from which the latter emerged as the clear winner, undermined the physical and moral well-being of the performers: almost overnight, young unknowns could find themselves knee-deep in dollars, weighed down by all the trappings of stardom; none was able to resist the temptation of fast cars, free-flowing alcohol, beautiful women and drugs galore. Many retired, others died, and some calmed down only to find themselves under the control of the same people who had tried and failed to get rid of them in the past. In 1960, the survivors of the 'class of 55' were no longer artists, only the fading stars of a dying musical genre.

The first blow

And yet, despite its defeat, rock'n'roll brought about something that even the Civil War had been unable to achieve: concerts meant that blacks and whites gathered together in public places, united by the same feeling of inter-racial solidarity. For the first time ever, Southern segration and Northern discrimination were openly challenged from both sides of the fence. At the end of the 1950s, a black preacher from Alabama called Martin Luther King began the fight that was to lead his people to civil equality . . . The second moral victory won by rock'n'roll is symbolized by the black leather jacket; following in the footsteps of Brando and Dean, Presley, Cochran and Vincent attacked white puritan culture with a mixture of informality, insolence, sensuality and freedom of expression.

The truly original aspect of early rock'n'roll therefore, is its importance as a socio-cultural, and not a musical, phenomenon; all rock was born of this union between existing black blues and a new white attitude: adolescent rebellion. Add to this the influence of white Southern music, the refusal of whites from the North and the West to miss out on any commercial opportunity, the strong belief that it was impossible for the socio-cultural establishment of the time to break officially with racial taboos, and the willingness of that establishment to govern any of the more unacceptable aspects of rock culture by watering them down (by any means, including scandal-mongering and defamation) and you have a list of the elements that caused a brief but enormously important tragedy: the birth of a new genre, rock'n'roll.

1958–1962:
the establishment triumphant

Rock'n'roll was the rebellion of American adolescence in an affluent society that was increasingly troubled by the problems of integration and adaptation created by the mass exodus from rural areas to the cities.

Casualties

However, rock'n'roll did not die merely because, in the space of a few years, those adolescents became adults. It also suffered the loss of some of its biggest stars: Buddy Holly, Richie Valens, Big Bopper and Eddie Cochran all died in tragic circumstances. Chuck Berry was imprisoned on a trumped-up charge. Elvis Presley had a close brush with an indecent exposure suit, and an assault and battery charge, only to draw the short straw and be called up for military service. Little Richard cracked under the strain of his hectic lifestyle and turned to religion; Jerry Lee Lewis's career was ruined because of his marriage with a minor; Carl Perkins spent six long months in a hospital bed after a serious car crash; Johnny Cash sank into alcoholism and a despairing Gene Vincent seemed set on a course of self-destruction.

Recuperation

To this curse, we should add the deliberate wearing down of a faltering genre whose young creators were too inexperienced to resist manipulation by sharp and unscrupulous businessmen. Show business pressure caused country music to steal a march on the blues in rock'n'roll from 1958. Black styles gradually gave way to sentimental and insipid cover versions like those of Pat Boone, while rock was given a much cleaner image: Roy Orbison, Ricky Nelson, the Everly Brothers and, on his return from military service, Elvis presented a reassuring picture of good little white boys returned to the bosom of white culture. From 1958, with 'All Shook Up' and 'Heartbreak Hotel' Elvis abandoned the wild and primitive music of his early recordings. With 'Love Me Tender,' the bell tolled for rock'n'roll, which gradually became easy listening music. Paul Anka with 'Diana', the emergence of the twist (Chubby Checker, Trini Lopez) and ready-made stars with carefully groomed media images (Frankie Avalon) distanced rock'n'roll even further from its original forms; it became more marketable, more acceptable and 'whiter' before the very eyes of its fans: many artists, including Jack Scott, Warren Smith, Charlie Rich, Merrill Moore, Billy Lee Riley, Johnny Cash and the Everly Brothers, took part in the reconversion of rock'n'roll to country music.

Female rock'n'roll saved the day with talented singers such as Wanda Jackson, Brenda Lee and Connie Francis who courageously took up where the pioneers Ella Mae Morse and Janis Martin left off. But, on the whole, from 1959, the rock movement was totally unrecognisable. The future belonged to smooth slow numbers (like the Platters' 'Only You'), sweet ballads (Presley's 'It's Now Or Never'), vocal duets with a gentle, polished sound, and the stylistically unimaginative twist (Trini Lopez's 'Let's Twist Again'), ever increasingly colourless transformations of the spirit and form of early rock'n'roll.

Age, bad luck, commercial demand, racism and puritanism thus got the better of the first wave of rock'n'roll. Today, with hindsight, we understand more fully the incredible ideological work accomplished by the Southern singers, both black and white. Their aborted revolution, coming as it did too early in a world that was hidebound by tradition, appears like a rehearsal for the world-shattering events of the following decade.

Chuck Berry

1928–   Singer and guitarist

There have been 'kings' of rock and roll; Chuck is the father

If racial segregation had not been in force, he would have been recognized as a major songwriter from his very early days.

From R & B to rock'n'roll

Chuck Berry was born in 1928 in Saint Louis, one of the capitals of the Old South. As a result of the bloody riots that shook the town in 1917, there was a strong feeling of hostility between black and white communities. The strictly adhered-to racial segregation isolated the black population in a squalid ghetto. Culturally, contact between the two communities was rare. Little Charles Edward Berry, who was fortunate enough to be born into a well-off family, was torn between these two worlds: he went to school, trained as a hairdresser, dreamed of driving white men's cars, of going to white cinemas and of going out with white girls. But he was black and so the usual ghetto pastimes had to suffice: going to piano-bars and dance halls, and listening to black radio stations that blared out blues and R & B hits all day long.

Influenced by New Orleans boogie-woogie and T-Bone Walker's guitar phrasing, anxious to make the link with white rock, which he considered to be the most rewarding financially, Chuck refined his style while playing with a talented pianist, Johnnie Johnson. Thanks to his boundless energy, the Johnnie Johnson Combo soon became the Chuck Berry Combo, and Chuck began to combine the elements that were to become the basis for future rock: piercing guitar intros, simple, but immediately recognizable, solos, catchy melody lines and foot-tapping rhythms, and humorous lyrics that evoke the Fifties' teenage experience.

In 1955, his first hit, 'Maybelline' sold a million copies, and he went on to record a whole string of rock gems. It was also at this time that he moved to Chicago and went on a series of national tours. Today, 'Johnny B

Chuck Berry *started out using a hollow-bodied electric guitar, orignally designed for jazz. His first recordings are distinctive for the full 'round' sound of this instrument.*

'Crazy Legs'

Chuck's first nickname was 'Crazy Legs' because of his incredible energy on stage, typified by the famous 'duck walk' which he still does today, despite his 60-plus years.

Goode', 'Roll Over Beethoven', 'Thirty Days', 'Carol' and 'Memphis Tennessee' are rock standards performed systematically in concert and often recorded by a wide range of groups. In the space of one year, while Elvis was storming the white world, Chuck Berry became the powerhouse of black rock; he entered the white charts in the company of Little Richard, Fats Domino, Bo Diddley and Ray Charles. He had fulfilled his lifelong ambition: he was rich and famous.

Fall and rise

However, rock'n'roll which, from its very inception, had always been linked with one scandal or another, was to lose one of its most influential songwriters when Berry was sentenced to two years' imprisonment on a rape charge for simply having crossed a Southern state line in the company of one of his white, female fans. His career in ruins, he was soon forgotten. By the time of his release, rock'n'roll had become a pale shadow of its former self.

Fortunately, an up-and-coming English group, the Rolling Stones, acknowledged his importance as a songwriter by performing and recording a number of his hits.

The Berry 'sound'

Chuck's sound was 'thicker' and 'rounder' than any of his Fifties' contemporaries. This was created by the kind of guitar he used. The Gibson 335 was the queen of guitars in Chicago blues. Popularized by the playing of BB King and John Lee Hooker, it has a hollow, smaller body. Because of this, it retains the resonance of jazz guitars but has its own drier, thicker sound.

This official recognition of the debt owed to him by rock was to bring Berry back in to the limelight. The British rock boom gave him a second chance at stardom, but Chuck was thoroughly embittered by the white world. Cheated out of what was rightfully his, slandered and broken, the bitterness of this misunderstood and persecuted genius was to translate itself into an immovable mercenary attitude towards the white rock industry. Chuck's resentment is still evident today: Taylor Hackford's film *Hail! Hail! Rock'n'Roll* (1988) shows a black artist whose quest for revenge on the white world will never end.

Chuck Berry Golden Decade vols 1, 2 and 3 (Chess 1967, 73, 74) is a combination of intelligence, creativity and humour.

Chuck Berry on Stage (Chess LP 1480, 1963) is a must, especially for collectors. A blend of original sound, the wild atmosphere of Fifties' concerts and a string of hits, namely 'Maybelline', 'Memphis', 'Sweet Little Sixteen' and 'Brown-eyed Handsome Man'.

Songwriter

In contrast to Elvis, who was only a performer, and to other black rock stars, Chuck Berry is a singer-songwriter. Moreover, he also plays rhythm guitar and certain solos. This makes him an all-round artist. He is the idol of Keith Richards (co-founder of the Rolling Stones with Mick Jagger and Brian Jones). In *Hail! Hail! Rock'n'Roll*, Eric Clapton, famous Sixties' 'guitar hero' and avid fan of the blues and rock, talks quite openly of the debt owed by all rock guitarists to Chuck. Give unto Caesar. . . .

Johnny Burnette

1934–64   Singer and guitarist

Shooting star

Despite his premature death, he is remembered for his original style.

He was born into a musical family; with his brother Dorsey and guitarist Paul Burlison he formed the Rock'n'Roll Trio, a group which managed to get a contract with Coral in New York. However, the record company was more interested in promoting Buddy Holly. The trio had a few minor hits, then separated in 1959, barely three years after getting together.

Johnny Burnette then attempted to go solo. He finally hit the jackpot with 'Dreamin'' and 'Sweet Sixteen' in 1960. Based on a clever mixture of rock'n'roll and easy listening, his style opened the way for a number of later groups. He drowned in 1964. His son is a well known country music artist in the United States today.

JB and the Rock'n'Roll Trio (MCA, 1976) contains his hits of the time, including 'Honey Hush' and 'Rock Billy Boogie'. Worth listening to.

> **Prestige**
> Johnny Burnette was the singer with the first group formed by Scotty Moore, Elvis's future guitarist.

Johnny Cash

1932–   Singer and guitarist

From rockabilly to country

He was part of that 'class of 55' which created a whole genre. However, he quickly gravitated towards country rock and easy listening.

Born in 1932 in one of the Southern States (Arkansas), he started out on the same musical path as all his generation's rock musicians. In 1955, he signed a contract with Sun, Sam Philips's company, met Elvis Presley and Jerry Lee Lewis and had his first hit with 'I Walk the Line' in 1956.

The 'ups' of his career were balanced by the 'downs', notably his various spells in 'drying out' clinics in the 1960s. He nevertheless enjoyed a succession of hits throughout the 1960s as he evolved towards traditional Nashville country rock music. He is still active today, and has more than 50 albums to his name, 10 of which are on the Sun label.

At San Quentin (CBS, 1969) is a superb album, recorded in the famous prison. Includes all his famous hits.

Classic Cash (Mercury, 1988). Twenty of the greatest hits by one of the biggest stars of quality country music.

Eddie Cochran

1938–60 Singer and guitarist

A brief but influential career

A guitar virtuoso, he also made a name for himself as a singer-songwriter. His death was a great loss to rock'n'roll.

Between Dean and Presley

He began to study the guitar when he was 12 years old, and first appeared on stage at the age of 15. Born in 1938 in Oklahoma City and brought up in California, he was influenced by the first hits of artists such as Presley and Haley. His fiery temper was well suited to 1955–9 rebel rock: his blond hair à la James Dean, jeans and bomber-jacket look, Chuck Berry-style stage movements, and rough, tense vocals ('C'mon Everybody', 'Something Else') alternated with sensual crooning ('Three Steps to Heaven', 'Teresa') all conspired to make him Elvis's most serious rival.

In fact, Cochran's first hits date from 1958 and 1959, at a time when pressure from both his manager and the establishment seemed to be forcing Presley to tone down his act. With 'C'mon Everybody' and 'Summertime Blues', and his wild versions of 'Long Tall Sally' and 'Blue Suede Shoes', he looked set to take over from the 'King' (Presley), whose talent had been neutered by the System, and the 'Killer' (Jerry Lee Lewis), who had fallen from grace because of scandal in his private life. But fate dealt fiercely and unrelentingly with the early stars of rock'n'roll: after the deaths of Richie Valens, Buddy Holly and the 'Big

Bopper' in a plane crash, Cochran too was killed in a car accident in 1960. His friend Gene Vincent, who was also in the taxi, escaped with his life.

Cochran's contribution

His influence on later rock'n'roll and rock groups was considerable: not only on the 'rock look' (lock of hair hanging in the eyes, dress, 'take it to the limit' attitude), but also in terms of musical arrangements, guitar solo structure, the important role of the drums, the rough voice, spoken narratives, and indeed the very sound of the group, marked by deliberate urgency and wildness. Eddie Cochran gave white rock'n'roll indisputable stylistic autonomy from the influence of black music and the 1955 rockabilly pioneers, and with his friend and fellow musician Gene Vincent, he led the way towards real rock.

The Legendary Masters Series vol 4 (United Artists, 1972). A choice selection of numbers.

The Very Best (United Artists) is also a good compilation.

Opposite effect

Eddie Cochran's career was launched by Frank Tashlin's 1956 film *The Girl Can't Help It*. His contribution to the soundtrack was a fast-moving version of 'Twenty Flight Rock'. Ironically, the film, a light comedy starring Dick Ewell and Jane Mansfield, was originally intended to ridicule rock'n'roll.

Bo Diddley

1928– Singer and guitarist

An 'African' beat at the heart of rock'n'roll

Although he was influenced by Chicago blues, R & B and white rock, he was able to create his own inimitable style.

Born in Mississippi in 1928, Ellas Bates moved to Chicago as a child. Like many others before him, he performed in the South Side clubs and became a respected singer and guitarist. During the 1940s, he took part in many small concerts, but was unable to break away from styles defined by the great founders of the genre. During his wait in the wings, he looked for a way to get himself noticed. His first attempt at the start of the 1950s, which involved singing obscenities and insulting the white world, failed miserably. From 1955 onwards, he was influenced by the rhythms and arrangements of the first white rock'n'roll records.

The 'Jungle beat'

He then decided to record a song with a beat that was close to his heart, which he called 'jungle beat' because it was inspired by the repetitive rhythms of the African drums; Bo Diddley's original jungle beat in 'I'm a Man' took the music world by storm. 1955 was a great year for this imaginative songwriter: 'Diddy Wah Diddy' and 'Pretty Thing' were highly placed in both black and white hit parades. Moreover, the cinema and television accorded him almost as much air-space as Chuck Berry and Little Richard. Bo Diddley became very famous, called himself 'Mr Jungle Man' and went on a series of successful

tours, during which he again entertained audiences with his originality, unexpectedly singing sugary ballads white-style. With a few rare exceptions, both Chuck Berry and Little Richard avoided singing country ballads. During the 1960s, while the 'class of 55' were wandering in a musical wilderness, Bo Diddley's career went from strength to strength. In 1957, Buddy Holly brought out a version of 'Bo Diddley/I'm a man', changing the risqué lyrics and calling it 'Not Fade Away', thus avoiding paying copyright dues. Then the Rolling Stones recorded the same song. Finally, his hit 'Who Do You Love' was added to the repertoires of most of the biggest bands in the rock boom. Even today, Bo Diddley still goes on the road in both the States and Europe, giving concerts whose sound can only be described as a mixture of African rhythm, rockabilly and white ballads. A real phenomenon.

Got My Own Bags of Tricks (Chess, 1971) is a double album of all his best known songs.

Bo Diddley (Chess, 1962) is undoubtedly the better album but extremely hard to find.

Surprise

Bo Diddley's quest for originality often led him to extremes of eccentricity. He even had a guitar custom-made for himself: of questionable taste, it was not only rectangle-shaped but bright white, and he added a rather incongruous car sticker on to this strange body . . . This is how this 60-year-old teenager appeared on the Parisian stage in 1983, complete with cowboy boots and hat.

Fats Domino

1928–   Singer and pianist

Magic fingers and velvet voice

By 1956, he had already been playing rock'n'roll in New Orleans for fifteen years, calling it 'rhythm and blues' . . .

The ghetto

From the 1940s onwards, he played boogie in bars in Southern towns, then settled in New Orleans where he became popular with black audiences. Racial segregation prevented him from reaching white audiences, but from the start of the 1950s he began to have an effect on white musicians who were captivated by his ability to adapt old, piano-style boogie to more modern arrangements (brass sound, drum beat and languorous vocals).

The 'covers'

Again because of segregation, his first true hit came about through a curious boomerang effect caused by cover versions: the white singer Pat Boone recorded a milder, more acceptable version of his black radio station hit 'Ain't That a Shame'. It was a hit for Boone, but paradoxically encouraged a large number of young whites to demand Fats Domino's original version.

In August 1955, Domino's original single entered the white charts, followed in September by Chuck Berry's 'Maybelline', launching a whole move-ment: from then on, black performers had access to an immense white American audience. In September, Little Richard's 'Tutti Frutti' also reached the number one spot in the white charts. The separate charts dictated by racial segregation were shattered, encouraging young black artists to enter white show-business.

Ratification

1956 was a glorious year for Fats Domino: his international hit 'Blueberry Hill' opened the doors of halls the world over. 'I'm Walking', 'Walking to New Orleans' and 'Your Cheatin' Heart' plus his modernized versions of old blues numbers such as 'Stack and Billy' and gospel classics ('When the Saints'), were all the rage.

The Domino 'style'

As well as his sweet voice and steady piano accompaniment, Domino's trademarks are his jovial facial expression and slicked-back hair. Thirty years after his first hits, he is still playing the same songs on stage.

Fats Domino (United Artists, 1972) is a double album of his greatest hits. A well balanced compilation.

Well deserved
Domino lived up to the nickname 'Fats': in 1985 in Paris, he broke through the stage by jumping heavily down from his chair to greet the audience!

Complete works
The Fats Domino Story (1949–1962) (United Artists, 1977) consists of six albums. The two following years are grouped into two records called *Reeling and Rocking*. *Live in Europe* tries to recreate the atmosphere typical of his concerts.

The Everly Brothers

1937– (Don Everly) and 1939– (Phil Everly)

Acoustic rock duet

Vocal harmony and beautiful melodies

Five years before the advent of the Beatles, they introduced a taste for soft and polished sound into rock.

A model duet

In 1958, when the first wave of rebel rock seemed to be dying out, Don and Phil Everly emerged with their clean, all-American look. Their carefully groomed image and well-crafted stage management and repertoire were at the other end of the rock scale from the hip-swaying of Elvis, Little Richard or Jerry Lee Lewis.

Yet they did not make their name by covering old songs, nor were they just another tame version of the original rock artists. Their style was genuinely original and their work truly professional; the two acoustic guitars (both Gibson J 200s) produced a steady, sophisticated sound, while their two strong but soft voices blended together perfectly, adding an element of calm that had been lacking in rock.

The first hit by early rock'n'roll's most famous duet was 'Bye Bye Love' which, in 1958, rocketed the Everly Brothers to the top of the charts. With 'Wake Up, Little Suzie' they became stars, for this single occupied the number one spot for several weeks. Other numbers followed ('Bird Dog', 'Til' I Kissed You', 'Ebony Eyes'), backed up by a selection of new variations on old standards, including a gentle rhythmic version of 'Lucille' and an incredibly melodic 'Be Bop A Lula'. Despite a long and brilliant career, the duet ceased to be productive after 1963. They separated in 1965, then got back together only to split again in 1973. Their comeback in 1983 at the age of 40 was greeted with enthusiasm by young and old fans alike; the resulting double album was a great artistic and commercial success.

The Everly bequest

They evidently influenced the Beatles, who inherited their preference for carefully arranged melodies and vocal work. But another, later duet formed by Paul Simon and Art Garfunkel is also indebted to them, as well as all the 'California sound' rock groups, including the Beach Boys, the Byrds, The Mamas and Papas, and even the Eagles. This gives some idea of their importance in rock history.

The Very Best of The Everly Brothers (Charly, 1964). A collection of the original recordings of their first hits. Irreplaceable.

The Reunion Concert (Big Beat Records, 1983). A double album which gives a reasonable overview of the duet's career, but with a more modern sound. The voices, however, have not changed at all.

Top twenty

With 40 million records sold and a number of compact disc editions now on sale, the Everly Brothers are still popular in the States. Slowly but surely, they have joined the élite ranks of the 20 best-selling artists in rock history.

Leo Fender

1909–   Inventor

He invented the archetypal rock instrument

An electrician fascinated by the problems involved in amplifying musical instruments, he changed the face of guitar making.

Fender lost his job as an accountant because of the Crash in 1929. He became interested in radio technology, specialized in wireless repairs, opened a shop and started to make amplifiers for the first electric guitars of the 1940s. The 'Champ' and the 'Deluxe', which both date from this period, are still produced today and were virtually unchanged before the 1980s!

*Eric Clapton and his **Fender**.*

Pressured by his guitarist clients, Fender studied the possibility of building a revolutionary guitar with a solid body. The first, not terribly convincing, prototype appeared in 1943; it was not until 1948 that the 'Broadcaster' (latterly 'Telecaster', which remains unchanged to this day) came on to the market. In 1951, Fender resolved bassists' problems by introducing the 'Precision Bass', which is still available today.

But the true revolution occurred with a model which emerged in 1954, the 'Stratocaster'. Still on sale today, the Stratocaster is the most frequently copied and sold electric guitar in the world. Collectors snap up the early models at exorbitant prices. This guitar, with its solid body, three pick-ups and adjustable tremolo arm, consists of two pieces of wood, neck and body, riveted together and was soon to become a must for rock'n'roll (Buddy Holly, Hank Marvin), Chicago blues (Buddy Guy, Johnny 'Guitar' Watson) and rock and pop guitarists (Jimi Hendrix, Rory Gallagher, Richie Blackmore, Eddie Van Halen, and Edge from U2).

The characteristic sharp and clear Stratocaster sound was ideally suited to nascent rock'n'roll. Its extraordinary versatility also allows for hard sound and means that the instrument still has a role to play in contemporary rock history.

Copy
To combat Japanese copies, the Fender company decided to produce its own false Fenders . . . in Japan! Marketed under the name 'Fender Squire', these copies look and sound reasonably like the original but cost a lot less.

Bill Haley and his Comets

1925–81 (Bill Haley)   Rockabilly/rock'n'roll group

'Rock Around the Clock', the first rock hit

Despite his 30 years and old-fashioned look, he launched rock'n'roll with his hillbilly orchestra.

Prehistory . . .

At the outset, Bill Haley sang traditional American music: he played at dances and parties without any great success. Influenced by older musicians of both colours (Hank Williams, Bob Wills, Bill Monroe, Joe Turner and Louis Jordan), he gradually changed his style, making the rhythm section of his band more powerful and introducing R & B-style guitar solos. Bass slapping is typical of Haley's rockabilly style. Presley's bassist also popularized this special technique.

First hits

In 1951, Haley cut 'Rocket 88' one of the very first rock numbers, then 'Crazy, Man, Crazy' in 1953. 'Rock Around the Clock' was released in 1954, but was only mildly successful. It was not until the song was used behind the opening credits of Richard Brooks's film *The Blackboard Jungle* that it became the symbol for a rebellious and violent generation. The film itself depicts the difficulties experienced by a young teacher (Glenn Ford) assigned to an under-privileged area. For many years, rock'n'roll was to be associated with juvenile delinquency and violence. Against their will, Bill Haley and Richard Brooks were at the root of this myth.

The following year, Bill Haley and his group distanced themselves further from

hillbilly by adapting one of the black radio station hits originally played by Big Joe Turner called 'Shake Rattle and Roll'. In 1957, 'Rip it Up' and 'Mambo Rock' kept them at the top of the charts but their popularity was already beginning to wane, for Bill Haley, born in 1925, did not have the teenage look of his younger rivals. Nevertheless, their British tour made Haley a rock legend. Until his death in 1981, the rest of his career was based on the deliberate exploitation of that image.

Rock Around the Clock: Bill Haley and his Comets (MCA, 1965) lists all their major hits as well as the title song: 'Shake, Rattle and Roll', 'Mamba Rock', 'Happy Baby' and 'Rock a Beatin' Boogie'.

On Stage (Vogue) is another well-planned compilation.

Rockin' Rollin (MCA) is a collection of five albums, the complete Bill Haley and His Comets.

Hit
'Rock Around the Clock' has been copied in 35 languages; there are 160 known versions to date. There were more copies of the single sold than almost any other in rock history (22 million copies).

Traditional
In 1949, Bill Haley's group was called 'The Four Aces of Western Swing'. Two years later they were billed as 'Bill Haley and the Saddlemen'. It was not until 1952 that he gave a more rock-sounding name, 'The Comets', to his group and gave up the 'cowboy song' style associated with his early days.

Johnny Hallyday

1943– French singer

The first French 'homegrown' rock king

The well-publicized ups and downs of his career, punctuated by the occasional unfortunate career move, have not detracted from his ability as a performer.

Following in Elvis's footsteps

1960: while rock'n'roll was on its last legs in the States, in France the movement was just coming to life. For Jean-Philippe Smet, a handsome boy with blond hair and an overall wild look, it all began with a radio show (*Paris Cocktail*), a few singles, which were really adapted (more than translated) cover versions of songs by Elvis, Cochran, Berry and Rick Nelson (amongst others) and three overheated concerts (Alhambra, Palais des sports, Olympia). Hallyday became the king of French rock'n'roll and the leader of a French-style rebellion symbolized by the ubiquitous black leather jackets, motorbikes, rough concerts and flashy lifestyle.

The 'system' was quick to cut the claws of this teen-idol; married off to a star of the 'ye-ye' movement (Sylvie Vartan), his talent was wasted in insipid films and light music.

The return

With the rise of the underground progressive movement and British pop, the 1960s were difficult for Johnny. It was not until the end of the 1970s that he fought back, taking advantage of the exhausted state of show-business in general.

With his new, more independent, career, his more original records and serious film roles, he has gained the respect of new generations.

Johnny Hallyday

Popularizer

French audiences often discovered the greatest American rock hits through Johnny's adaptations, sometimes before they had heard the originals themselves. He was therefore largely responsible for the popularity of rock'n'roll in France.

Buddy Holly and the Crickets

Rock'n'roll band

'Peggy Sue', tenderness and rhythm

This early rock'n'roll group's promising career was brutally interrupted by the tragic death of its frontman.

Born in Texas in 1936, Buddy attended one of Presley's concerts in 1954. By the following year, he was billed as his idol's supporting act for all the concerts in the region. Encouraged by the warm welcome they were given by the audiences, Buddy and his group, The Crickets, signed a contract and began recording in Nashville in 1956. Their first hit, 'That'll Be the Day', did not differ greatly from early hillbilly, but with 'Oh Boy' and especially 'Peggy Sue', cut in 1957, they moved into the true rock mainstream; with their pure guitar sound and polished vocals, the Crickets' style defied convention; moreover, Buddy Holly's lyrics showed both humour and an understanding of the Fifties' teenage experience.

In contrast with Presley's hillbilly and the rock'n'roll of such artists as Jerry Lee Lewis, Gene Vincent and Eddie Cochran, Buddy Holly never allowed the slightest sign of revolt to show through the lines of his music. With his neat jacket, bow-tie, horn-rimmed glasses and simple stage act, he played the well-behaved student to the hilt. The main concern of Buddy Holly and The Crickets seems to have been musical excellence. This was a rare attitude in the days of early rock'n'roll and certainly played a positive role, in that the high quality of the mix on 'Not Fade Away'

(borrowed from Bo Diddley), 'What To Do' and 'It's So Easy' forced the more rebellious groups to work on their sound. Today, it is difficult to estimate the extent of Buddy Holly's influence: by the time of his death in 1959, he had sold 10 million records, which placed him just behind the founders of the genre in the commercial stakes.

The tragedy

Buddy Holly's death stunned the music world, and his loss certainly had an effect on the development of rock'n'roll. By 1957, Buddy and a new line-up of the Crickets had begun to branch off into a musically interesting line, consistently refusing to produce light music but using country style arrangements and always searching for musical excellence in terms of vocals and guitar.

The Complete Buddy Holly (MCA, 1969) and **Buddy Holly, a Portrait in Music** (Warner) are good recent compilations with the original sound.

Fatal date

During a tour, four friends wanted to take the plane to save time and avoid a tiring journey by road; but there was not enough room on the plane. They drew lots. Eddie Cochran lost and had to go by lorry; laughing and joking, the three others, Buddy Holly, Richie Valens and Big Bopper got onto the plane. They were not to know that, on 3 February 1959, they were flying towards their deaths. It was a black day for rock'n'roll.

Jerry Lee Lewis

1935–   Singer and pianist

The first 'Killer' in rock history

Talented and extremist and capable of getting up to all kinds of stunts on stage, Lewis was one of the most outrageous figures in early rock'n'roll.

Born in the South, he was part of the first wave of rock: signed by Sam Phillips, he had begun his career as a pianist in Louisiana's brothels, where he was naturally influenced by the black boogie pianists.

The class of '55

He began recording for Sun in Memphis in 1955, and his first single, Sun no 259 ('Crazy Arms'/'End of the Road'), was mildly successful. His next single was a hit: the B-side, a cover version of the Commodores' 'Whole Lotta Shakin' Goin' On', made him a star of white boogie overnight. Ranked second only to Elvis in Sun Records's star line-up, Jerry Lee Lewis then cut 'Great Balls of Fire'.

His concerts whipped audiences into a frenzy. Excess is the name of the game in rebel rock. In a unique display of on-stage violence, Lewis belted out his hits, climbing on to his piano and pounding on the keys with his feet; sometimes, he would grab hold of the mike and sing standing on the piano stool. In a moment of furious excitement, flouting American legislation, he even downed a whole bottle of whisky in front of his worked-up audience. His teenage-idol physique and curly hair complete with one rebellious lock were the height of fashion, while he seduced his fans with his wild, whooping vocals and hammered out notes on the piano.

Scandal

While he was on tour in Britain, the news leaked out that he was married to his 13-year-old cousin. Although this was common practice in the South, the news shocked the whole world. His career was destroyed. He never fully recovered, despite a skilled attempt at converting to country in 1965.

Recognized today as one of the fathers of rock'n'roll, he is peacefully trying to recover from the effects of a life led in an unconventional fast lane, but still goes on tour. The passage of years and the excesses of his youth have left their mark on his face, but on stage, his energy is just the same.

The Great Ball of Fire (Sun) and **Whole Lotta Shakin' Goin' On** are his two original singles recorded in Memphis between 1957 and 1958 (re-mixed in 1969).

Live At the Star Club (Philips, 1964) is both indispensable and easy to find. Real rock'n'roll, featuring all the Killer's greatest hits.

Modest

In an interview with Taylor Hackford (who made the film about Chuck Berry), Jerry Lee admitted that, despite their long-standing rivalry, he greatly admired Chuck Berry's work. He also bestowed the title 'King of rock'n'roll' on him.

Outrageous

During one of his 1957 tours, Jerry Lee Lewis was more or less banned from all the hotels in the South; he had actually made a habit of breaking sinks and bath tubs with anything that came to hand, in order, he said 'to let off steam'!

Ricky Nelson
1940–85   Singer

From television to rock'n'roll

A teen-idol whose carefully publicized image elevated him to the rank of rock star, he was later to prove himself worthy of his status.

Born in New Jersey in 1940, he began to appear on his parents' TV show at a tender age. When he was barely 16, he shot to the top of the charts with a cover version of Fats Domino's 'I'm Walking'. His youthful physique and voice made him a sort of better-behaved Presley, and he rapidly became a rock'n'roll star. His hits 'A Teenage Romance', 'Be Bop Baby' and 'Teenage Idol' were all ideally suited to his teen-idol image. 'Poor Little Fool', 'Hello Mary Lou', 'Milkcow Blues' and 'You're So Fine' demonstrated his ability to blend syrupy ballads with a true rock influence. From 1964, his fame was on the decline and he moved into Nashville country rock, becoming one of its most prominent artists in the 1970s.

Ricky Nelson (United Artists, 1971) contains all his early recordings. The real sound of rock'n'roll.

Songs By Ricky (Imperial) is another, later compilation. Easier to find.

Cinema
A young gun-bearing Rick Nelson appears in the role of Colorado Ryan, the sharp shooter who helps out John Wayne in Howard Hawks's *Rio Bravo* (1958).

Roy Orbison
1936–88   Singer and guitarist

One of the lesser stars of early rock

He was famous in his time, but did not survive the difficult 1960s.

He was born in Texas in 1936. At the age of 20, he entered the charts with 'Ooby Dooby', his first single for Sun which sold 350,000 copies. Other hits followed: 'Only the Lonely', as well as 'Blue Angel' (1960), 'Cryin'' (1961), 'Dream Baby' (1962), 'Mean Woman Blues' (1963) and especially 'Oh, Pretty Woman' (Number one in 1964) consolidated his fame. But his rather unattractive physique and the pop fashion got the better of him. Before his untimely death, he attempted a comeback with Bob Dylan and George Harrison.

At the Rock House (Sun), **All Time Greatest Hits** (Monument, 1973) let us hear one of the golden voices of the 1950s.

Return
After 20 difficult years, Roy Orbison re-emerged thanks to his participation in the group The Travelling Wilburys.

Carl Perkins

1932–   Singer and guitarist

'Blue Suede Shoes' was his only smash hit

Misfortune ruined a promising career, but he remains one of the determining influences in early rock.

In 1954, he was signed by Sam Phillips and cut his first record for the Sun label: while not actually making him into a real star, 'Turn Around' and 'Movie Mag' distinguished him as a rockabilly hopeful. In October 1954, he cut the unforgettable 'Blue Suede Shoes', which immediately brought him into direct competition with Presley, followed by a series of hits including the famous 'Honey, Don't' as well as 'Everybody's Tryin' to Be My Baby' and a version of the blues standard 'Matchbox'.

The Perkins style

Perkins's rockabilly was livelier than Presley's, and also less rebellious, and his smart, 'country boy in the city' look endeared him to Hollywood and television producers; his singing was sharper, sometimes less exact than the King's, but his lyrics were more laid back and humorous. Unfortunately, at the height of his fame, Perkins was involved in a car accident that confined him to a hospital bed for six months – six vital months, for during this period Presley was to leap into the lead and head the movement that was only just beginning to be called rock'n'roll. By 1956, Elvis had become such an important figure in the media that the Sun record company seemed to be too small for him; in January 1956, he left Sun for RCA. Carl Perkins could therefore hope to replace him as the leading light of Sam Phillips' rock stable, but it was too late: Elvis was more handsome, more rebellious and more representative of the image America had of rock'n'roll. Perkins never came back to the forefront, but until the present day, has wisely cashed in on his rock'n'roll legend status: during the 1960s he moved closer to country music and frequently recorded at Nashville, where he was a respected artist. He is still working today, accompanied by his son, and is recognized as a major influence by such performers as Johnny Hallyday and Brian Setzer of Stray Cats fame.

Carl Perkins (Sun, 1969) and **Original Carl Perkins** (Charly, 1976) contain the hits recorded during his first career: 'Blue Suede Shoes', 'Honey Don't', 'Matchbox', 'Everybody's Tryin' To Be My Baby' and even an excellent version of the Platters' 'Only You'.

Class of 55 is a recent album which brings together three pioneers of the first wave of rock: Carl Perkins, Jerry Lee Lewis and Johnny Cash. Excellent.

Complete works

The complete Carl Perkins Sun recordings are available in a package which gives a better idea of his talent as a rock musician; an amazing blend of be bop, swing, rockabilly, rock'n'roll, country rock and western ballads.

Elvis Presley

1935–77   Singer

Symbol, legend and myth

Without him, the face of rock'n'roll would have been completely different. With his voice, Elvis brought about a fusion of seemingly irreconcilable styles.

Elvis Aaron Presley was born in Tupelo, Mississippi in 1935. His twin brother, Jesse Garon Presley, died the same day, leaving their mother desolate. It was probably this tragedy that created the uncommonly strong bond between Elvis and his mother. His childhood resembled that of all poor whites in the South: his father, an agricultural labourer, barely earned enough for the family to live on and was often out of work.

His youth

It was on the black radio stations of Tupelo that Elvis first came into contact with the

Sad

Grace Presley, Elvis's mother, didn't like her son to make films because she had seen him die at the end of Hal Kanter's *Loving You*. She felt this to be a bad omen. She made him promise only to make films with a 'happy ending' from then on. Elvis, of course, obeyed his mother.

Racism

1955: the head of a Southern anti-rock'n'roll league stated that his records were 'nigger music, bestial and vulgar'. Another declared 'The obscenity and vulgarity of rock'n'roll music is a deliberate attempt to lower white men and their children to the level of niggers. It is obviously nigger music.'

black music of the ghettos, the rural blues, which at the start of the 1940s were still very popular with the coloured populations of the segregationalist States. The black radio stations, of which there were few, attracted a tiny minority of Southern whites, the majority preferring to listen to so-called 'country' music, which is actually a mixture of a lively rustic music known as 'hillbilly' and its more urban equivalent, 'Honky-tonk'; we should also mention the extremely fashionable 'cowboy songs'. The whole makes up a very complex musical idiom, the 'country and western swing' which, along with the blues, was to be Elvis's main influence. It is impossible to give an explanation of the musical style popularized by Elvis, which was first called rockabilly (hence, rock'n'roll), without taking into account the simultaneous influences of the two traditional Southern music forms, black and white. All credit should go to Elvis for having been the first to accomplish what was thought to be an impossible task: he overcame cultural segregation by blending together two folk musics that had been pitted against each other since the tragic days of slavery.

Once his secondary education in Memphis was finished (his father had been charged with writing bad cheques and, like so many others, had moved to Memphis in search of work). Elvis left Humes High School and became a truck driver. Despite his success with women, he was something of a loner; he listened to boogie and wore his hair greased back and longer than was the fashion. His swarthy colouring and dark hair, his constant sensual sneer and eccentric, black-style clothes (bright shirt, dark tie, two-toned shoes) set him apart from his contemporaries.

Elvis had only two passions in his life: music and his mother; the two were inexorably linked throughout his career; his first recording was made for his mother and dedicated to her. At that time, Elvis was trying for a contract with Sam Phillips, founder of the Sun studios, who had been looking around for 'a white singer with a black voice' for more than a year. At first, Presley found this hard to believe and limited himself to suggesting cover versions of the Ink Spots and Bill Monroe. It was not until he played an adaptation of a Big Boy Crudup blues number 'That's All Right Mama' that he got his contract: on 6 July 1954, Sun record number 209 was cut with Crudup's 'That's All Right Mama' on the A-side. The B-side was Bill Monroe's 'Blue Moon of Kentucky': this first symbolic single sums up Presley's whole career. Two kinds of music, black and white, side by side and face to face. Guaranteed to provoke some sort of a reaction, the A-side was black and the white folk music was relegated to the B-side.

The explosion

This record was a phenomenon, for it broke with the trend for white teen-music started and popularized by Bill Haley. Elvis systematically developed a rockabilly style that owed much to black music; his whole appearance was more provocative. With his famous hip gyrations, breathy vocals, stray lock of hair, his clothes (black shirt, white tie, the opposite of 'good taste' at the time, and sequined jackets) he brought the wrath of the Southern establishment down on his head. Some towns banned his concerts; anti-rock'n'roll societies started to emerge. Without his knowledge, Elvis was filmed in concert by the vice squad with a view to taking him to court on a public indecency charge. However, this attack was too brutal and direct to have much of an effect: during radio interviews or television shows, Elvis always managed to get public opinion on his side. The country's youth, who were waiting impatiently for an equivalent to the cinema's recently emerged teen-idols Brando and Dean (the standard-bearers of teen-rebellion) to appear on the music scene, immediately took up Elvis's cause. He began to produce record after record with incredible speed. In 1955, sales and profits were up for Sun records.

The Sun period

Elvis's second single for the Sun label, number 210, was produced along the same lines as his first: on the A-side was a heavily black-influenced Ray Brown number 'Good Rockin' Tonight'. On the other side was a lively western swing-style ballad. Elvis's third single was again conceived along the same lines: 'Milkcow

Blues Boogie' is a reprise of the Texan bluesman Sleepy John Estes's song; 'You're a Heartbreaker' has a distinct 'white' air to it (Sun 215). The following record was made up of Arthur Gunter's 'Baby Let's Play House' and 'I'm Left, You're Right, She's Gone' (Sun 217); Sun 223 was also a hit, with an up-tempo Junior Parker piece, reminiscent of Chicago blues, on the A-side and 'I Forgot to Remember to Forget', a tribute to Charlie Feathers, the country music star who wrote the song, on the B-side.

1955 saw the confirmation of the birth of a genre, rockabilly, whose style and limitations were defined by Elvis's singles. At the same time, these early recordings showed the dramatic ambiguity of a period that was heavy with barely suppressed tension: attracted by black music and supported by Sam Phillips, a group of Southern-born youngsters attempted to bring about a difficult synthesis between their own traditional music culture (white gospel, western swing and hillbilly) and the blues, a musical influence that, despite the changes in attitudes towards racism, was still too shameful to mention.

The RCA–Parker period

From 1956, Elvis was Southern popular music; the small Sun studios began to seem too small: not only were they unable to

---

Jerry Leiber and Mike Stoller

How many times have we seen these names in small print on the album cover of the greatest classic rock hits? Their songs shot performers including Elvis ('Jailhouse Rock', 'Loving You', 'King Creole', 'Hound Dog'), Ben E King ('Stand By Me') and many others (The Coasters, The Drifters, King Curtis, The Isley Brothers), to stardom. They also worked with Phil Spector, the famous producer of the Ronettes and the Beatles, and gave him the idea for his 'wall of sound' which is characteristic of the recordings for which he was responsible ('Let It Be', 'Instant Karma', etc).

Films

Several documentaries of the King's life are worth watching: *This is Elvis, Rock and Roll Heroes* and *Rock and Roll, the Early Years* all contain interesting original recordings.

A music of contrasts: **King Presley** *on stage during his early hillbilly period.*

supply the demand for Elvis's records, but Sam Phillips believed that he had a stock of promising young hopefuls who could fill the gap created by Elvis's inevitable departure; however, neither Johnny Cash, Carl Perkins nor Roy Orbison could equal the 'King'. Elvis, complete with new impresario, signed with RCA and began to move towards national fame: the records and TV shows that came out of the first RCA period (1956–60) show a more subdued Elvis in the process of abandoning rockabilly for the more commercialized sound of rock'n'roll: 'Heartbreak Hotel', 'I Got A Woman' (a Ray Charles number), 'Money Honey', 'My Baby Left Me', 'Hound Dog' (originally sung by black singer Big Mama Thornton), 'Love Me Tender', 'It's Now

Or Never' (the rock version of 'O Sole Mio') and 'Jailhouse Rock' still worked despite the initial uncertainty as to whether they were white or black music.

In his films made between 1957 and 1958 (*Loving You*, *Jailhouse Rock* and *King Creole*) Elvis began to cultivate the problematic attitudes that were to become typical of rock'n'roll, but were absent from black music – 'teenage angst', and the 'generation gap'; to these should be added his provocative style of dress. At the same time, Elvis, who sold 10 million records in eight months and was personally responsible for 60% of RCA's turnover, became an institution run by 'Colonel' Parker. Little by little, the rebel of 1954 was drowned in the conformity of the new rock establishment.

The Hollywood period

After his military service (1958–60) spent in Germany, Elvis came home shrouded in the respectability of the perfect GI; a disciplined soldier, refusing all privileges his star-status might have brought him, and in love with the daughter of an airforce officer, under the guidance of the Colonel , he got his clean, all-American image down to a fine art. This was the end of the wild teenager with the sensual sneer, who sang lusty blues and gyrated his hips.

While rock'n'roll was stylistically losing momentum and fate was dealing it a series of harsh blows (the deaths of Richie Valens, Big Bopper, Buddy Holly and Eddie Cochran, the aimless drifting of Gene Vincent, the scandals in the private lives of Jerry Lee Lewis and then Chuck Berry), the 'Colonel' had Elvis sign an eight-year film contract, and he left for Hollywood. He gave up live concerts, and led a very quiet family life with his companion Priscilla, whom he married as soon as she came of age, and got bogged down in a series of trashy, repetitive films in which he played stereotyped roles. He never worked with any of the great directors again, despite the fact that he had filmed with Richard Thorpe and Michael Curtiz in his early days. For Elvis, Hollywood was an artistic graveyard, but his records, even though they had moved closer to country and light music, were still selling well. While the Beatles and the Rolling Stones were reaching for the stars, Elvis was growing older and fatter in Graceland, his Memphis estate.

The final awakening (1968–76)

Aware that his artistic career was foundering, Elvis reacted by terminating his last contracts in Hollywood. He organized his comeback during an extraordinary NBC TV show on the 13 March 1968; dressed in black leather, in a warm atmosphere touched with nostalgia which was not without a certain degree of self-derision, the King set the ball rolling again. His Las Vegas show was a huge success. Rock'n'roll record sales began once more to compete with pop sales, which in turn tailed off; Elvis, who was gradually distancing himself from his wife and Graceland, went back on the road, taking on marathon tours and massive concerts. His name appeared in lights in 130 towns and at 1094 shows across the country!

Overweight and long-haired, with impressive sideburns and country clothes, Elvis actively cultivated the 'deep America' style. In 1973 in Hawaii, he gave the first televised show to be transmitted by satellite to the rest of the world: that day, he had an

The Elvis 'look'

In the early documentaries, Elvis appears in his original outfits: white jacket, black shirt and a white tie and guitar for 'Heartbreak Hotel', a gold sequined jacket for 'Jailhouse Rock', a black flecked jacket, black shirt and white tie for his first television appearance ('Shake, Rattle and Roll'), and a black shirt without a tie for the Ed Sullivan Show. Then, from 1958, he moved towards 'country and western' fashions, a trend that was backed up in the 1960s by his move into light music and Hollywood westerns. In 1968, after a brief return to the black jacket of his younger days (NBC Special), he began to appear on stage in a clinging white bell-bottomed outfit, with long hair and western badges ('Suspicious Mind'), then in a white sequined costume with cape, distributing scarves to the crowd (the Hawaii show).

The Elvis sound

Throughout virtually his whole career, Elvis was backed by an excellent, blues-influenced guitarist called Scotty Moore. He plays on all the Sun and RCA period records until 1970.

audience of a billion. However, the King was reaching the end of his reign. Divorced from Priscilla, bloated from overeating, his nervous system ruined by drugs and tranquillizers, his interest seemed reduced to wrestling and boxing matches. At the age of 42, physically and mentally worn out, he was still giving massive concerts. A pitifully moving victim of the star system, the King died in a Memphis hospital, between two concerts, on 17 August 1977.

A Date With Elvis (RCA, 1959) is excellent.

Elvis, the Sun Sessions (RCA, 1976) includes all his hillbilly period hits. A must.

This is Elvis (RCA, 1983) is the original sound track of a biographical documentary which should not be missed, (available on video cassette).

Elvis Sings the Blues (RCA) demonstrates the extent of the black influence on the King.

Appraisal

At the start of the 1980s, before the arrival of Michael Jackson on the music scene, Elvis held almost all the rock records: more than 700 numbers recorded, 600 million records sold at the time of his death, 45 songs sold more than a million copies, a billion spectators tuned in to his Hawaiian concert, 1090 concerts attended by over 5000 people . . . and 100 Cadillacs. At the present time, the wheels of the Elvis corporation are still in motion: his ex-wife Priscilla has recently published a decent biography. Their daughter sings and would like to act. There is an 'Elvis Presley Boulevard' in Memphis, where the day of his death is a public holiday. Visitors to Graceland can see his stage costumes, his cars, furniture and grave. Throughout the whole world, posters of the King are among the most frequently sold. Now that his recordings are available on compact disc, sales are once again up. The impenetrable Elvis myth is a true gold mine.

Elvis in Hollywood

With 32 films made between 1957 and 1972, the King holds a sort of rock record.

But alas! Only a few of them (between 1957 and 1961) are worth noting: Robert Webb's *Love Me Tender* (1957), Hal Kanter's *Loving You*, Norman Tourog's *GI Blues* (1960), and above all Richard Thorpe's *Jailhouse Rock* (1975) and Don Siegel's *Flaming Star* (1960). In terms of music and cinematography, the other films are of no interest whatever.

Little Richard

Black singer and pianist

The unforgettable author of 'Tutti Frutti'

An extraordinary singer and showman, he added that flamboyant, crazy touch which rock'n'roll had lacked.

From R & B to rock'n'roll

Richard Penniman was only a small-time Georgian singer when he suddenly shot to fame in 1955 with 'Tutti Frutti'. His eccentric dress sense, manic, screaming vocals and hysterical stage act were an instant hit with young black and white rock'n'roll fans, but aroused the ire of racist associations which were quick to condemn any music they thought 'reduced whites to the level of niggers'. In spite of this, he churned out a series of hit singles ('Tutti Frutti', 'Long Tall Sally', 'Lucille', 'Keep a Knockin'', 'Good Golly Miss Molly', 'Rip It Up', etc).

Whether original numbers or cover versions, all Little Richard's hits are stunningly energetic and intense, with their clever mix of black vocals (falsetto, sudden screams and cries), R & B and boogie (piano, drums, brass section).

Little Richard's style influenced several major artists, including Jerry Lee Lewis, whose stage act was even more explosive, and Elvis (in his slower songs and loud clothes). Paul McCartney also acknowledged Little Richard's influence on the first Beatles records (for example, the version of 'Kansas City').

'Reverend' Penniman

A few years of celebrity proved to be too much for the delicate mental equilibrium of an artist whose colour and sometimes provocatively ambiguous sexuality had already placed him on the very edge of society. In 1958, he gave up 'earthly pleasures' and retired from the music scene. His mystic period lasted a number of years, then he emerged in 1964 with two more classics, 'Money Honey' and 'Hound Dog'. At this stage, his vocals were more influenced by soul music and the Memphis sound than by rock'n'roll. Many of his songs cut during this period sound like the first recordings of later artists such as Wilson Pickett and Otis Redding who were inspired by his Sixties' style (a blend of rock'n'roll, soul music, country ballads and Chicago blues). In 1973, he again turned to religion and since that time, has appeared only sporadically in rock documentaries.

Little Richard, Original Super Hits (Festival) is a collection of all his greatest hits.

The Georgia Peach (Charly) is a 1980 compilation of hits selected from the various stages in his career which gives an excellent idea of Little Richard's versatility.

Jealous?

For several months, Little Richard had a promising young unknown in his band called Jimi Hendrix. However, as the latter was already an eccentric as the star himself and was continually stealing the limelight, Little Richard fired him. Hendrix considered that he had learnt an enormous amount from this rock'n'roll legend, and therefore did not bear him any grudge.

Selfless

To prove that he really meant it, a short while before his first 'conversion', Little Richard threw a diamond ring worth thousands of dollars into the sea in front of a crowd of journalists. He later admitted regretting this extravagant and showy gesture.

The Shadows

English instrumental rock group

'Apache' was a worldwide hit

Before the Beatles emerged, they were the most famous English group in the world.

Formed in 1958 to back the singer Cliff Richard, in 1960 they broke away and formed an independent group. Hank Marvin's unique guitar style, combined with the clear, pure Fender sound, brought them instant success: 'Apache' and 'FBI' were international hits. The complete mastery the Shadows had over their instruments was to take them to the top of the charts on several occasions: 'Kon-Tiki' was number one in 1961, and 'Wonderful Land' and 'Guitar Tango' in 1962. Hank Marvin's influence over English and American (especially The Ventures') guitarists is undeniable.

Error

Hank Marvin owned one of the first Fender Stratocasters to arrive in Europe. Many other guitarists active at that time went on to play the same guitar: at first they thought that Hank Marvin had made it himself.

Tommy Steele

1936– English rock 'n' roll singer and entertainer

Known as the British Elvis Presley

A natural performer, with music hall roots.

After four years at sea, Tommy Steele was discovered in a Soho coffee bar while on leave, by Fleet Street photographer John Kennedy. With Kennedy as a manager, Steele soon signed a contract with Decca, leading to his first record release in 1956, 'Rock With the Caveman'. This top 20 single was followed only a month later with the no. 1 hit 'Singin' the Blues'. A further 18 hit singles followed before 1962, including 'Butterfingers', 'Water', 'Nairobi', 'Little White Bull' and finally 'Writing on the Wall' at a time when the initial impetus of rock 'n' roll in Britain was running out of steam.

Steele emerged as an all-round entertainer whose career has involved wide-ranging work on stage, and in film and television. Films included *The Tommy Steele Story*, *The Duke Wore Jeans* and *Tommy the Toreador*; after appearing in a variety of musicals and stage plays, he starred in and directed the stage version of the classic film *Singin' in the Rain*, from 1983 to 1985.

Greatest Hits (Spot, 1983) contains all his best known singles.

OBE

Steele's long and varied career, displaying enormous talent as an all-round natural entertainer, earned him the award of an OBE in 1979.

Gene Vincent and the Blue Caps

Rock'n'roll band

'Be-Bop-a-Lula' made Gene Vincent a star

With his band, he marked a turning point in both rock music and 'attitude'.

Professionalism

Apart from their evident desire to break with early rockabilly, Gene Vincent and The Blue Caps' rock music is striking for the quality and originality of their musical arrangements and guitar lines. The pure 'Blue Caps' sound was a distinctive blend of the uses of echo and vibrato effects and structurally complicated improvisations. In contrast with a number of groups which, in 1956, were happy to churn out imitations of Bill Haley and Elvis, Vincent and The Blue Caps were looking for a particular sound.

The hit 'Be-Bop-a-Lula' rocketed him to the forefront of the international scene; at one time, even the supremacy of the King himself seemed under threat. However, Gene Vincent was plagued by ill-health. During his military service he had severely injured his leg and it was only sheer willpower that allowed him to continue performing in spite of constant pain.

Violence

Music was his way of rebelling against an adult world which he judged to be absurd, and he bitterly resented the group's fall from popular favour. He became increasingly disillusioned with the media, who made fun of his lyrics and presented him as a sort of limping delinquent. His live performances, which had always contained an element of violence, became openly provocative: Gene would writhe around on the ground, partially undress in front of his hysterical fans, drink in public and drive at crazy speeds. 'Blue Jean Bop' was mildly successful, as was 'Bop Street' and then the last record that Gene Vincent cut with The Blue Caps, recorded non-stop in 96 hours in Nashville, during which he exhausted the other members of the group with his constant quest for perfection. Shortly after they had cut the record, the band left Vincent.

Bad luck

While America seemed to have forgotten him, Gene went on a successful British tour with his friend Eddie Cochran. 1959 drew to a close, 1960 began . . . In this fateful year, a terrible car crash set his health back irremediably and worse, claimed the life of Eddie Cochran. From then on, Gene was well set on a course to self-destruction; the rest of his life was spent in a series of love-affairs, monotonous concerts, and years of loneliness, alcoholism and drug abuse. By the time of his death in 1971, he was virtually forgotten.

Rock and Roll Legend (collection of four albums, Capitol, 1977) is the best of the many re-releases of Gene Vincent's work.

Image
Gene Vincent abandoned his jacket and tie in favour of black leathers for a televised BBC show, his face white underneath the make-up, blasting out his hits; he was never to shake off this wild-boy image.

New English sounds
and
American counter-culture
(1962–1970)

The Western cultural revolution

The 1960s was a period of intense creative activity, not only in terms of the arts but in all areas. It was a time of cultural and moral revolution, of artistic non-conformism, when little attention was paid to traditional rules and social mores, and faces were turned to all that was new, or revamped old forms. The heroes of this decade were Rimbaud, the black American bluesman, the rock pioneers, the beat generation, Henry Miller, Hemingway, Malraux, Baudelaire, Marcuse, the Indian gurus, Marx, Trotsky and Mao.

While the most powerful state in the world was engaged in the unwanted and bloody Vietnam war, the whole of Europe, with Scandinavia and France leading the movement, was more interested in the new moral code that was being proliferated through the cinema. As a direct challenge to traditional Hollywood values, a violent and stylistically new celluloid species was being developed. While Great Britain was providing the rest of the world with a radically novel music form which could be construed as the continuation of America's aborted rock'n'roll revolution, time went by. And along with the elapsed hours and minutes, the established order, the years of discipline, of austerity, the puritan years were consigned to oblivion.

The 'Old World' rejected

The global anti-authority ideology dominant in the 1960s was not spread to the younger generation by professional militants hovering at school gates or collaring workers at the end of their shift, but rather by the medium of rock music.

The music produced by the biggest songwriters during this period was but the artistic expression of a general call for change. By sheer determination and hard work, the survivors of the war had given their children the seeds of happiness, new consumer goods but also an overly strict moral code and far too many rules and regulations.

Torn apart by the two world wars, the wars in Korea, Indochina and Algeria, the African civil wars and the second secret intervention in Vietnam after the scare of the Cuban crisis, in the eyes of Western teenagers, the world in 1963 was not exactly a picture of success. By 1963, the younger generation had totally lost faith in long-standing Western social mores and codes: they found their world outdated and wanted a new way of life, but with the closure of the Iron Curtain on their hopes for the East, they were at a loss to find an alternative. Apart from rock.

However, rock was dead. Dead in America, where it had been swallowed and digested by show-business, and dead in Europe, where only the twist, sugary ballads and magazines peddling rumours of scandal in the stars' lives were guaranteed any degree of commercial success.

The magical mushrooming

From 1962, the miraculous Beatles relaunched the movement towards a creative reshaping of Western easy listening music. In their wake, the pop music explosion was to be the spearhead for an impressive number of styles, schools and rock movements. Throughout this extraordinary decade, the United States and Britain were to compete for creative supremacy, resulting in the birth not only of modern show-business, but also of a whole range of rock sub-genres, some of which are still active today: the 1960s gave rock its major trend called 'pop music', as well as the 'blues revival' and 'mod rock', the three principally British contributions, while the States retaliated with 'folk rock', 'protest song', 'country rock', 'blues rock', 'Southern rock', 'acid rock', 'progressive rock', 'jazz rock', 'soul music' and then 'heavy metal' followed by 'hard rock' . . .

The new English sounds

In the United States, rock'n'roll had been gradually undermined by stylistic clichés and the rules of the merciless star-system, and was firmly entrenched in an artistic rut. Britain was destined to take over the lead in the musical creativity stakes.

Beatlemania

In a very short space of time, an unknown group from Liverpool was to overturn the musical establishment: with apparent ease, they combined the rhythms and energy of early rock with the English vocal tradition, with its preference for polished melody lines and meaningless lyrics. From their very origins, the Beatles were a rock group, using typical equipment (electric guitar and bass) and adapting the rock 'look' to English tastes (dark 'mod' suits, straight, dark, long hair). The original pace-setters of the pop movement, the Beatles' success was as much due to their restrained non-conformism, rendered acceptable by its lack of political motivation, as to their extraordinary innovations in terms of musical style: the Beatles' early works, those endearing, sometimes naïve and precious light-hearted numbers, were held together by the exceptionally high quality of the compositions and arrangements, which compensated for the rather banal nature of the lyrics.

For as long as the Beatles' supremacy remained unchallenged, English pop was seen as teen-music, and as such, was actively encouraged by the English establishment. They were officially decorated, the darlings of the stockmarket, and honoured the length and breadth of the country, and that despite John Lennon's rebellious tendency for inappropriate jokes. In the wake of the Beatles, who had prepared the way for a movement they could not hope to control, a plethora of groups of a more or less ephemeral nature appeared, including Manfred Mann and Herman and The Hermits. Then the Who, The Kinks and Them directed pop music towards more daring musical innovations, resulting in a harder sound, more critical lyrics and a greater degree of non-conformism.

The Beatles stayed together until 1970. Their history is therefore intertwined with that of the 1960s, and for many people, they are still the symbol par excellence of that era. Their proclivity for experimentation far exceeded the musical movement they had started. They were responsible for changes in musical trends and direction and re-popularized forgotten techniques. In short, they were a sort of artistic yardstick, to which the whole music scene constantly referred.

With its own stock of stylistic possibilities exhausted, early American rock'n'roll, in a re-worked form, was fortunate enough to find a way of surviving through English pop.

The English pop movement

The post-war period showed the British the transient nature of their old Empire, and the superiority of the American life style. The 'Yanks' who were barely tolerated during the war while they were training on English soil for the imminent European invasion, became in the eyes of the next generation the living embodiment of good humour, of all that was cool, efficient and easy-going.

Contrary to their parents, English teenagers in the Fifties and Sixties were largely Americanophile; rock'n'roll, the twist, black soul music and the blues were the ideal replacements for the boogie and

And Europe?
An American music form, rock'n'roll was sung in English. Only English speakers ever really became known on an international scale: Johnny Hallyday, Eddy Mitchell and Dick Rivers were never famous outwith French territory. Adriano Celentano was never anything but an Italian rock musician. The Germans and Scandinavians remained within their linguistic boundaries. Due to censorship, the Eastern bloc countries were only able to take part in the rock movement thanks to the black market. It was not until later that European rock musicians decided to sing in English: Abba (Sweden) and the Scorpions (Germany) in the Seventies and Eighties prove just how wise this decision was.

swing brought across the Atlantic by American World War II conscripts.

However, in 1962, just when people were starting to wonder whether the seemingly impenetrable American rock'n'roll fortress would ever crumble, the breach caused by the Beatles encouraged small-time musicians all over the country to have the guts to give up their endless versions of 'Be-Bop-a-Lula'.

Within a short space of time, the pop movement attempted to topple rock'n'roll from its throne and succeeded with remarkable ease; the 'caverns' which had formerly been reserved for jazz and then rock'n'roll, opened their doors to the new wave of rock musicians. Despite their adherence to standard rock equipment (electric guitar, electric bass, drum-kit, semi-acoustic guitar, harmonica, etc), musicians like the Beatles developed a new kind of music, which was closer to English popular music, with its Welsh and Scottish roots, and its melodic traditions and choral work. By the end of 1961, there were 350 pop groups in Liverpool alone. Everybody was doing it: each big town produced its own star group which, thanks to a London contract or a television appearance, went on to gain national fame: Manchester, Birmingham and Tottenham contributed Herman's Hermits, The Spencer Davis Group, and the Dave Clark Five respectively to the pop movement. Surprisingly, at this stage London remained discreetly on the edge of the pop mainstream, the trend being for a 'fundamentalist' revival: in the capital, listening to the blues, rediscovering the roots of American folk and writing more politically-aware texts than those of the Beatles were the 'in' thing.

The Rolling Stones cultivated a rebellious bluesy style. Eric Burdon and Alan Price with the Animals turned to black music for their inspiration. The more eclectic Manfred Mann coupled a light music sound with political lyrics borrowed from Dylan ('Just Like a Woman', 'Mighty Quinn', 'With God On Our Side').

English pop music was therefore torn apart by two contradictory tendencies. On a stylistic level, some, of course, were happy to make use of the successful tried-and-tested Beatles recipe (clear sound, sober look and lyrics that on the whole were rather anodyne) while others (Alexis Korner, John Mayall, the Yardbirds and the Rolling Stones) tried to bring the wild rock'n'roll of the 1954–57 period back to life by using Chicago blues and R & B techniques.

Nevertheless, the innate experimental character of certain groups, including some of the more commercial ones (the Beatles and the Rolling Stones), prevented English pop music from slipping into mediocrity, which so many at the time predicted as its natural conclusion.

The 'Mod' movement

Besides the commercial pop music generally produced by middle class, city-dwelling young people, another trend emerged which, despite the fact that it never really made it to the top of the charts, was to leave an indelible mark on rock. This form was called 'mod rock' or 'mod music': the mods were young workers or unemployed people mainly from the vast London suburbs, although there were 'mods' in all British towns.

Working class in origin and form, mod music was stylistically a kind of poor relation of English pop music. A large proportion of young people from humbler backgrounds identified totally with its simplicity in terms of instruments, the harsh criticism relayed by the lyrics and the frank descriptions highlighting delinquency and the poverty of life on the dole in the massive urban housing estates.

Mod dress influenced the Beatles' first look (in their very early days, the Beatles were actually labelled 'mod'): kitted out in workers' Sunday best, with their old black suits, dark shiny shoes and longish hair cuts below the ear, they contrasted with the shorter-haired rock musicians. To a greater or lesser extent some of the biggest names in English rock, including Eric Clapton, Jimmy Page, Eric Burdon, Ringo Starr and Keith Richards, were involved in the mod movement.

However, although there were very few big mod groups, the most famous of these, The Who, changed the face of rock the world over. A small group of suburban rebels, they were the first to incorporate guitar- and amplifier-smashing into their stage act. The Kinks were another mod group, with their catchy riffs and cruel or erotic texts, while the Small Faces 'shocked the middle classes' with their unsightly grimaces and irreverent, critical lyrics.

Although it was marginalized, the mod movement redefined what English rock was all about: the non-conformism and deliberate provocation of stars who had 'made it', such as John Lennon and Mick Jagger, owed much to the hate for society expressed by those whom the 1960s economic recovery had not affected. The mods spoke up for that forgotten race. . . .

The 'blues revival'

Several years before the Beatles became the world's most famous pop group, at a time when the English rock scene was dominated by the Shadows and the great early rock artists, a number of purists, fans of old rural blues records, and avid collectors of Chicago-recorded imports, were patiently using their jobs as bandleaders and musicians to popularize the blues.

Alexis Korner, Chris Barber and Cyril Davies despised English pop and the watery rock churned out by Paul Anka, Trini Lopez and Chubby Checker. They preferred the more authentic sounds of BB King, Elmore James, Robert Johnson, Sonny Boy Williamson and all the other representatives of what they believed to be the one true certified root of all contemporary rock. Over and above the club owners and musicians already quoted as being part of rock 'prehistory' (in short, the 'blues revival'), mention must be made of John Mayall, whose avarice was only matched by his capacity for spotting real talent: erstwhile members of his band include (amongst others) Eric Clapton, Jeff Beck, Peter Green (future Fleetwood Mac member), Jimmy Page (future Led Zeppelin guitarist) and Mick Taylor (future Rolling Stone).

In fact, the importance of black American music was much clearer to English musicians, who were easily able to transcend racial taboos, than to the first American rock musicians who, as we have shown above, rarely acknowledged the extent of their debt to their unknown and unrecognized black counterparts. In a country where race was not yet a major issue, it was easy for Mick Jagger and Brian Jones, Eric Clapton, Eric Burdon and John Mayall, to shout from the rooftops that their music was basically black.

This honesty is to be praised, for it dragged unrecognized, underpaid artists such as Chuck Berry, Little Richard and all the Chicago bluesmen (who, without the intervention of the Rolling Stones, the Animals and the Yardbirds, would never have set foot on European stages) out of obscurity. The English blues revival purists' sense of fair-play allowed thousands of white Europeans to grasp the meaning and value of the first rock wave (from as early as 1967, the term 'rock revival' was in use) and perhaps to get an overall idea of its importance: thus they discovered that neither rock nor pop was really white. Once again, just as with jazz in the early years of the century, the black man's ghost had returned to haunt white music.

Still, in their heart of hearts, all the blues revivalists were rock artists. Most of the time they used blues melodies and instrumental structures and forms to further the aims of rock. Because of this, in Britain the blues were like a primer course prior to moving on to 'progressive' rock, to rock blues which gradually became 'hard rock' then 'heavy metal' through a simple exploration of fundamental blues structures. Thus, such diverse musicians as those of Pink Floyd (symphonic, 'spaced-out' rock), Led Zeppelin (hard rock), Cream (progressive rock) and even Jimi Hendrix, an American in London, were amongst the blues revival artists whose influence was far reaching. This was not only because of the incredible international success of the most famous group among them, but also because the United States jumped on the bandwagon and began promoting a number of groups whose intentions, at the start of the 1960s, had been exactly the same as their English counterparts: Paul Butterfield, Steppenwolf, the Grateful Dead, Jefferson Airplane, Canned Heat and . . . Bob Dylan.

Just as French new wave cinema awoke Hollywood from its artistic torpor, so the English pop movement launched by the Beatles (but not synonymous with them) provided a welcome shock and breathed new life into American songwriting.

The British 'Underground'

During the 1960s, few groups could have found an audience without the help of the 'Underground' which, in Britain, came in various and complementary forms: a prime example is the pirate radio stations which broadcasted songs banned and censored by the BBC from outwith British territorial waters. Radio Caroline was the most popular, and began transmitting from a boat anchored off the Essex coast from Easter, 1964. It was Radio Caroline that played the Pink Floyd number 'Arnold Layne' which had been censored by the official radio stations. Radio Atlanta, Radio City and London '390' played the same role for most of the pop groups to come under the eye of the censor.

Besides the pirate radio stations, there was the efficient work of clubs, pubs and piano-bars, which popularized in a rather rudimentary way the music of smaller bands, some of which went on to become famous.

The risky and difficult work carried out by the independent labels should not be forgotten; a collection of record companies came into being around this time whose intention was to give the least commercial bands a chance at a professional career. Transatlantic, Page One and later on Charly and Black and Blue did a lot for freedom of expression in rock music. The despotism of the established firms was such that, as soon as they could, the biggest names in English rock founded independent labels designed to permit them to work in complete freedom, and also to give new groups a helping hand.

Finally, on the fringes of the Underground were the official radio and television programmes which, although they were drawn to the exciting side of open provocation, had to remain within the guidelines laid down by officialdom. However, they constantly played a double game, attracting a younger audience without alienating adults. *Ready, Steady, Go!* was often criticized for its liberalism (which today would hardly seem worth mentioning) and was the making of several groups, as was the more conventional *Top of the Pops* and other programmes such as *The Saturday Club* and *Easy Beat*.

On the whole, the English pop move-

ment was able to expand thanks to a number of factors: the stylistic exhaustion of American rock, the tireless efforts of a few blues purists, the creative genius of four boys from Liverpool, the mods' proclivity for provocation, the cult of new sounds, the desire to shake up the 'Old World', the reappearance of the Underground element, applied this time to culture, and finally, in spite of everything, the continuing fascination exerted by the great New World myths: Elvis, glory, freedom of expression . . . and money.

Robert Moog

In 1964, at the age of 30, he patented a revolutionary machine which, through the electronic control of tension, could produce different sounds. At that time, the sounds produced were still monophonic, but little by little, Moog perfected his invention: the 'poly-moog', capable of emitting several notes and chords at the same time, brought the synthesizer up to the level of the traditional keyboards (piano, electric organ). At the present time, the range of sounds and pre-programming possibilities offered by the synthesizer are largely responsible for the tone of rock which, without the development of the former and the creativity of certain songwriters, would have arrested at the overloaded, hard rock sound. Pink Floyd and Jean-Michel Jarre were among the first to popularize the new instrument.

American counter-culture

The early 1960s were difficult for American culture as a whole: in a very short space of time, the United States lost the respect it had won after the military victory over the combined German/Italian/Japanese Axis forces in 1945.

The low ebb (1959–1961)

While American culture in terms of literature, cinema and music reached the summit of its popularity in Europe during the immediate post-war years and the 1950s, the following decade showed a dramatic decline in its fortunes: while Sartre, Malraux and even Camus laid claim to a certain American heritage (Faulkner, Dos Passos and Steinbeck were often quoted in *Les Temps modernes*), while the cellar-bars in Saint-Germain-des-Prés grooved to the sound of jazz and rock'n'roll had quickly caught on with the European younger generation at the end of the 1950s, while Hollywood had squeezed the life out of the world film-making industry by the early 1940s, by 1960 virtually nothing remained of this American cultural prestige. In the field of literature, the 'mighty' were falling silent: Hemingway committed suicide in 1961, Faulkner died in 1962, and although Steinbeck was awarded the Nobel prize in 1962, he had already written all his best works. He died in 1968, Dos Passos in 1970. During this time, the *nouveau roman* was invented, structuralism was all the rage and the debate on new ideas was definitely based in Europe.

In the world of celluloid, the situation was even clearer: throughout the 1950s, Hollywood hedged its bets by producing a series of costly epics and, despite the more adventurous efforts produced by the Actors' Studio, American cinema became hackneyed and dull. The French new wave, Scandinavian cinema and Spaghetti westerns rapidly discredited the American art form that had been stylistically undermined by self-censorship, that sad hangover from the MacCarthy witch hunts. Godard, Truffaut, Malle, Lelouche Bergman and Leone were the height of fashion. The films produced in Hollywood were box-office flops, and the American cinema was temporarily de-throned.

As far as the development of social mores was concerned, one might have thought that the rock'n'roll revolution of 1954–58 would have changed the American way of life, their very conception of the world. This was not the case. By 1960, the Cold War and fear of the Bomb caused the nation to withdraw shivering in to itself, and the puritan moral code did not evolve at all. The rock'n'roll artists' rebellious locks gave way to neat hair cuts, blacks in the North and the South were still confined to their ghettos and although women scored a few points against the phallocratic establishment, America was stagnating. In Britain, Sweden and the rest of Europe, rapid changes were taking place: contraception and free love were in fashion, while in America the very terms were still taboo.

Musically speaking, it was a disaster: faced with the overwhelming creativity of the English pop movement, the American music industry, still relying on its laurels won back in 1954, crumbled. The 'old school' rock musicians were either dead or had survived in a puppet-like state. The Beach Boys' sales dropped dramatically in the face of the Beatles–Animals–Rolling Stones invasion.

On a political level, that America was back-tracking in world affairs was obvious: in May 1960, the Soviet Union officially denounced the United States as 'international bandits' for having sent a U-2 spy jet (which they shot down, capturing the pilot) in to their air-space. On 12 October, Krushchev had the whole world laughing when he banged on the UN podium with his shoe. The communists were infiltrating Indochina: in March 1961, the United States sent military advisers to Laos, then, from December, troops to Vietnam. The situation escalated. In the meantime, there was a major military setback: the landings at the Bay of Pigs, intended to debilitate Fidel Castro, were a total failure. The Americans were humiliated again when the Russians won the race to put a man in space. American science, beaten by the first Sputnik in 1957, was once again pipped at the post in 1961 by Uri Gagarin. The Russians were scoring points in all fields: in August 1961, they got away with building the Berlin Wall and blocked all their common borders with

Europe. The end of 1962 was dominated by the Cuba missile stalemate. Using the threat of a nuclear war, Kennedy managed to have the Soviet missile installations dismantled.

Kennedy promised everything and gave nothing. The black problem continued to grow and to become more serious: James Meredith, the first black student at Mississippi University, and Martin Luther King certainly had the support of the central government, but in real life, black protest marches were often savagely broken up by overtly pro-segregation local police forces, and naturally turned into riots; and while blacks buried their dead beside the ashes of their churches burned to the ground by the Klu Klux Klan, militant pro-segregationalists chanted 'Never, never' and 'The Klan is here to stay'.

The 'new frontier' promised by Kennedy, that popular but politically clumsy and unlucky president, seemed very distant. The United States went into a decline, then sank into despair on learning of the shooting at Dallas which robbed them of a leader they adored despite his failures.

The victorious America of 1945 became a distant memory: the British took over in the realm of light music, the French in film and the Soviets were forging ahead politically and in the space race. It was time for the United States to shake itself out of its deadly torpor.

The awakening (1961–1965)

Once again it was youth in rebellion that provided the answer. Moulded by the individualistic values of a whole nation and impressed by the ideals of a culture that was originally Protestant and European, in a short space of time, 'Kennedy's children' were to put forward a profoundly novel replacement culture, based on anger, revolutionary ideology (more Utopian than Marxist) and a new form of humanitarianism. 'American counter-culture', a blend of a radical change in moral standards and in art, dreams of an alternative society, ecology, pacifism, concern for the Third World, the use and abuse of drugs and free thinking, was to reinstate the United States as the world leaders in culture. And these new ideas were to find their natural expression and vehicle in rock music.

The American counter-culture movement gave rock music its first real poets (Dylan), its first real militant campaigners (Joan Baez), and its first real geniuses (Hendrix) as well as its doomed champions of lost causes (Janis Joplin, Jim Morrison). At no other time in the history of American culture has the creativity of the whole younger generation been called into play: in all areas, the new did away with the old. Life in the most powerful country in the world was completely overturned by the determination and inventiveness of a protest movement which, in the space of one decade, turned the terms 'racial segregation' and 'sexual puritanism' into dirty words, knocked the political world from its pedestal, spoke out against the sacred 'world policeman' image of the United States and forced the rest of the dumbfounded Western world to acknowledge the new face of America, land of opportunity, freedom and the future.

By exploiting the rock media to the full, the Western cultural revolution changed the face of the world.

The protest song

As soon as they emerged, the folk and folk rock movements were seen as the continuation of the tradition of social and topical critique that seemed to have been started by Woody Guthrie who, incidentally, was still alive at the time (Bob Dylan went to see him on his death bed). In their political songs, their sometimes overtly socialist songs in support of left-wing causes, the new generation denounced racial violence and discrimination just as Woody Guthrie and his imitator, Pete Seeger, had done. Within the New York and Harvard (Dave Van Ronk, Ric Von Schmidt, 'Ramblin Boy' Elliott) folk groups, a few outraged intellectuals created the 'protest song' by systematically highlighting the imperfections and scandals of the American political system in their lyrics: Joan Baez, Phil Ochs, Tom Paxton, but especially Bob Dylan, then the Byrds were to be the leaders of this movement which, in 1962, hardly seemed justifiable. However, from 1964 with the aggravated civil rights struggle and the military intervention in Vietnam, the politically engaged folk lyrics were to be proved right . . .

The fundamentalists: the folk movement (1961–1965)

The American spring began with a return to the wellspring of all music. Weary of the media's incessant plugging of rock'n'roll, or rather what was left of it by the 1960s, a small group of New York intellectuals began to look for the American people's folk music roots.

The group soon split into two distinct movements with different objectives and musical preferences, but whose common aim was to highlight traditional folk by reassessing old records. One half was attracted to white folk and unearthed old 78rpm records dating from the turn of the century, then went out looking for any violin and banjo players from the Twenties, Thirties and Forties who might still be alive. The other half was more interested in the black roots of North American folk, and it was through the efforts of some of its members that some of the big names in the blues who, between 1940 and 1960, had been swept aside by swing and rock'n'roll were brought back into the public eye and given an unhoped-for chance at a seconc musical career.

In general, these students, amateur musicologists and journalists writing for progressive papers printed in the North Eastern States were ill-received by the Southern population: the whites were wary of these Yankees who, moreover, were often Jewish and suspected of harbouring Communist sympathies. Always on their guard, the blacks couldn't understand why they were being asked to fetch the old blues singers home after a lifetime of playing in both Northern and Southern cities, nor why these long-haired whites were bothering interviewing and recording them.

The intellectuals associated with *The Village Voice* newspaper and a number of other specialized or limited-distribution magazines carried out important work: not only did folk clubs form with incredible frequency from 1960, but record companies systematically reissued the works of all the forgotten folk artists. Woodie Guthrie's *Dust-Bowl Ballads* is to folk what *The Grapes of Wrath* is to literature. With his album *Songs of the Spanish Civil War*, Pete Seeger (whose father was a famous Thirties' music-ologist) illustrated the political awareness tendency that was to influence a whole generation of 'protest singers' led by Dylan,

Baez and Tom Paxton. Furthermore, old folk songs were added to contemporary performers' live repertoires and recordings.

The Folkways catalogue rapidly became a national, then worldwide, white folk music guide: Bascom Lunsford's *Smoky Mountains Ballads, The Ritchie Family of Kentucky, Progressive Bluegrass and Other Instrumentals, Old Harp Singers* and *Doc Watson and his Family* give an idea of the vocal and instrumental techniques fashionable in American rural areas between 1920 and 1950. *American Moonshine and Prohibition, Depression Songs, American Folk Music Vol 2,* and *Social Songs* lie within the framework of the social critique trend in folk and draw together the battle songs of the unemployed and trade unionists during the Roosevelt years. *Child Ballads in America* and *Old Time Songs for Children* are collections of children's songs. *American Banjo* and *Old Time Fiddler Convention* were a tribute to the skills of the Mid West artists.

Along with white folk, Folkways also re-released the works of some of the rural blues performers, starting with *Big Joe Williams and His Nine-String Guitar,* then Big Bill Broonzy, Memphis Slim, Snooks Eaglin' and Brownie McGhee.

However, for the blues the most comprehensive catalogue was produced by the Biograph company. From its central office in New York, Biograph tracked down and recorded forgotten artists, while releasing reworked albums on to the market.

All the great early bluesmen including Blind Lemon Jefferson, Blind Willie McTell, Skip James, Mississippi Fred McDowell, Furry Lewis, Gary Davis, Blind Blake, Papa Charlie Jackson and Johnny Shines were listed in the Biograph catalogue. Most often their recordings dated from the Twenties and Thirties, but they were very successful.

The Arhoolie company did the same for the rural bluesmen, thus putting the finishing touches to the picture of black rural music as it was between the two world wars.

In Great Britain, Sonet popularized rural, then Chicago, acoustic blues. In France at the start of the 1960s, Vogue brought out blues compilations featuring many of the great songwriters. In Germany, Fontana cut the unforgettable *American Folk Blues Festival* series of recordings whose quality is still outstanding even today, particularly considering they are the only audial records of the black bluesmen's first European tours.

The folk movement was not limited to a nostalgic appreciation of old black or white music; some great musicians capable of equalling their idols emerged: John Hammond marvellously reproduced the Robert Johnson style, and Stefan Grossman those of Gary Davis, John Hurt and Son House; Eric Von Schmidt and Dave Van Ronk (Bob Dylan's first mentors) were equally at ease with the folk repertoire and the acoustic blues, and Pete Seeger, frequently partnered by the legendary Leadbelly, could fill concert halls across the country. A whole crowd of young white musicians threw themselves into exploring the dry techniques of the acoustic guitar, which was the folk movement's instrument par excellence. Bob Dylan, Joan Baez, Tom Paxton, Arlo Guthrie (Woody's son), Country Joe McDonald, Peter, Paul and Mary, Paul Simon, the Byrds guitarists, the future Eagles and so many others began their careers with a technical return to their musical roots, going on to influence and rejuvenate all Sixties' rock.

Once again, an extremely important music movement was to draw most of its energy from the direct confrontation between the black and white roots of American folk.

The nonconformists: folk rock (1965–1970)

The transition from acoustic blues and folk to the rock musical idiom did not go unchallenged, nor was it without its own particular pitfalls: for it to be possible, all the pulling power of absolute stardom was necessary, for in the eyes of the Greenwich Village fundamentalists, superposing a new electric sound on to genuine folk numbers was tantamount to sacrilege. According to them, it was better to sell 4000 copies of a 'genuine' album (as was the case for Bob Dylan's first LP) than to have a smash hit based on an electric guitar sound (which again was the case with Dylan's 'Mr Tambourine Man', which the Byrds recorded using electric instruments).

Not one major folk artist dared electrify his music before Dylan. The latter did this at the Newport festival, was booed for 20 minutes but carried on, playing the electric intro to his song, backed by the Paul Butterfield Blues Band, over and over until the crowd finally fell silent. Won over, the audience changed its tune and gave its wholehearted approval to this daring innovation by which the musical energy of rock and the finesse of folk poetry were fused together. Dylan's first electric albums (*Bringin' it all Back Home* and especially *Highway 61 Revisited*) were major hits. A new genre was born: it was called 'folk rock' because it owed its harmonies and lyrics to the folk movement, but used reworked rock-style sounds and rhythms, and also the range of rock instruments (electric guitar and bass, drums, electric organ, and the clear/fuzzy harmonica sound passed on from the rural/Chicago blues) that, from then on, were seen as traditional. With Dylan, The Byrds are the best representatives of folk rock. Their sound was truly perfect, and better, more polished in terms of instrumental arrangements and vocals than Dylan's. However, they had neither the prolific songwriting abilities nor the supreme originality of the ex-king of folk who, with his anti-commercial rasping voice, unpredictable behaviour and basic arrangements, still headed the movement, at least for as long as he wanted to.

Other talented groups affected folk rock with their professionalism and skill. Folk rock was the only properly American genre to compete with the wave of English pop (Beatles–Animals–Stones): the Lovin' Spoonful, a group of folk rock musicians from the East Coast (The Byrds were from California), had a number of hits, particularly 'Do You Believe in Magic', 'Daydream' and 'Summer in the City'. The Mamas and the Papas took up where they left off and linked up with Californian music ('California Dreamin'', 'Free Advice', 'Dedicated to the One I Love'). Sonny and Cher (the latter has recently made an astonishing comeback with a Hollywood film career) were big folk rock stars with 'I Got You Babe' (number one in the charts in July 1968) then 'The Beat Goes On'.

Neil Young also took part in the folk rock movement before forming the famous Crosby, Stills, Nash and Young quartet in 1969, after having been the front man for Buffalo Springfield from 1965 to that date. However, it was not until the 1970s, by which time he had completely assimilated all the musical influences absorbed during the 1960s, that his talent really exploded in to life.

Simon and Garfunkel were perhaps the genre's greatest creative team: their vocal work is still more or less unmatched and their melodies are still famous throughout the whole world. Although at first they followed the folk 'hard line', Paul Simon, that musician without equal, instigated the discreet and flexible use of rock instruments, without ever fully abandoning the acoustic guitar. With Bob Dylan, the Byrds and Neil Young, he wrote some of the most beautiful ballads in the history of American contemporary popular music.

The experimentalists: psychedelia and the hippy movement (1966–1970)

January 1967: 460 000 young Americans aged from 19 to 23 were fighting in Vietnam. Losses were much heavier than expected: 2000 had already been reported dead or missing. The gravity of the situation began to dawn on an increasingly concerned nation, and the younger intellectuals refused to cooperate.

In this general atmosphere of protest, it was the West Coast which led the way and experimented with all the forms of struggle against a 'system' whose military blunders and unwillingness to face the realities of racial integration and changing moral standards had caused it to lose all credibility.

The student protest movement began at Berkeley University near San Francisco. Political groups with left-wing sympathies organized mass pacifist rallies during which draftees burned their call-up papers in public. Their next step was to organize open air concerts where politics and folk rock rubbed shoulders with North Beach squatters who claimed to be the inheritors of Kerouac's beat generation. Little by little, what had been a protest against the hollow American dream became a protest against all forms of war, against the established educational system, puritan upbringing and environmental pollution. Under the influence of protest song lyrics (Marxism remained outwith the protest mainstream, and was only represented by a marginal terrorist group known as the 'Weathermen'), and in the communicative fervour created by 'be-ins' and 'love-ins' a new, revolutionary ideology began gradually to take shape. Rather than issuing any challenge to the powers that be, this ideology was directed towards immediate, profound reform in individual and social pre-conceptions and behaviour.

The hippy movement was born during the first love-in at Golden Gate Park, San Francisco, which was an explosive blend of free concert (performed by the Grateful Dead), political rally (attended by a member of the Black Panthers and various left-wing groups) and psychedelia: the use of 'natural' (particularly marijuana) and chemical (mostly LSD) drugs gave these youth gatherings an extremely provocative aura, which was accommodatingly relayed by national network media to an increasingly shocked and unprepared America.

The musical side of the hippy movement, which is also known as 'flower-power' (because of the pacifist connotations) or psychedelia (meaning literally 'spiritual revelation') was represented by what is usually called 'West Coast' rock, because it was mainly Californian. Characterized by its 'anything goes' attitude, its strong avant-garde tendencies and the use of all sorts of instruments intended to distort the too traditional rock'n'roll and folk-rock sounds, the 'acid rock', or psychedelic rock, of the second half of the decade bridged the gap between the political and

Jazz rock

The three original rock chords could not hope to suffice groups of such exceptional abilities as Pink Floyd, King Crimson, Soft Machine or Genesis. Talented soloists (John MacLaughlin, Larry Coryell, Chick Corea and Jeff Beck) threw themselves into a thorough exploration of the possibilities offered by jazz rock, a genre which was still relatively unknown because of its elitist aspects. All the truly skilled rock musicians were tempted by the harmonic and rhythmic complexity of jazz. Thus, rock musician Jimi Hendrix and jazz musician Miles Davis attempted a merger between their two totally different musical spheres. While interesting, the blend was not an easy one; in the main, rock fans, used to simple melodies and catchy rhythms, rejected the musical complexity of jazz rock. Popular with initiates in the first half of the 1970s, jazz rock gradually disappeared. Today as a genre in its own right, it is practically non-existent, but it survives as part of the musical repertoires used by many successful groups in the form of Pink Floyd's 'spacey' rock, Prince's electrofunk and the cool jazz dear to Sade and Ricky Lee Jones.

spiritual demands of young people and rock tradition. The psychedelic movement gave birth to several big bands. In 1968, 500 groups claimed the privilege of belonging to this category around San Francisco Bay alone!

The most famous of these was Jefferson Airplane, a group of musicians from totally different backgrounds who were variously influenced by the French symbolists (Baudelaire, Rimbaud), the surrealist painters (Dali, Miro), and the New York avant-gardists (Warhol) as well as Dylan, the blues, the Rolling Stones and jazz.

Having played at the Monterey festival in 1967, and then at Woodstock, the group managed to survive the move into the 1970s and was one of the strongest influences on the whole rock movement. Their biggest hit 'Somebody to Love' (1967) was quite definitely in the 'love-generation' tradition, and they were frequently questioned by the police because of their 'obscene' suggestions and their fondness for taking acid while on stage.

The Grateful Dead symbolized the very essence of the flower power movement. Not only did they live in a commune, but they also refused to become part of the commercial star system, giving free concerts and contributing what profits they made to left-wing causes. With their liberal ideology and preference for psychedelia, Bob Dylan, the blues, soul music and the Beatles, the Dead are an extraordinary musical melting pot,

and are part of a rock culture, to which they contributed a number of excellent songs and a certain unchanging coherence in their attitude towards their fans (they are the only band still to allow bootleg recordings to be made at their concerts).

With the quality of their lyrics, the personality of their leader Jim Morrison and their constant sound experimentation, The Doors were perhaps the most prestigious of the West Coast groups. Faced with uncompromising reality (one million soldiers in Vietnam by 1970, the invasion of Cambodia and Laos in 1972, the assassination of Martin Luther King in 1968, and the deaths of their idols Hendrix and Joplin in 1970 and Jim Morrison the next year), their illusions shattered, the most idealistic of generations sank into despair, pessimism and violence. The Doors were the ultimate expression of these feelings. The whole rock movement was changed by their open use of drugs and alcohol, their frenzied lyrics which echoed the poetry of Baudelaire and Rimbaud, their sexual provocation (Jim Morrison's suggestive gestures and on-stage strip-teases, etc), their theatrical stage-management and the syncretism in their songs.

The West Coast also became famous for producing so-called alternative or avant-garde groups which, despite their different aims, shared a rejection of all that had already been 'seen and done'. Quick Silver Messenger Service shot to fame with *Happy Trails*, an alternative and curious blend of psychedelic music, rock and Chicago blues; Janis Joplin, a young Texan who had moved West, gave white rock its first black-sounding voice.

Frank Zappa and The Mothers of Invention showed what systematized eclecticism had to give to the rock movement. With his tendency towards avant-gardism, his totally unexpected use of non-rock instruments, orchestras (like the Beatles on *Sergeant Pepper*, but more disorganized), baroque Italian music scores, Boulez compositions, fuzzy guitar sounds and synthesisers, Zappa, who at one time left the rock scene for a career in the theatre, defies categorization.

Andy Warhol, 1930–1988
The East Coast response to the Californian scene was typically intellectual and centred in New York, where a group of artists from diverse backgrounds gathered around an extraordinary creative genius, Andy Warhol. Involved in sculpture, painting, the theatre (he was often linked with the 'Living Theatre' and the 'Hair' troupe), hard drugs and a dubious sexual milieu, Warhol adopted the Velvet Underground as his protégés (today, the group is considered to be the father of punk and new wave). The Velvet Underground featured prominently in the psychedelic movement; Lou Reed, one of the biggest names in Seventies rock, was a member of the band which also featured Nico, a former model, who went on to cut several solo albums. Andy Warhol died in 1988.

'Deep' rock: the blues boom, swamp rock, Southern rock and country music

New York and California do not make America. The folk and psychedelic movements came as a sharp and unwelcome shock to the rest of the United States.

A number of musicians from the Central and Southern states preferred to take refuge in a different kind of fundamentalism from the folk movement and directed their energies towards the creation of a rock form that relied more on the actual music than on topical lyrics, without, however, completely giving up social criticism. Indeed, with groups such as Steppenwolf and MC5, that critique was sometimes extremely acerbic.

The equivalent of the English blues boom took place in the United States when a number of influential songwriters emerged who remained faithful to the spirit of black music while adding all the new energy produced by the hard and solid sound of rock: Johnny Winter, a Texan rock musician whose two major influences were Chicago blues and the Rolling Stones, found fame with an extraordinarily accomplished cover of Chuck Berry's 'Johnny B Goode'. The Los Angeles group Canned Heat were devoted to the John Lee Hooker style, to which they added instantly recognizable atmospheric guitar and harmonica sounds ('On the Road Again'), which gave birth to a genre which was soon known variously as 'boogie blues', 'boogie rock' and 'rock blues'.

Not to be outdone, the South produced Creedence Clearwater Revival: a veritable hit factory, CCR was one of the most famous Seventies' American groups. From as early as 1969, they were producing the heavy, powerful sounds of 'swamp rock' which, with its familiar rhythms (inherited from rock and the blues) and tunes with simple, catchy lyrics was close to the hearts of American Southerners. At the same time, Tony Joe White appeared on the 'swamp rock' scene; in 1969 Presley, who since 1968 had been trying to get out of his particular musical rut, cut a version of White's 'Polk Salad Annie' which marked the start of his long-term affair with traditional Southern rock.

'Swamp rock' and the 'rock blues' were quickly fused together to give what was first called 'Southern rock'n'roll', which reached the height of its popularity during the 1970s with groups such as the Allman Brothers and Lynyrd Skynyrd which, with Jimi Hendrix and Led Zeppelin, are considered to be the forefathers of heavy metal and hard rock. The pounding rhythms, screaming vocals and skilled guitar or harmonica playing were, with

the exception of the works of one left-wing group, Steppenwolf ('Born To Be Wild', 1968), accompanied by simplistic and conservative lyrics; the members of MC5 ('Motor City's Burning') and Bob Seger, who all came from the predominantly working class city of Detroit (the world's largest car-manufacturing centre) produced rhythms that were close to future hard rock and lyrics that described the workers' experience in the cities.

Country music

Encouraged by Elvis's country and western hits or simply hoping to dissociate themselves from the new musical trends, a certain number of rock, folk and easy listening performers retreated to Nashville, which rapidly became America's popular music capital. Taking their stereotyped 'Western' look to extremes (cowboy hats and outfits, custom-made guitars, etc), whether they attributed greater importance to guitar (Chet Atkins, Doc Watson) or vocal (Dolly Parton, Emmylou Harris, Barbie Benton) techniques or even just plain on-stage energy (Willie Nelson, Sleepy Labeef), the Nashville artists clung on to their white roots, but gradually drifted towards easy listening music. Their glitzy Las Vegas shows, flashy patriotic statements and puritanical views on city decadence completely erased the true spirit of rock from commercial country music. With few exceptions (Johnny Cash, Jerry Lee Lewis, J J Cale and Crosby, Stills and Nash), commercial country artists never managed to transcend the limits of light music.

The ghetto song: Soul music

Black Sixties' music was never explicitly topical; black artists had had great difficulty in attracting a white following and were understandably afraid to compromise their position. The misadventures of Chuck Berry and Little Richard had taught them a lesson.

Yet it was during this period that the black struggle for civil rights had escalated to become the country's major problem. Two distinct but complementary trends evolved whose common aim was to win equal civil rights for blacks in all countries. The majority group was pacifist and more 'presentable' and run with great determination, the second was more violent and oriented towards the organization of illegal demonstrations. Martin Luther King on the one hand, and Malcolm X and his Black Muslims, Bobby Seale, Joel Carmichael and the Black Panthers on the other, used their own particular methods to attack the racist establishment. King and Malcolm X were assassinated at the end of the 1960s; Seale and Carmichael fled to Algeria to avoid heavy sentencing.

Black music from this period reflected subtly the struggle for civil rights; some songs had two meanings: thus Martha and the Vandellas 'Dancing in the Streets' was perceived as a call to riot (demonstrators modified the lyrics to 'fighting in the streets'). Otis Redding's 'Respect' was more than just a love song, it was a request for blacks to be considered as human beings, a call for respect. Aretha Franklin's 'Freedom' needs no comment, neither does 'I'm Black, I'm Proud' by James Brown, one of the first black militants.

Whether they were signed to Motown in Detroit or Stax in Memphis, all the big soul artists gave their moral support to the civil rights workers both in private and in public, sometimes to the detriment of their own musical careers. Veined with sensitivity and that curious mixture of joy and sorrow passed on from the early blues, the music produced by these artists was of an extremely high quality in terms of score arrangements, their skilled blend of sax, guitar, bass and electric organ and the particular sound that each studio sought to give its productions.

Berry Gordy for Tamla Motown aimed to get into the charts with his laid-back sound that moved soul one step closer to easy listening without compromising the music's black spirit. Produced by him, James Brown, The Miracles, Mary Wells, Marvin Gaye, the all-female groups like the Crystals, Martha and the Vandellas and the Supremes (with Diana Ross) and the all-male groups (the Four Tops and the Temptations) reached number one in the charts on numerous occasions.

The Atlantic company's sister label, Stax, was based in the South in Memphis. This company's more uncompromising outlook led it to promote a sound with a genuine blues/jazz tone, but the quality of the artists signed to Stax was immediately recognized, first by black, then by white audiences. The biggest names in soul (which the white music industry called Rhythm'n'Blues) recorded for the Stax label: hits were cut by instrumental groups (Booker T and the MG's, the Mar Keys), all-male bands (the Drifters, Sam and Dave), soloists of both sexes (Aretha Franklin, Otis Redding, Wilson Pickett, Percy Sledge, Ben E King), musicians such as King Curtis and duets including Rufus and Carla Thomas.

After the strictly segregated black and white charts were finally merged in 1963, black performers reached the top of the hit parades and were sometimes placed even ahead of the Beatles and Bob Dylan. These artists were instrumental in encouraging other people to be proud of being black, and forced the white world to recognize that blacks were quite capable of working independently while influencing all rock music. Each of the groups mentioned above had at least one of their songs borrowed by the biggest names in white rock in both Britain (the Beatles, the Rolling Stones, the Who, Them, the Yardbirds and the Animals) and the United States (Dylan, the Beach Boys, Creedence Clearwater Revival, the Doors, Jefferson Airplane, the Grateful Dead, Canned Heat, and in more recent times Springsteen, John Cougar Mellencamp and even country and western artists such as Chet Atkins and Johnny Cash).

The festivals: the end of the dream (1967–1970)

Starting in the 1950s, musical gatherings organized along the European lines of Montreux and Antibes had popularized the folk movement. The Newport (Rhode Island) festival became the model for many others in the United States, but remained a simple open-air concert.

With the exception of the Californian protest movement in the 1960s, these gatherings gradually became political rallies (in support of the civil rights movement and the anti-Vietnam war campaign) or the perfect opportunity to highlight new life-styles (the use of drugs in public, free love, ecology, etc). There were more and more of these festivals during the second half of the 1960s.

Artists from all sorts of musical backgrounds performed together on stage during these festivals, sometimes with astonishing results: Otis Redding played with the Grateful Dead, Tina Turner sang with Mick Jagger and Country Joe McDonald played with Jimi Hendrix. All the sounds and trends of 1960s rock were represented at them.

Amongst others, Otis Redding, Jimi Hendrix, the Who, the Byrds, Canned Heat, Jefferson Airplane, Booker T and the MG's and the Mamas and the Papas appeared at the Monterey festival from June 16–18, 1967. There were 50 000 spectators.

At the August 1968 Miami Pop Festival, 90 000 spectators saw Fleetwood Mac, the Grateful Dead, Steppenwolf, Chuck Berry, Marvin Gaye, the Box Tops and the Turtles live on stage.

At the Newport '69 concert held at Northbridge, 150 000 people came to see Creedence Clearwater Revival, Joe Cocker, Ike and Tina Turner, The Byrds, Johnny Winter, Booker T and the MG's, Jimi Hendrix and Taj Mahal. There were also some violent clashes with the police.

On 4 and 5 July 1969, the Atlanta Pop Festival, held in the capital of the Old South, drew a crowd of 140 000 to see Canned Heat, Led Zeppelin, Johnny Winter, Joe Cocker and Creedence Clearwater Revival. This was the first big hard rock festival, and could even be considered as the baptism of a style that was to dominate the 1970s.

The 'Woodstock Music and Arts Festival' was the biggest and most famous of all the Sixties' rock festivals. With its 450 000-strong audience and its three days of almost non-stop music, it has become a symbol: there were three deaths (due to exhaustion, a cardiac arrest and an overdose), three births, tons of hash, thousands of sugar cubes laced with LSD, couples, children, adolescents and deserters. It was a sort of rock high mass which, all things considered, was extremely peaceful: after all, most American towns with a population of 450 000 have more cases of theft

and assault in one day than were reported in the course of Woodstock's three.

A political festival (many hoped that Dylan, who owned a house at Woodstock, would put in an appearance, but were disappointed) and celebration of Sixties' culture (psychedelia, alternative ideals, pacifism and racial solidarity), Woodstock was also an extraordinary demonstration of the eclectic and tolerant nature of Sixties' rock. Although the different schools had already been defined and there was open rivalry between the genres, they all managed to co-exist peacefully. The biggest songwriters present at Woodstock remember it mainly as a joint concert that was extremely fruitful in terms of music. Santana represented Latin rock; Canned Heat, Ten Years After and Johnny Winter, rock blues; Jefferson Airplane and the Grateful Dead, psychedelic rock; and Joan Baez and Country Joe McDonald, protest song. Joe Cocker and The Who represented the English rock branch, and Crosby, Stills, Nash and Young, country rock.

After the Louisville, Texas, festival in 1969, which attracted an audience of 120 000, the movement seemed to run out of steam. The last straw was the unfortunate free Rolling Stones concert at Altamont, during which a black fan in the audience was stabbed to death by Hell's Angels. Despite the 300 000-strong crowd and the impressive list of performers, Altamont confirmed a rumour that had been in the air at Woodstock: the decade of dreams was drawing to a close, and another, more realist, was dawning. Rock counter-culture was not even able to respond to the ban put on rock festivals after the Altamont incident.

The Allman Brothers Band
Country rock bank

The pioneers of Southern rock

At the end of the 1960s, the Allman brothers developed a form of rock music that was somewhere between R & B and country music.

Born in Nashville, Duane and Gregg Allman went professional in 1965. Under various names (Allman Joy, 31 December) they played the clubs of the Deep South and built up a solid reputation thanks to their studio work with artists of both colours (Wilson Pickett, Aretha Franklin, Eric Clapton, John Hammond, and Chet Atkins). Little by little, Duane's masterly slide-guitar playing and Gregg's 'black' voice brought them fame. Their unforgettable cover versions of such classics as 'Stormy Monday' and 'Statesboro Blues' influenced all subsequent Southern rock artists. Sadly, Duane Allman was killed in a motorbike accident in 1971, and the following year, the group also suffered the tragic loss of Berry Oakley. Dicky Betts and Gregg tried to keep the band together, but the heart had gone out of it.

At Filmore East (Polydor, 1971) is as much of a must as **The Road Goes On Forever** (Capricorn, 1975) and **The Best of A.B.B.** (Polydor, 1981).

Friendship
Shortly before his death, Duane had played on Clapton's album 'Derek and The Dominos'. Visibly affected by the death of his friend, at his funeral, Clapton played an extraordinary version of 'Statesboro Blues' which was never officially released.

The Animals
English blues boom band

The unforgettable 'House of the Rising Sun'!

Mad about the blues, Eric Burdon and the other members of the band cut passionate versions of several blues standards.

This small, Newcastle-born group showed Europe and even the United States the true power of the blues. Burdon's hoarse, wild vocals and Alan Price's arrangements (Price also played keyboards) made the Animals one of the most popular and impressive groups in the British beat boom. Top of the charts on both sides of the Atlantic in 1964, 'House of the Rising Sun' was covered by many other artists, influenced the Rolling Stones, and launched the 'blues boom' wave. The group had another smash hit with 'Please Don't Let Me Be Misunderstood' then disappeared from the music scene in 1967.

Animals Anthology (1964–65) and **Best of Animals** (ABKCO, 1973) sum up the spirit of 60's heavy rock.

Greatest Hits Live (IRS, 1983) is a recording of the concert the group gave when they got back together in 1983. Interesting.

Covers
Burdon and the Animals drew their hits from the best songwriters of the era, including Little Richard, Ray Charles, Sam Cooke, Bo Diddley, John Lee Hooker and even Chuck Berry and Fats Domino.

Joan Baez
1941– Folk singer and guitarist

She set her talent to work for humanitarian causes

Inexorably associated in everyone's mind with the Sixties' protest movement and Bob Dylan, she has her own strong image and style.

The queen of folk

Baez, who made her debut at the 1959 Newport festival when she was still a student, met Bob Dylan at the 47 Club in Cambridge, Massachusetts. At that time, Dylan was only one of a horde of Greenwich Village beatniks. Seduced by his lyrics and non-conformism, she persuaded him to appear on stage with her.

This university tour, backed up by their joint appearance at the 1963 Newport festival, was to make her the most famous of the politically engaged female singers. The press were quick to understand that her relationship with Dylan, who now had his own, expanding following, was not just professional. Little by little, their on-stage partnership developed into a real artistic collaboration; Dylan wrote songs for her which she recorded in 1968 ('Any Day Now') and accompanied her on her long anti-racist and anti-war tours in 1964 and 1965.

Baez, who had discovered Dylan, ended up living in his shadow. She disapproved of the excesses to which his facetious and extremist nature led him (dangerous motorbike races, drug and alcohol abuse) and of his unfaithfulness. The couple, who were the very embodiment of the protest movement, broke up when Dylan, who was attracted to rock and sick of his political leader label, decided to start living like a star.

A well planned career

Despite her later marriage with a conscientious objector, Joan Baez never completely broke away from Dylan. One of the themes on her successful 1975 album *Diamonds and Rust*, is still expressive of her love for him.

The purity of her voice, the simplicity of her melodies which never really stray from folk despite an audible country influence, the topical nature of her lyrics and the classic, rather austere, beauty of her face were largely responsible for her successful career. With her unwavering commitment to pacifist and humanist causes she has taken part in virtually all the topical concerts in the last three decades.

Farewell Angelina (Vanguard, 1975), **Any Day Now** (Vanguard, 1969) and **Diamonds and Rust** (A/M, 1975) all testify to the extensive influence of Dylan's personality and style on her work.

Double-edged compliment
Joan Baez found Dylan's individualism hard to understand. She felt that his straying from the straight, militant path was due to an irresponsible streak in his nature. She would lecture him on this point and constantly tried to draw him away from his life as a superstar back towards a total political engagement. He ended up giving her an ambiguous nickname: 'the most beautiful nun'.

The Beach Boys

Surf music band

The most famous American group of the 1960s

*They gave rock new sounds and
complex vocal harmonies.*

Their roots

The initial line-up was organized around the three Wilson brothers, Brian, Dennis and Carl, with the added talents of Mike Love and Al Jardine. Under Brian's guidance, the group worked particularly hard on their vocal arrangements, using harmonies extracted from nascent rock. There is no doubt that the Beach Boys were strongly influenced by the works of that pioneer duet, the Everly Brothers.

The Californian Beach Boys soon gained a national and then international reputation as the only truly all-American band. Their cover of Chuck Berry's 'Sweet Little Sixteen', rebaptised 'Surfin' USA', made them stars. This song launched surf music and, more importantly, brought the centre of rock music from the Deep South to the sun-drenched, swinging beaches of California.

The victory of a style

In a very short space of time, the Beach Boys' music, a celebration of the sun and fun lifestyle of Californian youth, became immensely popular. The group's vocal work delighted fans and the quality of sound produced under Brian Wilson's direction was such that it is still astonishing today. Hit followed hit with amazing speed: 'Surfer Girl', 'Fun, Fun, Fun', 'I Get Around', 'Barbara Ann' and of course, the enormously successful 'Good Vibrations'. In the three years between 1963 and 1966, the Beach Boys left an indelible mark on American popular music.

By disassociating themselves totally from the black music of which their English counterparts were so fond, the Beach Boys were the only group to compete successfully with the wave of British bands (the Beatles, the Animals, and the Stones). The Beach Boys then can be seen as the only truly white expression of American contemporary popular music.

The fall

The group was rapidly worn out by its extended tours, the stressful recording sessions, drug abuse and internal quarrels. By the start of the 1970s, they were all but forgotten. On paper, the group still exists, but, despite a number of commercially successful songs such as 'Rock'n'Roll Music', the original creativity and drive has totally disappeared.

The Beach Boys 62–65 (double album) and **66–69** are the compilations to buy, as well as the legendary **Pet Sounds**, cut for Capitol.

Scores
The Beach Boys reached number one in the charts several times with 'I Get Around', 'Help Me, Rhonda', and 'Good Vibrations'. They got to number two with 'Barbara Ann', number three with 'Surfin USA' and number five with 'Rock'n'Roll Music'. Their other works were also commercial hits, with 80 million records sold in the 15 years of their career.

Eclipse
A perfectionist and tortured by anxiety, Brian Wilson found the unqualified success of the Beatles' album *Sergeant Pepper* hard to swallow, particularly as it had been released before what he considered to be his group's best work, an album provisionally called *Smiles*. In a fit of despair, Wilson blocked the release of his album. Shortly afterwards, he left the group and spent 20 years in self-imposed exile, before re-emerging in 1988 with an astonishing and unexpected solo album.

The Beatles
English pop group

Biggest myth in rock history

They were able to go commercial without compromising their tendency for experimentation. Their music became a movement on a world scale.

Much has been written about the Beatles' story, their shared love of English folk music, and their ability to create simple melodies or musical arrangements for extremely complex pieces. Born in Liverpool's poorer quarters, the four Beatles shot to millionaire status. They were awarded medals, were worth a fortune on the stockmarket and broke all existing world records for sales. They used drugs, started new fashions in clothes, founded independent studios, starred in films (one of which, *Yellow Submarine*, was a cartoon), introduced Europe to Indian music, made it fashionable to have a 'guru', brought the wrath of the censors down on their heads (because of the *White Album*) and, after a decade at the top of the charts, split up, casting their millions of fans into despair.

More than just a 'hit factory' (although this was undeniably part of their mystique), the Beatles incarnated a certain 'pro-gressive' spirit in rock music. In fact, they had begun their joint musical career by playing American rock hits in Liverpool and Hamburg bars, both because it was the fashion at the time, and because John Lennon identified totally with this wild and uncontrolled form of music. However, Paul McCartney was more demanding in terms of the arrangements and melodies (at least in the first few years of the group's existence) and insisted on choral work that was reminiscent of traditional English folk. The Beatles evidently had little trouble in incorporating the results already achieved by the Beach Boys and the Everly Brothers in this field into their own work. They developed a new sound, the distinctively pure and clear 'Liverpool sound'. Free from any 'heavy' influence in the early years, the Beatles sound was much closer to the Shadows than to black rock.

Rock and easy listening

The Beatles' music was to be accepted by a much larger audience from all age groups; in contrast with the Stones, with their bad boy image and loud, simplistic music, the Beatles popularized an art that really was within everyone's reach, a popular music form in the true sense of the term, that was soon to be called 'pop' music.

Thus the Beatles were not really a rock group (even if, deep down, some of the members were rock musicians); their musical intention was far from any kind of revolt. And while it is true that they started the fashion for long hair, for the 'mod' haircut, they had no desire to become inextricably linked with the growing teenage rebellion movement.

This does not mean to say that they avoided all forms of non-conformism, quite

Hair
Today, that the Beatles hair in 1963 could ever have been considered long, is astonishing. Yet, the two or three extra centimetres had an incredibly far-reaching influence on Sixties' fashions . . .

Apple
Fed up of being at the mercy of other studio owners, in February 1968 the Beatles founded their own label called Apple. Apple soon became a multi-media organization, controlling vast financial resources, producing films and records and discovering new talent. The original idea was to create a kind of anti-business, but the incompetence of its appointed heads was such that the company was soon in financial difficulties. Apple was later to release the ex-Beatles' solo albums.

the contrary. But they made sure to keep their distance from the mood of violence that typified the early 1960s.

The Beatles' aim was perhaps to bridge the gap between rock music, the restless younger generation's newest form of cultural expression, and light music, which was more popular with the older generation and was less of a challenge to the existing system. A study of the Beatles' songs proves that their lyrics are neither topical nor controversial. Some are allusive or contain elements of social criticism, but when protest song was at the height of its popularity in America, the Beatles did not release one political song. And while a few years later the Rolling Stones saluted the French students who took part in the May 1968 riots with 'Street Fighting Man', the Beatles sang 'Revolution' to declare that they, on the contrary, did not want one.

Here we touch on the real reason for the break-up of the group; the well-publicized quarrels and differences of opinion between the Beatles' wives were but the surface cause. It is clear that within the group, two conceptions of the world were opposed on the battlefield of songwriting. On the one side, there was Paul McCartney, a talented singer, songwriter and bassist, with a strong preference for popular melodies and sophisticated choral work and little interest in world affairs, and on the other, John Lennon, who constantly reiterated his predilection for rock'n'roll, harder sound,

violent vocals and more topical lyrics. The reason for the disappearance of the biggest group in rock history should be sought in this basic, irreconcilable difference, rather than in the arguments caused by the arrival of Yoko Ono, John's avant-gardist companion who was all too often blamed for the demise of the group.

Due to their shared experimental tendencies, 'to rock, or not to rock' was one of the most frequent and important questions to crop up throughout the group's career. Their first albums contain light music tempered with rocky rhythms and an electric sound. By the time of their first releases, they had already come a long way from the rock'n'roll-influenced repertoire they had used in Liverpool and Hamburg cellar bars. A few years later, the famous album *Sergeant Pepper* was symptomatic of their search for a tighter, more orchestral sound that was far from the rock being produced at that time. On the other hand, the *White Album* demonstrated both their return to more basic rock rhythms and their giving up of the pure sound popularized by the blues boom, Jimi Hendrix and nascent hard rock. Later, after they had gone their separate ways, each member of the Beatles was to pursue a solo career in his own particular field: Paul McCartney never lost his taste for tight vocal work and was highly successful with his new group, Wings; John Lennon recorded an out and out rock'n'roll album (*Rock'n'roll*) and an inflammatory double album called *Sometime in New York City*; George Harrison gave free rein to his mystical tendencies and produced 'My Sweet Lord'; and Ringo Starr proved himself as a singer and producer before attempting a career in the movies.

Thus, the blame for the Beatles' separation should be put on their innate inability to agree on artistic matters, and not, as is all too often the case, on the pressures created by the star system.

Nonetheless, the Beatles, without being a rock group, have had an extensive and far-reaching influence on rock music that continues even today. The variety of their output and the daring of their imaginative innovations prove the depth of their artistic and creative talents.

The Beatles' career

The Beatles' first album was recorded in a day. Thus the date, 26 November 1962, is an historic one, for it marked the explosive

Influences

It is no exaggeration to state that the Beatles wrote the most famous songs of the century. Beatles songs have been covered by some of the biggest stars in the music world: Wilson Pickett brought out a version of 'Hey Jude', Joan Baez 'Let it Be', Otis Redding 'Day Tripper', Joe Cocker 'With A Little Help From My Friends', Rod Stewart 'Get Back', and more recently U2 'Helter Skelter'. This, of course, is but the tip of the iceberg.

Imitated

Beatlemania is still alive and kicking today: groups like the Bangles or Bananarama have a Beatles ring; and Todd Rungren's speciality is accurate copies of their style, sometimes with surprising results. Even the 'Boss' himself, Bruce Springsteen, often rounds off his concerts with 'Twist and Shout'.

entry on to the rock scene of a group that was to overturn totally all the habits and standards created by the mainly American songwriters in the previous decade. The Beatles' arrival was to shift rock music's centre of gravity. From 1962 onwards, England became home to Western youth's new musical culture.

A careful step by step examination of the Beatles' music will give us a better understanding of the various evolutive stages in their stylistic development.

Please, Please Me. Cut in March, 1963, it was their first LP. Produced by George Martin, with a rather conventional sleeve, on which the Beatles really look like 'good boys'. Nothing particularly exciting so far. With its neat little three-minute numbers, this album was hardly rock'n'roll. However, 'Love Me Do' and 'Please, Please Me' assured the album's success. The one concession to rock, undoubtedly imposed by Lennon, was the unforgettable 'Twist and Shout' with its jumpy rhythm, screaming vocals and pounding guitar sound.

With the Beatles (November, 1963). Despite their free use of other people's works, the group still managed to include some of their own striking creations on this album, notably 'All My Loving' and 'I Wanna Be Your Man'. And despite a well-crafted cover of Chuck Berry's 'Roll Over Beethoven', *With the Beatles* is somewhat disappointing and mainly interesting for its value as an historical record of the group's development.

A Hard Day's Night (1964) is the soundtrack for the film of the same name, which naturally ensured its progression up the charts. This was the album that shot the Beatles to fame and crushed the sales records formerly held by such 'classic' rock musicians as Elvis and the Beach Boys. Three numbers included on this album are among the best produced by the Beatles throughout their long career. They are: 'A Hard Day's Night', a true rock number, which never slips into the clichés of a genre that was being suffocated by the twist; 'Can't Buy Me Love', which runs much along the same lines; and 'And I Love Her', which demonstrates Paul McCartney's ability to transform a sickly ballad into a tender love song. The rock v. light music duel (Lennon v. McCartney) carried on, albeit secretly, for all the songs were jointly credited to the two front men . . .

Beatles for Sale (Christmas, 1964) is a change-over album. 'Eight Days a Week'

and 'I'll Follow the Sun' are quality compositions. That the Beatles were still trying to move in on the rock mainstream is demonstrated by their cover versions of Little Richard's 'Kansas City', Carl Perkin's 'Honey Don't' and 'Everybody's Trying to be My Baby' and Chuck Berry's 'Rock'n'Roll Music'.

Help! (July, 1965) could be considered the best album of their first period: 'Help!', 'Ticket to Ride' and the extraordinary 'Yesterday', which has since become the group's theme song, make this album an anthology of styles from pop to lachrymose ballads.

Rubber Soul (December, 1965) is less interesting, despite 'Drive My Car,' 'Norwegian Wood', 'Nowhere Man' and especially 'Michelle' and 'Girl', which all indicate the group's increasingly high standard of vocal work.

Revolver (August, 1966) is stylistically more impressive, even if the songs on this album were not all smash hits. 'Yellow Submarine' will always be famous because of the animated film of the same name, and 'Eleanor Rigby' and 'Good Day Sunshine' are chrystallized images of their perennial indecision between rock and light music. 'Love To You' is interesting because it highlights the imaginative and innovative side of the band which, under the aegis of George Harrison, had begun to introduce an oriental touch in to its music.

Equipment

The Beatles built their sound around specialized equipment: McCartney's Hohner 'bass-violin' has accompanied him throughout his long career. Lennon liked electric Epiphones and Rickenbackers, but preferred an acoustic Gibson (both six- and twelve-string). After playing Rickenbackers for a number of years, Harrison changed over to Gibson 335s, Les Pauls and SGs. The whole group tended to use British Vox amplifiers, ensuring the company's longlasting fame. Ringo Starr always used a Ludwig drum kit.

Overview

For those who just want a quick overview of the Beatles' output, we recommend two double albums: *The Beatles (1962–1966)* and *The Beatles (1967–1970)*. Anthologies are often the target of much criticism, but the basics are all there.

From left to right: **George Harrison**, **Paul McCartney**, **John Lennon** and **Ringo Starr**.

This photo of the Beatles in rehearsal shows the extent to which the haircut that bears their name was actually rather tame and conformist, especially when compared to the later, extremist fashions associated with hard and punk rock. Nevertheless, these few extra centimetres were considered to be outrageous at the time; thought to be dirty and badly dresssed (the photo shows Lennon and Harrison typically dressed in their dark, mod suits), they were soon totally outdone by the Rolling Stones, but were always to be associated with the fashion for long hair.

Sergeant Pepper's Lonely Hearts Club Band (June, 1967) was a turning point, not only for the Beatles but for the whole of rock music. It was the album of the decade, perhaps even of the whole generation. In any case, it is an undisputed masterpiece of inventiveness and professionalism; it was thanks to this album that rock music finally won the respect of classical musicians and acquired the status of an art form in its own right. *Sergeant Pepper* is striking for the quality of its arrangements, the more ambitious nature of the lyrics and the variety of influences incorporated in to the music. Recorded in the utmost secrecy in a four-month period with the collaboration of a full philharmonic orchestra, and engineered by the talented producer, George Martin, the album was a veritable bombshell on the music scene. It was the end of a long journey, but it was also the end of an era: to blend early rock'n'roll, new innovations and an oriental influence with psychedelia and concrete music seemed an impossible challenge. And to attempt to turn that blend into a commercially successful musical genre was like challenging fate.

And yet, examined side by side, the ragtime songs ('When I'm Sixty-Four'), rock'n'roll hits ('Sergeant Pepper'), the sentimental ('With a Little Help From My Friends'), philosophical ('A Day in the Life') and psychedelic ('Lucy in the Sky with Diamonds' – note the capital letters!) ballads form a coherent whole, an artistic testament. Without falling into rock or light music clichés and without making any concessions to the demands of commercialism which would have forced them to cash in on their superstar status and thus compromise their musical integrity, the

Beatles gave a whole musical genre a second chance. In one single album, they proved that the true spirit of rock still lived on . . .

Magical Mystery Tour (Christmas, 1967, double EP soundtrack album) was a relative failure, despite the obvious quality of such numbers as 'The Fool On the Hill', 'Hello Goodbye' and especially 'Strawberry Fields Forever', 'Penny Lane' and 'All You Need Is Love'.

Yellow Submarine (November, 1968) is a disappointment because of its neutrality: there are no references to Vietnam (the Americans had just started bombing North Vietnamese towns), nor to the huge American pacifist movement, or the Paris, Berlin and Mexico riots. The only call for peace is a re-mix of 'All You Need is Love', but this is a small gesture compared to what the Stones, MC5 and Steppenwolf were producing during the same period ('Street Fighting Man', 'Motor City's Burning' and 'Born To Be Wild' respectively).

The 'White Album' (November, 1968) was the Beatles' first double album. With *Blonde on Blonde*, Dylan was the first to package two LP's together, but the Beatles had often passed over this format, even in the case of *Sergeant Pepper*. This time, Lennon and McCartney felt the need to give the public the most numbers possible, for they were aware of the group's impending split. There is a striking variety of music types on this album. The gulf between McCartney's style (ballads, vocal work, light music, the perennial three-minute number and sophisticated arrangements) and Lennon's preferences, exacerbated by the growing importance of Yoko Ono in his life, (simpler rock numbers, more topical lyrics, and a harder, more solid sound) had widened considerably. A third influence was provided by George Harrison, who had gradually shrugged off his simple lead guitarist image and was contributing an Eastern ('Within You, Without You' on *Sergeant Pepper*) and mystic element.

Thus, this double album contains all the reasons for the future separation of the Beatles. It was only an established business contract that allowed these stylistically incompatible songs to exist side by side. On the one hand, there were pleasant but inconsequential songs such as 'Hey Jude', 'Ob-La-Di, Ob-La-Da', 'Martha My Dear' and 'Honey Pie', and on the other, pure rock numbers that come close in sound to future hard rock, such as 'Helter Skelter'

and 'Revolution', classic rock songs like 'Back in the USSR' and 'Everybody's Got Something to Hide', and even some blues ('Yer Blues').

Abbey Road (1969) put an end to the rumours of the group's imminent break-up because the Beatles were bringing out another album. 'Come Together' was the only hit.

Let it Be (May, 1970) was the last album they released together. The melancholic ballad 'Let it Be' and 'Get Back', their last real rock number, were smash hits.

Sensational

With their very first hits, the Beatles posed a threat to American rock supremacy: they reached the top of the charts with four consecutive songs between February and July, 1964. Their American and European tours whipped the massive crowds into a frenzy unmatched by the concerts of the King himself.

Eccentricity

The Beatles often tried to dispel their well-behaved teen-idol image: several of their record sleeves were censored: the American version of *Yesterday and Today* shows them holding broken dolls and bloody pieces of meat. The 1968 double album is white because they had intended to pose nude for the cover.

John Lennon returned his MBE to the Queen in protest against Britain's backing of the Nigerian government during the Biafran war in 1969.

Cinema

Encouraged by the example of Elvis, but jealously watchful of their independence, the Beatles took part in a number of musicals, which contributed to the survival of rock during its most unstable period: *A Hard Day's Night* (Lester, 1964), *Help!* (Lester, 1965), *Magical Mystery Tour* (directed by the Beatles themselves in 1967) and *Yellow Submarine* (Dunning, 1968) were all released during the Beatles' heyday; in the 1970s there followed *Let it Be* (Lindsay-Hogg, 1970) *All this and World War II* (Winslow, 1978), *I Wanna be Your Hand* (Zemachis, 1978) and *Sergeant Pepper's Lonely Hearts Club Band* (Schultz, 1978).

Jeff Beck
1944– British guitarist

One of the forgotten 'guitar heroes'

One of the most talented British guitarists, Beck was gradually marginalized by his eclectic and experimental style, but he is still a model musician for many contemporary guitarists.

He became famous when he replaced another great guitarist, Eric Clapton, as the Yardbirds' lead guitarist, but he felt that the classic rock blues produced by the band were musically too simple for him.

He left for a solo career, and began to experiment with new harmonies passed on from jazz and Eastern music as well as a range of sounds produced by all kinds of effects boxes which, along with Jimi Hendrix, he was the first to use. Adopted by other musicians, the results of these experiments gave momentum to the young fuzz rock (which later became heavy metal and hard rock) and psychedelic movements.

In 1967, he formed the Jeff Beck Group with Rod Stewart on vocals and Ron Wood on guitar and bass, but preferred to withdraw from the music scene to spend more time experimenting with new sounds. He still continues to release albums today.

The Jeff Beck Group (68–69) (Pathé, 1972) and **Wired** (CBS, 1976) are both absolute musts.

The 'talking box'
Jeff invented a device about which much has been written. The talking box is a tube which links the guitarist's mouth with his guitar which in turn is connected to a synthesizer, giving the impression that the guitar is singing the guitar lines with a human voice.

The Bee Gees
Mainstream British rock group

They changed with the times

Their undeniable success is matched only by their complete lack of originality.

The three Gibb brothers were born in England, emigrated to Australia in 1958, then came back to Britain in 1967 to begin their long and carefully planned career: with their Beatles and commercial American rock sound-alikes, they were often highly placed in the charts, but hit the jackpot with the flower power number 'Massachusetts'. 'I Started a Joke' was an immensely popular single with disc jockeys.

After a brief separation, the brothers, with great foresight, got back together just in time for disco mania, releasing their hugely successful singles 'Saturday Night Fever' and 'Staying Alive'. Barry Gibb's later work with Barbra Streisand ('Woman in Love' and 'Guilty'), Kenny Rogers and Dionne Warwick show the brothers' musical versatility.

Bee Gees Gold (RSO, 1976) is a decent compilation.

Failures
The Bee Gees (their name is from the 'Brothers Gibb') had an unfortunate experience with a concept album, *Odessa*, in 1969, and also with their iconoclastic disco version of the Beatles' 'Sergeant Pepper'. These two failures cost the brothers a lot, both financially and psychologically.

Mike Bloomfield

1944–81   White blues guitarist

Virtuoso

When the blues went out of fashion, Bloomfield virtually disappeared from the music scene.

Born into a cultured Chicago family, from a tender age Mike took a lively interest in the black music that was so popular in his home town. By his teens, he had already learnt B B King's guitar techniques. Recruited as the first white American blues band's lead guitarist, he played on Dylan's historic single 'Like a Rollin' Stone' (on the *Highway 61 Revisited* album) and backed the king of folk rock at the Newport festival which marked his definitive break with the acoustic folk movement. Bloomfield's career got bogged down in a blues rut and, as a rather solitary artist, isolated by his purist ideals, the 1970s were extremely difficult for him. Worn out by life, he died in 1981.

The Live Adventures (CBS, 1979) is worth buying, but is hard to find.

Between the High Place and the Ground (CBS, 1979) is a well-crafted blend of technical mastery and emotion.

The decline
Disgusted by the commercial nature of Seventies' rock, Bloomfield made his living by writing the soundtracks for second-rate porn movies.

The Paul Butterfield Blues Band

White blues band

Pioneers of the blues boom

Trained by watching and playing with the leading black musicians in Chicago's South Side, this white blues band influenced all Seventies' rock.

Today we can sum up just how very important Butterfield's band, with their passionate love of the blues, was in the development of Sixties' and Seventies' rock.

Their hour of glory came when they accompanied Dylan at the 1965 Newport festival. With Paul Butterfield on harmonica and vocals, Mike Bloomfield on guitar and Mark Naftalin on keyboards, the band backed Dylan with a powerful and modern rhythm, then carried on in pursuit of their own independent career. However, they continued to be instrumental in the evolution of some of the most famous artists of the time, such as Eric Clapton and Jeff Beck, and even some of the groups which were making a name for themselves, including Fleetwood Mac and the Rolling Stones.

East West (Elektra–WEA, 1966) is a rare pearl.

Live (WEA, 1971) is a must.

Gratitude
Thanks to the backing of certain major songwriters such as Little Walter and Muddy Waters, the Paul Butterfield Blues Band was the first white blues band to tread the boards of Chicago's black blues clubs.

The Byrds

Folk rock group

Their search for new sounds and techniques was endless

With its highly experimental nature, this band was the first to link folk rock music with the arrangements produced by rock'n'roll.

Their first hits

The initial Byrds line-up was centred on two exceptionally talented musicians, Roger McGuinn and David Crosby. Attracted by the rich melodic variety offered by white folk which they hoped to amplify electrically without compromising the advances in the field of choral work obtained by the Everly Brothers and the Beach Boys, the Byrds had a smash hit with their version of the Dylan number 'Mr Tambourine Man' in April 1965, which sold more than a million copies.

This master stroke was their 'open sesame' to the world of show-business, and

Break up

With their 1965 version of 'Mr Tambourine Man', the Byrds made Bob Dylan famous. Relations between the two were excellent until Dylan, the creator of 'protest song' grew weary of his political leader label and withdrew into a neutralism that was ill-received by his admirers, including the Byrds who continued to play at pacifist rallies until the 1970s.

The Turtles

This Californian folk rock group, which reached fame with their unforgettable 'Happy Together' (1967) also brought out an extraordinary cover version of Dylan's 'It Ain't Me Babe'.

they were soon topping the charts worldwide with another cover version, this time of Pete Seeger's 'Turn, Turn, Turn'. With this single, the Byrds played a central role in the creation of an exceptionally successful genre; folk rock joined quality lyrics with a modern scoring which was resolutely adapted to the fashion of the times. For their albums, they recorded other Dylan tracks ('All I Really Want to Do', 'Lay Down Your Weary Tune') side by side with daring and innovative numbers. The band continually looked for new sounds, each of their songs pushed back the limits of the whole of rock music.

Further and further

The band was quick to orientate itself towards the unexplored areas of music, starting with 'space rock'. This new style was easily recognizable for its use of the most up-to-date technology, machines that, in effect, were the forefathers of today's synthesizers. 'Fifth Dimension' and 'Younger than Yesterday' can be considered as the first truly synthesized rock songs. There is a direct link between them and the progressive, visionary rock produced by Pink Floyd. Furthermore, changes in the band's line-up and the recruitment of Gram Parsons resulted in the release of one of country music's major albums, *Sweetheart of the Rodeo* (1968). In addition to this, the band was also responsible for the album *Eight Miles High* with its audible oriental influence. Despite a successful world tour at the start of the 1970s and the release of an interesting album (*The Byrds*) in 1973, the band, exhausted by the endless squabbling between members, lost its creative momentum.

Mr Tambourine Man (double album, CBS, 1965) is a collection of the band's early numbers.

History of the Byrds (double album, CBS, 1973) is a representative compilation of all their work.

Canned Heat

Boogie blues band

The most authentic of the white blues bands

An association of rural blues fans and Chicago blues players, this Californian band popularized a particular style.

Return to the fountainhead

Canned Heat was conceived by two expert musicologists, Bob Hite and Al Wilson. Between them, they owned several thousand albums known as 'race records', extremely rare jazz, boogie, and acoustic rural blues recordings from the Twenties and Thirties and unabridged copies of the works of some of the greatest Chicago songwriters. In the blues tradition, Bob Hite, the singer, took the name 'the Bear', because of his size and bushy beard. Al Wilson called himself 'Blind Owl' becausaue of his large glasses. These two front men recruited world class musicians (guitarist Henry 'Sunflower' Vestine and bass player Larry 'the Mole' Taylor). The band was all the rage in West Coast clubs with their electrically amplified blues, a skilful blend of true blues and the energy produced by rock music.

In the autumn of 1968, their single 'On the Road Again' (composed by Jim Oden) set them on the road to stardom. It was the first white blues single to break the million copies sold barrier. The shockwave created by the catchy harmonica backing (adapted from a John Lee Hooker riff), the hypnotic instrumental arrangements and Al Wilson's falsetto, fluid vocals was such that it even reached Europe.

The glory

In the following year, they appeared at Woodstock, and their song 'Goin' Up

Country', which had also sold over a million copies, was chosen to be used behind the opening credits of the first documentary made about this historic gathering of Sixties' rebellious youth. In 1970, Canned Heat persuaded John Lee Hooker to collaborate on a joint album with them. The result was *Hooker'n'Heat*, and in 1973, Little Richard himself accepted a similar invitation which produced *The New Age*. However, the creative momentum had gone. Rock was becoming more and more commercial, and the accidental death of the irreplacable Al Wilson completely broke what was left of the band's spirit. Bob Hite also died prematurely in 1981.

The band's influence was far-reaching: such diverse performers as John Mayall, Eric Clapton, even the Rolling Stones, then all the Southern rock musicians (Molly Hatchett, Lynyrd Skynyrd and, more recently, ZZ Top) owe a great deal to Canned Heat.

Boogie with Canned Heat (Liberty, 1968) is a veritable diamond mine, with 'On the Road Again', 'Amphetamine Annie', 'One King Favor' and 'Fried Hockey Boogie' featuring amongst the titles.

The Very Best of Canned Heat (EMI. Manhattan, 1987) is the best CD compilation.

Collectors
Canned Heat records are hard to find. We recommend all of the following: *Canned Heat 70, Concert Live in Europe* (Liberty), *Future Blues* (Liberty), *Halleluja* (Liberty) and *Living the Blues* (Liberty). Those unable to find the above could try *History of Canned Heat* or *The Very Best of Canned Heat* (United Artists).

Eric Clapton

1945– English singer and guitarist

Blue-eyed boy of the 'blues boom'

This master, whose career is remarkable for its troughs and peaks, has influenced all contemporary rock guitarists.

'God'

Between 1964 and 1970, Clapton was the figurehead of rock music; an inventive and precocious virtuoso, he perfected an amazing and new technique on the guitar; his fluid and laid-back style, coupled with what, for the time, was an incredible speed, earned him the nicknames 'God' and 'Slow Hand' (due to the smooth and flowing movement of his hand on the neck of the guitar). He began his career with the Yardbirds, and in 1963 accompanied the Chicago harmonica player Sonny Boy Williamson on his British tour (*Sonny Boy Williamson and the Yardbirds*, L and R Records, Bellaphon, 1980). He then

Admiration

Jimi Hendrix only agreed to the English tour which made him famous because he was promised a meeting with Eric Clapton.

Tastes

According to Clapton, the best records in his collection are *Best of Muddy Waters* and *Best of Little Walter*. This explains a lot.

Useful

Some records on which Clapton has played have become monuments in rock history: 'While my Guitar Gently Weeps' with the Beatles, the third side of the double album *Sometime in New York City* with John Lennon, the soundtrack of *Tommy* with The Who, the concert in aid of Bangladesh and *The London Sessions* with the blues artist Howling Wolf.

joined John Mayall's group, The Bluesbreakers, with whom he recorded an unforgettable album (*Blues-breakers with Eric Clapton*, Decca, 1965) which won over a great majority of the Sixties' rockers to the blues.

The Clapton Style

First and foremost, this 18-year-old guitarist had set about learning the blues; from adolescence onwards, he taught himself to sight-read the music of the black blues players from the South (like Robert Johnson, Big Bill Broonzy, Blind Blake and Brownie MacGhee) and from Chicago (like Muddy Waters, John Lee Hooker, Jimmy Reed and Elmore James) note by note. However, his true idol is the guitarist Freddie King, whose style owed much to B B King, but who used 'pure' sound to its full potential. Clapton later recorded an extraordinary version of 'Further on up the Road' (*Freddie King, 1936–1976*, Polydor, 1977) with him.

While he remained faithful to the blues, Clapton's interest in the new effects boxes that were appearing on the market inclined him more towards sound experiment which was the ultimate in fashion at the end of the 1960s; Clapton and Hendrix were the first to use a 'wah-wah' pedal, and the distortion effects of 'delay' and 'chorus'. His blues were to take on a distinctly psychedelic tone immediately after he joined Blind Faith in 1968, following the demise of Cream, that legendary group whose meteoric rise brought Clapton phenomenal fame (*Cream, Wheels of Fire*, Polydor).

With a new group, Derek and the Dominos, he recorded a superb double album which drew together all the musical trends of the time: slow and fast blues, endless solos with his friend and colleague Duane Allman of the Allman Brothers, pop melodies and psychedelic arrangements. The resulting compositions, 'Layla', 'Key to the Highway' and 'Have You Ever Loved a Woman' emerged as music's *ne plus ultra* at the end of the 1960s.

Phoenix

The death of his friend Duane Allman, excessive use of hard drugs and personal problems (his love affair with the wife of his best friend George Harrison, the former Beatle, threw him into a crisis of self-doubt and recrimination) upset the delicate balance of a personality struggling with the pressures of sudden fame.

Clapton the star broke down and, despite a number of remarkable hits like cover versions of J J Cale's 'Cocaine' and Bob Marley's 'I Shot the Sheriff' (which, incidentally, popularized reggae), stopped writing, withdrawing totally into himself. The 1970s were difficult for this god with feet of clay, who was reduced to selling all his guitars to pay for drugs and spells in detoxification centres. Only one album recorded during this period, *E C Was Here*, showed any unique talent, characterized by an obsessional desire for a return to the blues of a bygone age in those dark days when rock had stagnated to become just one more commercialized form amongst a mass of others.

Five years later an emotionally stable and drug-free Clapton made an impressive comeback with the ideal tour, which resulted in *Just One Night*, one of the best blues records by a white artist since the 1960s. At the beginning of the 1980s Clapton, the most influential guitarist since Jimi Hendrix, was again a force to be reckoned with.

Today he produces highly polished albums on a regular basis, accompanied by tours and personal appearances, all of which have brought him back into the public eye and boosted his professional self-esteem: Clapton the god has become Clapton the man, and it's better that way.

John Mayall Bluesbreakers with Eric Clapton (Decca, 1965), a must like **Derek and the Dominos: Layla** (double album, Polydor, 1973) to get an idea of his early career.

Slowhand (RSO), **E C Was Here** (RSO,

1976) his best album produced in the Seventies.

Just One Night (double album, RSO, 1980), a masterpiece.

Backtrackin' (double album, Polydor, 1984), an excellent compilation covering his whole career, to which some prefer **Time Pieces** (1979), which is more concise but also pleasant to listen to.

Cream

The 'power trio' formula (guitar, bass, drums), popularized by Jimi Hendrix, made Cream a leader in rock avant-gardism. In two meteoric albums, Eric Clapton, Jack Bruce and Ginger Baker became one of the myths of the Sixties: 'Sunshine of your Love', 'Strange Brew', 'Badge', and 'Crossroads' became progressive rock classics.

Fresh Cream (Polydor, 1967), *Disraeli Gears* (Polydor, 1967) and *Wheels of Fire* (Polydor, 1968) influenced rock history.

Easily influenced

Photographs of Clapton taken from the start of his career to the present day show the various changes in his image. From 1964 to 1969, he played a Gibson like his mentor Freddie King, wore his hair long and dresssed like an English 'mod' in tight suits. Then, after he met Hendrix, he had his hair permed, sported multi-coloured fringed jackets and used a Fender Stratocaster. During the 1970s, when he admired Dylan, he appeared on stage in a black jacket and played a black Stratocaster like his idol of the time. During the 1980s he became slightly more autonomous, but his friendship with Mark Knopfler of Dire Straits has somewhat influenced both his image and his style. Clapton could never be accused of narcissism. He is a rock legend but has always been modest. The last album *Journey Man* (1989) shows him bearded with long hair, self-confident and at ease.

Eric Clapton

Joe Cocker
1944– British vocalist

The black voice of white rock

His speciality was and still is soul music.

He had his first hit with a cover version of the Beatles' 'With a Little Help from My Friends' to which he brought a strong R & B influence, particularly in terms of vocals. In 1968, he became a star.

His 1970 tour, *Mad Dogs and Englishmen* resulted in an album and a film. 'The Letter', 'Cry Me a River' and 'Honky Tonk Woman' were all Top Ten hits.

During the 1970s, Cocker gradually slid into a tragic drug- and alcohol-induced oblivion from which he only emerged in 1982, with the theme song from the award-winning film *An Officer and a Gentleman*. The recent success of 'Unchain My Heart' consolidated the comeback of one of British rock's most enchanting voices.

Mad Dogs and Englishmen (double album, CBS, 1970) is also available on video cassette and CD.

Sheffield Steel (Capitol, 1983) and **Unchain My Heart** (Capitol, 1986) show that he has lost none of his talent.

Cinema
Cocker sings one of the principal songs on the soundtrack for the film $9\frac{1}{2}$ *Weeks*, 'You Can Leave Your Hat On', to which the heroine, played by Kim Basinger, does her torrid strip-tease.

Leonard Cohen
1934– Canadian singer and guitarist

Writer, poet and singer

He was perhaps the most poetic and sensitive of the Sixties' singer-songwriters.

In purely musical terms, Cohen never really managed to break away from folk melodies and can therefore not be called a rock star.

However, there was a time when, with his highly polished poetry and melancholic melody lines, he was generally considered as Dylan's most serious rival. He relaunched the fashion for intimate, personal lyrics, championed the later stages of protest song and became a widely respected artist.

His records are distinctive for his wistful style, his slow, almost hypnotic diction and his deep, drawn out vocals.

Greatest Hits (CBS) is a well-crafted compilation.

Songs of Leonard Cohen, **Songs from a Room**, **Songs of Love and Hate** (CBS, 1968, 1969, 1971) are indispensable to fans of this Canadian singer-poet.

Love
Cohen's love songs, including the hits 'Suzanne' and 'So Long Marianne', were his most commercially successful compositions.

Donovan
1946— British folk singer and guitarist

Following in Dylan's footsteps

He initially made a name for himself as part of the folk movement, but soon branched off down a different musical track.

Born in Glasgow, Donovan and his family moved to London when he was ten. With his anglicized Dylan look, his break came with an appearance on a TV music programme. Like Dylan, he was later to 'go electric' and enter the American charts with numbers such as 'Sunshine Super-man' which was number one in August 1966.

'Mellow Yellow' confirmed his extra-ordinary (but ephemeral) popularity. From 1967 to 1969 Donovan was very active musically, and seemed determined to remain at the forefront of the rock scene.

However, his style gradually and inevitably had to give way to the increas-ingly sophisticated score arrangements being popularized by 'spacey' and hard rock and the massive concerts organized by the supergroups. He appeared at the Wight festival before disappearing from the music scene.

The Universal Soldier (Epic, 1966) and **Open Road** (CBS) are still on sale today. **Greatest Hits** (CBS) is a good CD compilation.

Anti-militarism
Donovan frequently attacked war and the military establishment with numbers such as 'The Universal Soldier' (1966–67) and 'Little Tin Soldier', a stance which was confirmed by his appearance at Amnesty's Secret Policeman's Ball and the Los Angeles Peace Sunday Festival in the 1980s.

The Doors
Californian psychedelic group

To the very limits of poetic experience

With his deceptively angelic looks, Jim Morrison, poet and singer, contributed exceptional melodies and lurid lyrics to rock music.

It is very difficult to classify music and lyrics as original as those produced by the Doors. Their sound, which was influenced by what was then called psychedelia, and their lyrics, obviously composed under the influence of hard drugs, had that luminary, sometimes devilish aura typical of extremist creative spirits. A member of the student protest movement, Jim Morrison was both well educated and intelligent. In order to develop a music form that was similar to West Coast acid rock (Jefferson Airplane, the Grateful Dead, Quick Silver Messsenger Service) but, in terms of actual content, was closer to early Dylan or MC5, Morrison drew his creative energy from an uncompromising rebellion and a total rejection of all established systems.

However, the Sixties' spirit died the moment the Doors became a cult group. Doors lyrics are variously nihilist ('The End'), or overtly erotic ('Light My Fire'), they vindicate drug use and develop the theme of disenchantment with the system in

Jim Morrison

general ('Summer's Almost Gone'). *Absolutely Live* and *L A Woman* show that the creative talent which inspired their first album, *The Doors* (1967) had not burned out. 'Riders on the Storm' is all the more moving because it was released posthumously, Jim Morrison having died of a lethal cocktail of drugs and alcohol in Paris in 1971. As was the case with Hendrix, Jim Morrison's accidental death plunged the rock world into despair: where would the craziness stop? Were all the best performers going to share the same fate as their fellow musicians Brian Jones of the Rolling Stones, Jimi Hendrix and Janis Joplin?

From 1972, Richards and Clapton attempted to free themselves from the slavery of drug addiction, sometimes with extreme difficulty. Morrison provoked a new awareness of the problems associated with stardom, for his loss was one of the most severely felt in Seventies' rock.

The Doors (Elektra–WEA, 1967) is a must.

L A Woman, An American Prayer and **Morrison Hotel** (WEA, 1970, 1971, 1978) are very characteristic of the band.

Acid
'If the doors of perception were cleansed, everything would appear to man as it is, infinite' . . . the band took its name from this line by William Blake, which also demonstrates their proclivity for sensory experience. Morrison and Ray Manzarak, a student of film studies at the University of Los Angeles, shared a weakness for strong hallucinogenics, heroin and alcohol, emulating their idols, the doomed French poets Baudelaire, Rimbaud and Verlaine.

Improvisation
This was the band's speciality, which almost became an institution in terms of lyrics (The End', 'An American Prayer'), melodies and score arrangements ('Celebration of the Lizard') as well as the actual stage presentation. Jim Morrison's stage act is one of the most elaborate ever to be developed.

Symbol
The song 'The End' was used behind the opening credits of Coppola's *Apocalypse Now!* (1979); in general atmosphere and its despairing lyrics, the song is ideally suited to the image commonly held of the last days of a bloody war.

Provocation
Aware of his beauty and encouraged by his admiring fans of both sexes, Morrison was wont to strip on stage. However, he had a brush with the police when he exposed his private parts during a concert in Miami in 1969. The video recordings of this event still exist: the police interrupt the show, climb on stage, handcuff the singer and remove him by force.

Bob Dylan

1941– Folk and folk rock singer and guitarist

Rock's first true poet

An unpredictable and tormented character, staunchly individualist and supremely original, Dylan continues to inspire other musicians today.

There is no question that throughout his career Dylan, whether mockingly, or out of vanity or necessity, has told a number of fantastic tales about his adolescence, his personal problems and the exact conditions under which he wrote the best of his works. Thus, any biography of this artist is necessarily incomplete and inconclusive, not only because the details of his private life are deliberately rather vague, but also because Dylan is still alive and, therefore, still capable of surprising us.

The folk period, 1961–1963

The son of modest Jewish shopkeepers, Robert Zimmermann was born in the small midwestern town of Duluth. Not long after his birth, the family moved to Hibbing, a mining town close to the Canadian border where Bob attended school. Early rock'n'roll and motorbikes seemed to be his sole interests in life, although he had a relationship with Echo Helstrom (the girl from the song 'The Girl from the North Country'). After his early teenage rock'n'roll period, he discovered folk music and was fully converted after reading *Bound for Glory*, singer and guitarist Woodie Guthrie's autobiography, which proved his belief that topical lyrics were superior to those of rock.

Crowned an intellectual thanks to his decision to drop out of university ('you don't learn anything interesting'), he left for New York. The legend begins . . . Did he, as he stated to the students slumming it in Greenwich Village to 'give his image an

boost', really lead the life of a wandering singer in the rural areas of the Deep South? Was he really acquainted with Big Joe Williams? In short, did he really discover the blues 'on the job' and not in New York record shop stacks? We will never know for sure.

One thing is certain, he did actually arrive in Greenwich Village, the hang-out of New York intellectuals, in early 1961 at the age of 20. At that time, he could only just play the guitar, had the most basic of

Taking advantage?
Those who take Dylan's religious crises seriously might be interested to hear a quote from the master himself: 'There is money to be made on the road to heaven . . .' Self-explanatory.

Speciality
Throughout his career, Dylan has been the self-appointed commentator on political news items, to which he attempted to draw attention. A few examples are:
'Talking' John Birch Society Blues', on white extremists;
'Only a Pawn in Their Game' on the assassination of a black leader;
'Oxford Town' on police repression;
'Who Killed Davy Moore?' on the death of a boxer in the ring;
'Hurricane' on the incarceration of a boxer accused of murder;
'Ballad of Donald White' on juvenile delinquency;
'The Lonesome Death of Hattie Caroll' on the murder of a black servant by her employers' son;
'Ballad of Horace Brown' on a suicide in a poor black quarter;
'North Country Blues' on the closure of mines and unemployment;
'George Jackson' on the murder of a black leader in prison; and
'John Wesley Harding' and 'Knockin' On Heaven's Door' present 19th-century outlaws in a positive light.

harmonica-playing techniques and swore by his idol, Woodie Guthrie. Shown the ropes by skilled musicians (Dave Van Ronk and Ric Von Schmidt) who also gave him a roof over his head, Dylan made quick progress, assimilated the techniques and influences current in the Village at the time and managed to get a few gigs in the capital and Cambridge.

Thanks to Jack Elliot's backing and a number of successful performances (he played Gerde's and Club 47 as the supporting act for such greats as John Lee Hooker), he was automatically accepted into east coast beat circles. Before a year had gone by, he had played on a track for a Harry Belafonte album and had brought himself to the attention of John Hammond, who got him a contract with CBS.

Dylan's first record was released in October 1961. Marked by what he had learnt from Dave Van Ronk ('House of the Risin' Sun') and Ric Von Schmidt ('Baby Let Me Follow You Down'), with a strong Woodie Guthrie and rural blues influence, it was an extraordinary tribute to the music of the past; purist in the extreme, the record was a commercial failure, but won Dylan the respect of the 'Village' critics.

The leader, 1963–1965

One year later, Dylan was producing work that was 'whiter', more original and more modern in tone: his second album, *Freewheelin'*, contains the song 'Blowin' in the Wind'; it was the polished Peter, Paul and Mary version of this song that brought Dylan to public prominence. From then on, the situation changed with incredible speed. Between 1963 and 1964, he gradually emerged as the undisputed leader of the nascent protest movement with extremely popular topical songs attacking the army ('Masters of War'), the Ku Klux Klan ('Only a Pawn in Their Game'), the police ('Oxford Town'), the legal system ('The Lonesome Death of Hattie Caroll'), political and economic leaders ('With God on Our Side' and 'North Country Blues' respectively) and finally, society as a whole ('The Times They Are a-Changin'').

The protest generation now had its prophet, a sort of uglier, but shrewder and fiercer, James Dean.

First split, 1965–1966

Suze Rotolo, who featured with Dylan on the sleeve of *Freewheelin'*, was replaced by the beautiful high priestess of folk, Joan Baez. Seduced by the talent of the man who was to become her lover and her protégé, and heavily involved in the pacifist and civil-rights movements, she dragged Dylan along in her wake, but little by little it was he who became the star, for he had great difficulty in playing the part of 'Mr Joan Baez'. Moreover, his innate unpredictability and constant self-derision made it impossible for him to take his role as the king of protest song (imposed on him by the media) seriously.

At this time, one of Dylan's greatest assets, that ability to assimilate all kinds of influences with incredible speed, surfaced: contact with the music being produced by the Beatles, the Stones and the British blues rock artists, and the example of the Byrds' transatlantic success (with 'Mr Tambourine Man', one of Dylan's own compositions) encouraged him to amplify his folk. Sacrilege . . . for his Village admirers, it was his fall from glory: Dylan appeared on stage at the pure folk Newport festival with a Stratocaster! For 20 minutes, while the crowd heckled and booed, Dylan and the Paul Butterfield Band patiently played the introduction to 'Ballad of a Thin Man', waiting for the noise to stop, which it eventually did. Round one to Dylan. He lost many of his original fans, but on the other hand, he won some over from the Beatles, Animals and Stones followings.

However, the changeover to electric amplification was not his only break with the past. Slowly but surely, Dylan's art underwent a profound modification. He gave up the topical songs characteristic of his début in favour of poetry abounding with daring metaphors and symbolism and a jerky syntax, virtual automatic writing, that would not disgrace the pen of a surrealist. At the same time, he broke with

Topical songs

Popularizer of protest songs, songs which analyse the more dubious aspects of 'The System', Dylan has produced a large number of texts of this type: 'Blowin' In The Wind', 'Talkin' World War III Blues', 'A Hard Rain is Gonna Fall' and 'With God on Our Side' are all to do with war. 'Like a Rollin' Stone' and 'Ballad of the Thin Man' are on conformism and education. 'It's Allright, Ma' is an overview of all that can go wrong in society.

Bob Dylan

the left-wing groups, fell out with Tom Paxton and the Byrds, left Joan Baez, led the life of a rock star, started to take drugs and cultivated a deliberately provocative style that was designed to win over the younger generation. Symbol of the free spirit, at this stage Dylan was close to being engulfed by the 'System'. The 'king of protest song' became the 'electric prophet', the 'heavenly tramp'. It was time for another change . . .

Withdrawal, 1966–1971

The release of *Bringin' it All Back Home* and *Highway 61 Revisited* marked the high point of Dylan-the-poet's career. By the beginning of 1966, he had already sold over 10 million records. However, his personal life was but an endless, uncontrolled series of all kinds of excess.

On 29 July 1966, he was involved in a serious motorbike accident, which seemed to be the shock he needed to bring him down to earth. A year's convalescence gave him time to think . . . He turned to the Jewish religion, got married and rarely left his Woodstock home, much to the consternation and bewilderment of his fans.

The album *John Wesley Harding* marked his return to simple lyrics and folk music. But a year later, he released *Nashville Skyline* which intimates his entry into the hyper-reactionary world of white country music.

At the Isle of Wight festival in 1969, he openly ridiculed the audience. In that same year, he failed to appear at Woodstock, but did a TV show with Johnny Cash. This was the last straw. Dylan lost most of his fans and plunged into the facile jet-set life. It could not last.

The return of the rebel, 1971–1976

Musically out of his depth and incapable of producing anything to equal the dazzling lyrics that had rolled effortlessly from his pen between 1964 and 1966, Dylan fell back on contemporary causes célèbres: in 1971, he took part in the massive concert in aid of Bangladesh, cut a single about the prison murder of black leader George Jackson, and wrote the sound track for Sam Peckinpah's film *Billy the Kid*, in which he had a small, rather enigmatic, part. He completely turned his back on show-business, preferring to organize a tour of small clubs, which he called the Rolling Thunder Review. Paradoxically (but inevitably), by the end of the tour, the small clubs had become stadiums filled to capacity.

After the huge success of the world tour with The Band, which was consolidated by the release of *Before the Flood* in 1974, the Rolling Thunder Review was no longer fun, but had become a chore. In 1976, he was back in the studio to record another topical song, 'Hurricane', which was instrumental in obtaining the release from prison of a black boxer unjustly accused of murder.

The next step, 1977–1985

1977 was the year of his divorce from Sara; five children, lots of memories and huge alimony payments forced him back on the road: his film *Renaldo and Clara* was a flop, but the tour went well. The double album *Live at Budokan*, recorded in Japan, was a hit. In Paris, under the twofold pressure of fashion and his audience, he gave what amounted to a hard rock concert.

Musically burned out, Dylan again looked around for new styles: shortly after his conversion to Christianity, he met Mark Knopfler, the talented lead guitarist of the British group, Dire Straits. *Slow Train Coming* (1979) is steeped in his new militant spirit (which, incidentally, was strongly opposed by his original fans) and is a masterpiece in terms of the arrangements, many of which must be attributed to Knopfler; following this, apart from the album *Real Live* (from the 1984 tour) and a well-crafted return to rock (*Infidels*, 1986), Dylan seemed to be looking for a new lease of life. Towards the end of 1988, he gave an aggressive 'basic' rock concert in Los Angeles, backed by two young musicians whose overall style owed much to punk. How far was he going to go?

Dylan's 'art'

His guitar technique is not particularly sophisticated. Dylan is adequate on the acoustic guitar, but mediocre on the electric. He is first and foremost a songwriter. His harmonica-playing may be instantly recognizable, but it is also very basic. In short, he has always preferred to surround himself with high class musicians rather than work on his technique. Al Kooper, Mike Bloomfield, The Band musicians, Carlos Santana, Mick Taylor and Mark Knopfler have all come to his aid.

As far as his lyrics are concerned, the quality has been uneven throughout his long career. His first songs are lucid, topical and use little imagery. Then, from 1964, he made free with the techniques developed by the symbolists and surrealists. His poems become complex, obscure, cabbalistic, even. He used a stream of baroque images and striking metaphors to evoke both his personal problems and socio-political reality. His last militant period (the Christian one) was an attempt at blending religious fervour, social message and symbolist poetry . . .

Dylan's melodies have also clearly evolved: in the 1970s, Sixties' folk and folk rock gave way to stronger rhythms and an altogether harder sound, boosted by black backing vocalists and violins inherited from white folk music. At the start of the 1980s, he seems to have been most impressed by the Dire Straits sound. More recently, he has returned to a crude and primitive style, notwithstanding various experiments with the Jamaican rock sound.

Dylan respects nothing, not even his own 'classics'. His many changes in direction could be attributed to a constant search for new sounds, innate eclecticism, or even pure opportunism. Everyone agrees on this point: Dylan only has to walk around a studio where 10 musicians are working on 10 different pieces, to be able to produce his own piece which synthesizes the rest within the hour.

This extraordinary talent, present in the earliest days of his career, has never left him.

The Dylan 'persona'

From his earliest days as a performer, Dylan has systematically cultivated his reputation for unpredictability, and actively encouraged the confusion surrounding everything that concerns him: he refused to take a particular political stance, although it was he who created the fashion for political commitment, then made a 180-degree turn at a time when all the other musicians were playing at being rock stars. A non-practising Jew, then anti-religious, he returned to the bosom of Judaism, then converted to Christianity, and finally sneered at the whole of religion. He played at being unconventional, but got married and had five children. He refused the role of leader, but considered himself a genius, then later stated that he was not sure of his talent. He despises his fans (he never says either 'hello' or 'goodbye' in concert), but keeps abreast of changing tastes. He takes part in charity concerts but demands astronomical fees, although he sometimes plays for nothing at all.

Freewheelin' (CBS, 1962), **Bob Dylan: The Times They Are a-Changin'** (CBS, 1964) are representative of his folk débuts.

Bringin' It All Back Home and **Highway 61 Revisited** (CBS, 1964) are both musts.

Blonde on Blonde (CBS, 1966). Some believe this album to be his masterpiece of the 1960s.

Before the Flood (Asylum, 1974) is more typical of the 1970s.

Slow Train Coming (CBS, 1979) contains perhaps his best arrangements.

Live At Budokan (CBS, 1978) is a good double album; the more recent **Real Live** (CBS, 1984) makes good use of the presence of ex-Rolling Stone Mick Taylor.

Oh, Mercy (CBS, 1989) shows a certain return of the creative spirit.

Hope

The organizers of the Woodstock concert had chosen that site precisely because Dylan had a house there. It was to this house that he had withdrawn with his family for the year of his convalescence after his motorbike accident. Everyone thought he would appear as a guest star. His appearance would have crowned the event. Dylan never turned up, and many of the people present were left extremely disappointed.

Jimi Hendrix

1942–70   Experimental rock singer and guitarist

Comet

The three years of his public career were enough to throw all the accepted basics of rock music into question. An inventive and hyper-sensitive virtuoso, Hendrix is still considered to be one of the most important figures of rock history.

Début

Jimi Hendrix's looks (above average height, slim build, frizzy hair and yellow-brown skin) were inherited from his black father and his Cherokee Indian mother. His mother died when he was still quite young, and it was his father who bought him a guitar and taught him the basics of jazz and the blues. Jimmy (who was not yet 'Jimi') was soon the star of various amateur bands, then joined the 101st Paratroop regiment. Based in Texas, he came into contact with a number of well-known artists, whom he later supported on tour when, after two years as a paratrooper, an injury sustained during his 26th parachute jump forced him to leave his regiment. This was where he had his real 'lessons', with performers such as B B King, Ike and Tina Turner, the Isley Brothers and even Little Richard, Otis Redding and Sam Cooke.

In 1966, he started up his own band called Jimmy James and the Blue Flames and played the Greenwich Village clubs in New York. After seeing Jimmy perform, Chas Chandler, the Animals' bassist, persuaded him to go on a British tour. Hendrix accepted, mainly because he was promised a meeting with Eric Clapton. A drummer and a bassist were recruited in England. Hastily thrown together, the most famous trio in rock history gave their first concert on 18 October 1966 . . . at the Olympia, as Johnny Hallyday's supporting act! They received mixed reviews, for at that time, Hendrix was technically far superior to his companions; however, the group slowly took shape and their first single ('Hey Joe'/'Stone Free') rose to number four in the British charts. Two months later, in March 1967, their second single ('Purple Haze'/'51st Anniversary') broke with the more commercial style of 'Hey Joe': 'Purple Haze' was in keeping with the psychedelic, drug-oriented culture popular at the time, but it was the radically new sounds that made up the record which attracted attention to Hendrix.

His eccentric dress sense and violent stage act (he played guitar with his teeth, and sometimes actually set fire to it) impressed many English musicians (Pete Townshend of the Who, Eric Clapton and Eric Burdon worshipped him and tried to emulate his style), and the British public succumbed totally to the charms of his sexy lyrics and style. Hendrix shot to fame: his million-dollar contract meant an abundance of drugs, alcohol and women, but brought tension, nervous exhaustion and quarrels in its wake.

Peak

In a short space of time, the group's first album, *Are You Experienced?*, became a best-seller (it beat all the other British blues and rock bands to the number two spot in the charts, behind the Beatles' extraordinary

Cover versions
Hendrix particularly admired Chuck Berry, B B King and Little Richard. His versions of their great hits are very far from the originals, but they often genuinely surpass them: 'Johnny B Goode' (Chuck Berry) is technically extraordinary; 'Rock Me Baby' (B B King) is striking for its speed and up-tempo rhythm. His versions of Dylan's 'Like A Rolling Stone' and 'All Along the Watchtower' free the energy implied in the originals.

103

Jimi Hendrix

Sergeant Pepper). Their second album, *Axis: Bold As Love*, released at the end of 1967, was hailed as a masterpiece of the art of electric guitar playing. During the winter of 1967–68, the Jimi Hendrix Experience gave 47 concerts in the space of 54 days, then withdrew to the studio to record another monument to Hendrix's skill: *Electric Ladyland* includes the famous 'Voodoo Child', an exercise in style which has become the ultimate test of a guitarist's skill.

Then, despite their commercial and artistic success, the group broke up due to internal conflict, and an exhausted Hendrix began to see his stream of creativity run dry. His mental balance was gradually upset by drug abuse, trouble with the police and an unhappy private life. Moreover, he had had enough of playing guitar with his teeth and setting fire to it, and of rubbing himself suggestively against his amp. Those showy gestures which had made him famous overnight, had become a chore.

In spite of this, he continued to play at the big Sixties' concerts, which his mere presence rendered worthy of a place in the history books. He played at Berkeley, the Isle of Wight and, above all, Woodstock, where he gave an unforgettable rendition of 'The Star-Spangled Banner', the American national anthem. With its distorted sound, Hendrix's version brings to mind the bombings of the Vietnam War.

Decline

The start of 1970 was not auspicious: Hendrix had an ultra-modern studio built in New York, where he hoped to carry his

Drugs

Although he took tranquillizers and stimulants designed to help him maintain the fast and furious pace of his exhausting career, and even though he took LSD, Hendrix could not exactly be termed a 'junkie'; all those who knew him confirm that he never used heroin or morphine, that he was not familiar with cocaine and that he never injected any drug whatever. His death (which some maintain was murder) was probably a tragic accident: exhausted by insomnia, Hendrix is believed to have taken too many tranquillisers on a full stomach and died, choked by his own vomit.

'Wild Thing' is a reprise of a song by the English band, the Troggs, who reached number one with it in the States.

search for new sounds even further. His performance at the Isle of Wight festival in August was disappointing. Exhausted, prematurely aged by the excesses linked with stardom and disappointed by the fundamentally conventional nature of British rock, Hendrix took a lethal cocktail of barbiturates and died in hospital without ever regaining consciousness on 18 September 1970. He would have been 28 on 27 November.

Jimi Hendrix's contribution

His main claim to originality was the special relationship he had with his guitar. Before the advent of this artiste, the guitar was seen as an instrument capable of producing certain sounds, the simple intermediary between intention and result. In Hendrix's hands, the guitar really realised its full potential: it became an independent object, free, sensitive and almost animate. To a lesser degree, this phenomenon already existed in the styles of the Chicago bluesmen, and guitarists such as Beck, Clapton and Page. With Hendrix, the rock musician's existential relationship to his instrument came into being.

A whole dimension of Hendrix's music would be missed if we neglected to underline the fact that his work was essentially experimental in character. Hendrix launched and reinforced the search for new sounds and the development of equipment designed to modify 'natural' guitar sound.

With the particular demands he made on his guitar, Hendrix invented or bettered a range of special effects: distortion (thick and fuzzy sound), phasing (whirling, vibrato effect), wah-wah (alternation between high and low notes which gives the impression that the guitar is 'speaking') and feedback control (high, piercing tone which builds up to a crescendo). A guitarist without equal, Hendrix is still a role model today, and was instrumental in the development of heavy metal and hard rock (whose guitarists continually borrow his solos). The harmonic complexity of his work naturally drew him close to jazz rock. Furthermore, it was only with Hendrix that classical and jazz musicians began to take rock seriously.

Soundtrack Recording from the Film Jimi Hendrix (double album, WEA) is a must, as is **The Jimi Hendrix Concerts** (Arabella, 1981).

Beware!
Shortly after Hendrix's death, record companies outrageously cashed in on his fame by re-releasing a series of records on which the star played merely for seconds. Other albums released at this time are studio sessions which Hendrix himself never completed, but which were rounded off by other artists after his sudden death. The last category brought out were the numbers he had cut when he was a simple R & B guitarist, and are of no interest whatever . . . The only worthwhile buys are the four albums he recorded during his career and the two compilations mentioned above.

Jefferson Airplane

Californian psychedelic band

Leaders of the 'love generation'

With their blend of folk rock, synthetic sounds, jazz and blues, they became the very embodiment of the hippy movement.

The band unexpectedly shot to fame with 'Somebody to Love', which was basically a 'classic' folk rock number. However, with the combined skills of guitarist Jorma Kaukonen, bassist Jack Casady and vocalists Paul Kantner, Marty Balin and Grace Slick (a former model), the band gradually became more experimental and adventurous, moving closer to 'spacey' rock and the fusion between jazz and rock.

Despite numerous changes in the band's line up, Kantner and Slick continued to work together and were rejoined by Balin after changing their name to 'Jefferson Starship' in 1974, carrying on the Flower Power and psychedelic traditions they had popularized by their appearance at the Monterey Festival in 1967.

Surrealistic Pillow (RCA, 1967) and the excellent CD compilation **The Jefferson Airplane Collection** (RCA) give a good idea of their work.

New paths
Despite the band's success, Kaukonen and Casady left in 1969 to form Hot Tuna, whose album *Burgers* marked their return to acoustic blues and country music.

Janis Joplin

1943–70   Rock blues singer

One of the most famous victims of 'drug culture'

As the first female Sixties' rock star, Janis was under constant pressure. She was unable to withstand the loneliness and disillusionment that went hand in hand with fame.

Born in Texas, Janis, with her rebellious views and refusal to accept the conservative, segregationist policies of her home state, was something of an outsider. She moved to California, where her 'black' voice and blues repertoire were instant hits with San Francisco's club audiences. It was not until her first major concert in 1966 that she became more widely known. Her powerful, raunchy voice set to sophisticated arrangements with a heavy blues and British rock influence made her the biggest female star on the Californian rock scene.

Despite her commercial success and critical acclaim, Janis was emotionally insecure and became heavily involved in the hard drug scene which eventually claimed her life. The music world was devastated by the loss of one of the finest blues singers in rock history.

Cheap Thrills (CBS, 1968), **I Got Dem Ol' Kozmic Blues Again Mama** (CBS, 1969), **Pearl** (CBS, 1971) and the compilation **Greatest Hits** (CBS, 1973) are all available on compact disc.

Posthumous

'Me and Bobby McGee', Janis's only real hit, was released on the *Pearl* album shortly after her death. The song was written by an obscure country singer who was later to become a film star, by the name of Kris Kristofferson.

Janis Joplin *in the H Alk and S Findlay film* Janis *(1974). She was the link between the blues made famous by Bessie Smith and Billie Holiday and the white rock industry. Sadly, she too died a victim of the loneliness of stardom that claimed the lives of so many other great female blues singers.*

The Kinks
English pop group

Catchy riffs and wild lyrics

Their popularity was based on their non-conformist look, their simple and catchy rhythms and incisive lyrics.

Ray and Dave Davies, Pete Quaife and Mick Avory took advantage of the fashion for pop and R & B created by the Beatles to bring a radically new music form to the ears of the British public. As demonstrated by the riff on 'You Really Got Me' and Ray Davies's rough and ready vocals, this music was obviously designed to upset established rock traditions. Hit followed hit with almost magical regularity: 'Set Me Free', 'Tired of Waiting for You' and especially 'Sunny Afternoon' (1966) and 'Waterloo Sunset'.

Davies's lyrics adapted American protest song to the British situation: Kinks songs starkly describe the lives of the British populace and the teenage experience. The band only just survived the 1970s and attempted a comeback in the 1980s.

Low Budget and **One for the Road** (Arista, 1979–80) show that the energy was still there, but tempered with a hard rock influence.

Document Series (double album, Pye Records) and **Hit Singles** (CD) are a good choice unless **Something Else** (Reprise, 1968) or **Greatest Hits** (Reprise, 1966) is available.

> **Longevity**
> Because of the length of their career (or, some say, through lack of inspiration), the Kinks have also experimenteed with hard rock, disco and new wave. Should they be condemned for their eclecticism?

John Lennon
1940–80   English singer and guitarist

Symbol and martyr

He refused to remain simply a former Beatle.

Lennon was a long-time admirer of Elvis, was heavily influenced by Dylan and would have liked the Beatles to be much more politically orientated. Failure to bring the other members of the group round to his point of view resulted in these four talented artists going their own ways, but Lennon's solo work shows that the split in no way detracted from his musical ability. His relationship with marginal Japanese artist, Yoko Ono, aroused much criticism, as did his sometimes violently radical opinions. He was assassinated by a crank on the eve of his long-awaited return to the music scene. A terrible loss . . .

Imagine (Apple–EMI, 1971) is quite simply a masterpiece, the record of the decade. Without exception, all Lennon's other albums are worth buying.

Rock and Roll (Apple–EMI, 1975) shows exceptional energy.

> **Grading**
> In its hit-parade of the 100 all-time best singles, the magazine *Rolling Stone* placed Lennon's 1970 single 'Instant Karma' in the number one spot.

The Mamas and the Papas
Californian vocal folk group

'California Dreamin'' popularized the hippy movement

Their music was a skilful blend of folk rock and polished vocal harmonies.

Their career was brief but influential: between 1965 and 1968 (when the group broke up), marked by the sounds produced by the Everly Brothers and the Beach Boys, whose popularity was on the wane, these two men and two women (one of whom was the outstanding vocalist, Mama Cass) had a series of hits with a jaunty, catchy kind of music that epitomized the nascent hippy movement's joie de vivre.

Not only did they shoot to fame with hits such as 'California Dreamin'', 'Dedicated to the One I Love' and 'Monday, Monday', but John Phillips also organized the unforgettable concert at Monterey in 1967, and thus, the Mamas and the Papas were the driving force behind the whole 'Flower Power' movement.

As their first albums are now impossible to find, we recommend **16 of Their Greatest Hits** (RCA, 1986), a CD compilation.

Leader
John Phillips, one of the 'Papas', wrote and produced Scott McKenzie's single, 'San Francisco', which became the theme tune for the hippy movement and was one of the biggest hits released in 1967.

John Mayall
1933–   English singer, guitarist and harmonica player

Talent spotter

'Head' of the rock blues school, he set many other artists on the path to fame and glory, but never 'made it' himself.

With Alexis Korner, another veteran of the British blues, who was the first to spot the Rolling Stones, John Mayall was the man who brought so many of the biggest names in the blues boom to the forefront of the music scene. Mayall recruited skilled young players for his group the Bluesbreakers, training them and often providing them with their lucky break; after leaving the band, John MacVie, Mick Fleetwood and Peter Green formed Fleetwood Mac, Mick Taylor joined the Rolling Stones, Jack Bruce and Eric Clapton founded Cream and Larry Taylor became the bassist for Zappa, then Canned Heat.

John Mayall did not lack talent, but his experimental flair prevented him from becoming famous in his own right.

Bluesbreakers with Eric Clapton (Decca, 1965), **Crusade** (Decca, 1967), **A Hard Road** (Decca, 1967), **The Turning Point** (Polydor, 1970) and **Back to the Roots** (Polydor) are all absolutely indispensable.

Modesty
Mayall continues to surround himself with talented musicians today: during his last concert in Paris, he gave a memorable show by keeping to the back of the stage and giving a hand-picked group of young hopefuls the chance to prove themselves.

The Moody Blues
English pop group

From progressive rock to easy listening

They invented symphonic rock and prepared the way for Pink Floyd.

Surprisingly, their promising début did not lead on to a brilliant career. Now seen as the precursors of synthesized rock, their number one British hit, which came at a time when the charts were ruled by the Beatles–Stones–Animals trio, showed a strong classic R & B influence.

Then the Moody Blues bravely threw

themselves into sound research, using special effects and machines that were capable of producing unusual sounds. 1967 was the year of *Days of Future Passed*, an album that marked a turning point in their career, and which influenced more than one major band (including Pink Floyd).

By 1969, the band had absorbed the combined influences of classic/jazz/symphonic and synthesized rock and were producing all-purpose music, enjoying the huge commercial success of their albums.

Days of Future Passed (Deram, 1967) was their true masterpiece of 'art rock'.

Peter, Paul and Mary
East Coast vocal folk group

They popularized the songs of Bob Dylan

Made famous by their cover versions of 'Blowin' in the Wind' and 'The Times They Are a-Changin'', they did not outlive the folk movement.

Without them, Bob Dylan might well have remained an obscure singer-songwriter. Dylan was more of a poet than a commercially viable singer, and, despite their evident quality, his lyrics were often difficult for ordinary music audiences to understand. With their clever vocal harmonies set to flowing guitar lines, Peter, Paul and Mary brought his songs within reach of the general public.

Furthermore, their predilection for white folk music was ideally suited to early Sixties' tastes, a fact that was amply demonstrated by the success of their versions of 'If I Had a Hammer' and 'This Land is Your Land'. They had a further hit with their one rock song, 'I Dig Rock'n'Roll Music'.

10 Years Together (Warner, 1970) is fortunately still available.

Manager
Peter, Paul and Mary had the same impresario as Bob Dylan. Was it in order to promote his protégé that Albert Grossman advised the trio to release more commercial versions of his numbers?

The Rolling Stones
British rock group

The biggest of the 'supergroups'

Musically faithful to the blues, they exploited and popularized the non-conformist, rebellious attitude that typified Sixties' youth, and have continued to influence rock music for over two decades.

In the beginning were the blues

Legend has it that the two founders of the group, singer Mick Jagger and guitarist Keith Richards, met by chance on a train and struck up a conversation because one of them was carrying a Chuck Berry record. Both were students, one in economics and the other in fine art. With their shared passion for black music, they soon met again in Alexis Korner's R & B club, where they had come to watch the band. It was in this club that they met another like-minded musician, Brian Jones, whose suggestion that they start a band was to shape their entire future. They enticed bassist Bill Wyman and drummer Charlie Watts away from a jazz band. The line up was completed by the addition of Ian Stewart, former blues pianist in Korner's club.

Their first concert was for an audience of 172, on 26 December 1962. Their music, which was clearly directly inspired by the Chicago bluesmen and black rock musicians, gradually attracted a larger following. Female fans went wild for pretty boys Jagger and Jones and their more rugged-looking fellow band members Richards, Wyman and Watts, with their long hair and eccentric clothes. The Stones were soon playing gigs in London clubs (the Marquee and the Crawdaddy), before going on to greater things.

Their lucky break came when guitarist George Harrison of the Beatles (who were already famous) happened to catch one of their performances and persuaded them to record a single. On 10 May 1963, they went into the studio for the first time and cut a cover version of Chuck Berry's 'Come On'. The single entered the charts in June, and by September, the band had embarked on their first British tour.

The career of the Rolling Stones (who took their name from a number by Chicago bluesman Muddy Waters) had begun. Not only are they the longest lasting rock band ever, but in the course of their 28 years of fruitful and influential musical association, they have cut 28 albums and sold billions of records. One million fans came to see them during their 1981 American tour alone.

The Stones style

While the Beatles were mainly a vocal group composing polished melodies, the Stones were more concerned with producing an authentic blues sound. They made good use of the rock beat, composed few slow numbers and hardly any ballads. In contrast with the Beatles, they deliberately tried to provoke a reaction from the country's youth with their outrageous statements, sordid private lives, use of all

Other albums

The Rolling Stones no 2 (Decca, 1965)
Out of Our Heads (Decca, 1966)
Between the Buttons (Decca, 1967)
Their Satanic Majesties Request (Decca, 1967)
Sticky Fingers (R S Records, 1973)
Exile on main Street (R S Records, 1973)
Goats Head Soup (R S Records, 1973)
It's Only Rock'n'Roll (R S Records, 1974)
Black and Blue (R S Records, 1976)
Emotional Rescue (R S Records, 1980)
Tattoo You (R S Records, 1980)
Undercover (R S Records, 1985)
Dirty Work (R S Records, 1986)
Steel Wheels (R S Records, 1989)

Compilations

For evident commercial reasons, there are a considerable number of compilations of the Stones work. The best of these is quite definitely *The Singles Collection, The London Years* (ABKCO, 1989), a collection of 60 songs accompanied by a booklet of the appropriate lyrics and photos.

The Rolling Stones at the start of their career.
From left to right, **Bill Wyman**, **Brian Jones**, **Charlie Watts**, **Mick Jagger** *and* **Keith Richards**.
    Whether they liked it or not, they became role models for rebellious Sixties' teenagers: their casual look, deliberately provocative behaviour and liberal morals made them the powerhouses of the struggle against the 'old world', of which they later, inevitably, became part.

kinds of drugs, non-conformist attitudes and dress, delinquent behaviour, and, above all, their virulently critical and overtly sexual lyrics. To the adult world, they were inveterate rebels, while to rebellious Sixties' teenagers, they were genuine intellectual leaders.

However, the history of the greatest rock group ever should not be reduced to the eccentricities of its members, to the vitriolic genius of Brian Jones, Mick Jagger's (false) androgyny, Keith Richards's (real) drug problem and Bill Wyman's preference for (very) young girls. A particular look and outrageous behaviour cannot be solely responsible for the 28 years of their successful career. There had to be something more: the members of the band, with their different but complementary talents, were bound together by their almost fanatical love of early blues and rock music, and by their respect for their fans.

Musical development

Despite their constant proclivity for the blues, the Rolling Stones' music developed audibly, and was marked by certain key events which changed the course of their career.

In June 1964, they toured America (just after the famous Beatles tour) and by the time they came home to Britain, were

---

Money, money, money . . .
20 000 tickets were put on sale by mail for the 1981 New York concert. The organizers received two million cheques.

Films
The Stones made three musical documentaries: Jean-Luc Godard's *One Plus One* (1968), David and Albert Maysles' *Gimme Shelter* (1970) and Hal Ashby's *Let's Spend the Night Together* (1981).

Censored
Andy Warhol's sleeve design for *Sticky Fingers* was judged obscene and was subsequently banned in a number of countries. Moreover, the Stones were often forced to censor their own work for live performances by changing the lyrics. 'Let's Spend the Night Together', 'Brown Sugar', 'Star, Star' and 'Honky Tonk Woman' were all adapted for their American televised appearances in the 1960s and at the start of the 1970s.

---

internationally acclaimed. In a short space of time, they became the Liverpool four's only credible rival.

The summer of 1965 saw the release of their smash hit 'Satisfaction' which made them world-famous. At the same time, the Stones began to prove themselves as songwriters, whereas before they had mainly confined themselves to bringing out cover versions of black rock musicians works.

During 1965 and 1966, their rebel image was reinforced by a series of clashes with the police during their tour of the major European cities and various charges of assaulting police officers, public indecency and drug possession, etc.

1967 was the year in which guitarist Brian Jones, suffering from depression, conceded the leadership of the group to singer Mick Jagger. In 1969, only days after he left the band, Jones drowned in a swimming pool.

He was replaced by master guitarist Mick Taylor, who guided the band back to a true blues sound (he had just left John Mayall's Bluesbreakers). Until 1974, Taylor was responsible for the Rolling Stones' musical credibility and originality. His improvisations, directly inspired by Chicago blues and Chuck Berry melody lines, contributed to the success of the albums released during this period.

The departure of Mick Taylor, who was tired of taking a back seat while it was his guitar work that shaped the Stones' sound, could have disorientated the Jagger–Richards tandem which had headed the band for so long. Instead, they immediately recruited the lead guitarist from the Faces (Rod Stewart's group), Ron Wood, who accepted his background role without question. With Mick Taylor gone, Jagger was able to experiment with styles that were far removed from the music initially produced by the band, which, by the mid-1970s, had become a vast commercial machine. In keeping with what was fashionable at the time, the Rolling Stones tried out funk ('Miss You') and even disco with 'Emotional Rescue'.

The 1976 world tour was a major triumph, and placed the Rolling Stones firmly at the head of the rock movement.

The 1981 tour was a record breaker: there were over 20 000 people at every concert in Europe and allegedly up to 90 000 in the States; in the space of a few months, more than a million fans had seen their idols.

In 1986, the group released *Dirty Work*

then, weary of sharing the same stage for 25 years, individual members began to spend more and more time on solo projects. Two years later, they were back together again and, having cut *Steel Wheels* (1989), they went on a major tour of the same name.

The Rolling Stones (Decca, 1964) is their first album and is comprised mainly of cover versions of black American music. Excellent.

Aftermath (Decca, 1966), released immediately after the hit single 'Satisfaction', was their most important release during their pop period. However, there is an audible blues (the eleven minute long 'I'm Coming Home') and rock ('It's Not Easy' and 'Stupid Girl') influence. The album was mainly successful thanks to two pop-rock ballads ('Under My Thumb' and 'Mother's Little Helper') and an elegant slow number ('Lady Jane').

Big Hits (High Tide and Green Grass) (Decca, 1966) is a compilation of their early releases including 'Satisfaction', but also their first real hit 'Come On', as well as the famous 'Paint it Black' and the curiously Elizabethan 'Lady Jane', with its sophisticated, baroque melody.

Beggar's Banquet (Decca, 1968) Released at the end of 1968, this album is both a summation of their work until that date and their most confident output; it also marks a turning point in their musical style. 'Sympathy for the Devil' and 'Street Fighting Man', in support of rebellion, were cut alongside obsessive ('Parachute Woman'), and historic ('Prodigal Son', written by Robert Wilkins in 1929) blues, nothing but the blues. With *Let It Bleed*, released shortly afterwards, *Beggar's Banquet* is a truly great blues album, with a clear acoustic sound. After Brian Jones was replaced by Mick Taylor, the band rapidly moved towards a harder sound that was closer to Chicago blues and hard rock; from 1970, the Stones could no longer be called a pop group, Keith Richards having thrown himself wholeheartedly into the wild style suggested by Mick Taylor.

Through the Past, Darkly (Decca, 1969) draws together all the 1968 hits, including 'Jumpin' Jack Flash', 'Let's Spend the Night Together' and 'Honky Tonk Woman'.

Let It Bleed (Decca, 1969) Newly recruited Mick Taylor's presence can be heard on all the tracks on this heavily blues-rock influenced album.

Get Yer Ya-Ya's Out (Decca, 1970). This is the Stones first major live album and

is a testament to their on-stage technical abilities: the numbers are all strikingly tight and well balanced. This is probably the best record to come out of their 'first period'. It contains live versions of many of their better known original compositions including 'Jumpin' Jack Flash', 'Stray Cat Blues', 'Midnight Rambler' and 'Sympathy For the Devil' (which Jean-Luc Godard used for his film *One Plus One*), as well as unforgettable covers of Chuck Berry songs 'Carol' and 'Little Queenie'; their version of Robert Johnson's soulful 'Love in Vain' is stunning in its authenticity.

Love You Live (R S Records) is a double album and represents their style in the 1970s. Recorded during their 1976 tour, it contains all their hits and gives a useful overview of their most fruitful period, for they never again reached such astounding levels of creativity.

Some Girls (R S Records). Released in June 1978, the album was a smash hit, mainly due to 'Miss You', which was the most popular discotheque track of the summer. Although the other songs on the album ('Some Girls', 'Just My Imagination', 'Shattered', 'Beast of Burden') were also interesting, they were somewhat eclipsed by the huge success of 'Miss You', a rather cheap disco number with rock overtones provided by a harmonica and heavy guitar sound.

Still Life (R S Records–EMI) was taken from their 1981 tour. An excellent recording, it highlights the Stones' ability to develop their sound according to new music trends: even the older numbers are given a more modern tone, overlaid with a metallic sound which shows a strong punk influence (Richards appeared on stage wearing a torn T-shirt).

The Stones' ages

Singer Mick Jagger was born in 1943, guitarist Keith Richards in 1943, bassist Bill Wyman in 1936, Mick Taylor in 1949, Ron Wood in 1947, Brian Jones in 1942 (he died in 1969) and drummer Charlie Watts in 1941.

The man in the background

Ian Stewart, keyboards player and later, road manager, for the band was excluded by their managers because he didn't have the right rebellious look. He was friends with all the members of the band, who were deeply saddened by his death in 1986.

Carlos Santana
1947–   Latin rock guitarist

He has an extraordinary ability to fuse different styles

He succeeded in rock with that which Nat King Cole had attempted in jazz.

Carlos Santana was born in Mexico. His childhood, and the Latin American music with which he grew up, gave way to an adolescence heavily influenced by rock music; after he had emigrated to California, he became a master of the electric guitar, performed in local clubs and then all over the San Francisco area. He was soon part of the burgeoning hippie movement and, if his first album made him famous, his appearance at Woodstock made him an international star.

His flowing improvisations, versatile and energetic rhythm section and lyrics frequently sung in Spanish make his music not only unusual, but a genre in its own right.

Santana, Abraxas and Amigos (CBS, 1969, 1970, 1976) are all musts.

Developments
Santana's experimental, adventurous temperament lends itself to many forms of music: he played jazz rock with John MacLauchlin ('Love Devotion Surrender') and folk rock with Dylan on his world tour in 1984.

Simon and Garfunkel
Folk rock duet

Following in the footsteps of the Everly Brothers

They are famous for their beautiful lyrics and polished melodies.

Paul Simon and Art Garfunkel had their first hit with 'Sounds of Silence'. Their soundtrack for the film *The Graduate* made them international stars. A whole series of subtly written and performed songs made up the quality of their voices is quite exceptional on melodic arrangements adapted to suit the fashion for folk rock. Their partnership, which ended in the mid-1970s, resulted in a considerable number of what can only be called masterpieces. 'Mrs Robinson', 'Bridge Over Troubled Water', 'The Boxer' and 'Scarborough Fair' swept the art of vocal harmony to

heights earlier groups (the Everly Brothers, Peter, Paul and Mary, and even the Beach Boys) were never able to reach using such simple methods.

Simon and Garfunkel's Greatest Hits (CBS, 1972) sums up their joint career.

Live In Central Park (Geffen, 1982) is a unique moment in the whole of rock history.

Apartheid
Paul Simon who, from the very first, was the driving force behind the duet, has also had a brilliant solo career. One of his most recent albums, *Graceland*, on which he plays with black South African musicians, launched the fashion for Zulu-rock (Johnny Clegg, Savuka, etc).

The Soft Machine
English progressive rock group

Original and impossible to categorize

Each of the members was so creative that the band eventually split to allow them their solo careers.

It is almost impossible to describe the stylistic elements of a band which was popular, but whose changes in direction and constantly shifting line-up were such that they alienated most potential fans apart from a hard core of rock lovers who were attracted to avant-garde music.

Variously influenced by pop, symphonic rock and jazz, erstwhile members of the psychedelic movement (hence the surrealist, Dali-esque name), Soft Machine are impossible to categorize and did not survive the 1960s.

Soft Machine: 1 & 2 Architects of Space Time (Atlantic, 1968, 1969) and **Third Soft Machine** (CBS, 1970) are 'monuments'.

Instability
Amongst their other claims to fame, Soft Machine had one of the most unstable line-ups in the history of rock; with every new record or tour, one or several members of the band were replaced, which could have had disastrous consequences for their popularity. Over 20 musicians were officially part of Soft Machine.

Steppenwolf
Rock underground group

Born to be Wild

With a wolf as their emblem, they challenged American complacency. Their burning intensity never cooled.

Of European origin, the members of Steppenwolf (the name comes from Herman Hesse's novel) met and founded the band in Canada. Singer John Kay shook the foundations of the rock music establishment with his heavy, threatening vocals, while the band produced lyrics that were to become the theme for rebels at the end of the 1960s who were disappointed by the range of flash-in-the-pan trends that characterized the mid-1960s. In 1968, Steppenwolf had a hit with 'Born to be Wild', which became the bikers' anthem and was a veritable vindication of violence. The overall sound was basically a harder version of blues rock, close to future hard rock. 'Monster' was even more politically radical, calling for a revolution. After the release of 'Monster' Steppenwolf embarked on one of the longest tours in the history of rock, playing in more than 1000 towns to a combined audience of 2 million.

Devastated by the end of the protest movement, the band split up in 1972.

Monster (MCA, 1968), **Steppenwolf Live** (MCA, 1971) and **Steppenwolf** (CD, MCA, 1980) are all musts.

Easy Rider
The sound track for Dennis Hopper's underground film made 'Born to be Wild' the American bikers' anthem. Ironically, the biker movement was led by the infamous Hell's Angels, whose militarist and xenophobic ideology was anathema to Steppenwolf.

Ten Years After
English blues rock group

Forefathers of hard rock

Alvin Lee's talent took the whole band to the heights of fame.

Like many other English musicians, with Chicago blues as their starting point, the members of Ten Years After had a brief, but intense, period of fame after their performance at the Woodstock Festival in 1969. 'Going Home', an up-tempo blues rock number sprinkled with long guitar solos (which were much admired by the rest of the rock world), was the most popular piece produced in the few short years of their career.

The album *Sssh . . .* (1969) was a big hit and their subsequent releases, as well

as their countless American tours, show their gradual progression towards more pounding rhythms and a harder sound on which several later rock groups based their sound.

Ssssh . . . (Deram, 1967), **Rock and Roll Music to the World** (CBS, 1972) contain their best work.

Slide
Alvin Lee used to produce a wild slide effect by frantically rubbing his guitar against the metal foot of the mike stand. This rather unorthodox method was a favourite with the audience.

The Velvet Underground
New York avant-garde rock band

An explosive cocktail

Sixties' symbol and myth.

Members of the group were involved in all areas of the arts in the 1960s and were attracted to all that was new and experimental (commune life, drugs and alcohol, new wave cinema and avant-garde rock music). The classic line-up revolved around singer Lou Reed, singer Nico, Sterling Morrison, John Cale and Maureen Tucker, and played a considerable role in defining rock for the following decade.

The music they produced was, and still is, obscure and difficult to define. In

keeping with the New York intellectual tradition, their music, a blend of psychedelia, classic rock, hard sound and pre-punk arrangements (10 years before the Sex Pistols!), and deliberately outrageous lyrics, was garishly publicized.

The Velvet Underground & Nico (Polydor, 1967) is a must.

Lives
Lou Reed went on to become a star. Sterling Morrison teaches literature in Texas. Maureen Tucker has five children and works with computers. John Cale has cut solo albums and Nico died in 1988.

The Who
English mod group

Wild Sixties' rock band

More important than the originality of their music, the Who defined a new, primitive and destructive rock attitude.

In 1964, four friends living in London's western suburbs decided to form a rock band. All four were R & B fans and attracted by the showmanship of black artists. They coupled the energy of the blues and rock'n'roll with a spontaneous tendency for extremism and protest in general. The Who will always be linked with alcohol and drug abuse, verbal abuse and a wild stage act. Pete Townshend was the first to ritually smash his guitar against the amps, while master drummer Keith Moon would destroy his kit at the end of every concert. They kept up this extremism at least until the death of Moon in 1978.

My Generation (Decca, 1966) and **Live at Leeds** (Polydor, 1970) are their best albums.

Tommy (MCA, 1969) and **Quadrophenia** (MCA, 1979) are the soundtracks for the films of the same name, the latter having been made of the 1973 album.

Shocks
Not only did the Who write the famous 'hope I die before I get old' refrain, but they also developed the rock opera concept with their hugely successful film *Tommy*.

Johnny Winter
1944–   Blues–rock singer and guitarist

An outstanding performer who returned to his roots

He made a name for himself as one of the best white guitarists.

In his native Texas, it was not the done thing to play black music. Despite an obvious handicap (he was albino) and despite the strictly observed rules of racial segregation, he managed to get gigs in black clubs in some of the South's major cities. His rock music bore the distinctive stamp of the rural (he was one of the best white blues guitarists of his time) and Chicago blues. His wild versions of Chuck Berry and Rolling Stones classics made him famous. Never particularly strong, his health was totally undermined by a serious drug problem, resulting in a career that can only be described as erratic, punctuated by various comebacks (new releases and tours). In more recent years, Winter's obvious fondness for the blues has not prevented him from joining the ranks of hard rock guitarists.

Nothing But the Blues, Still Alive and Well and **Serious Business** (CBS, 1977, 1973, 1987) prove that, despite changes in technique, Winter was able to keep faith with the spirit of the blues.

Gratitude
'Without the arrival of cute English guitarists like Clapton and Jagger, etc, I don't think the blues would have become so big. We can't expect them to play the blues as if they were Mississippi born and bred, but they have developed their own style, and it's great.'

The Yardbirds
English blues rock band

A breeding-ground for talent

At one time or another, all the great English guitarists were members of this band.

Formed in 1963, this legendary group was originally made up of musicians drawn together by their shared love of black music. A happy combination of circumstances set them on the road to stardom: not only did they get a residency in the extremely popular Crawdaddy Club, but they also had friends in the right places (blues boom musicians Alexis Korner and John Mayall, and the Rolling Stones, who shared their musical preferences and started out almost at the same time). Their tour with Chicago blues legend Sonny Boy Williamson, who was travelling in England at the time, earned them the respect of the music world. After the international success of 'For Your Love', Clapton left the band and was replaced by Jeff Beck. Beck in turn was replaced by Jimmy Page who, after the Yardbirds broke up, founded Led Zeppelin.

Greatest Hits (Epic, 1967) is a good compilation.

Changes in direction
With Clapton on guitar, the Yardbirds produced blues (*With Sonny Boy Williamson*, Fontana), with Beck, psychedelic rock (*The Yardbirds, Featuring Jeff Beck*, Motors) and with Page, pre-hard rock (*Little Games*, Epic).

Frank Zappa
1940– Progressive rock singer and guitarist

Controversial personality

Some see him as a genius, others as a fake; he is impossible to define.

Of Greek and Italian extraction, the Groucho of rock has been attracted to all sorts of music including the classical and folk genres. He is also interested in avant-garde theatre, symbolist and surrealist poetry, and is equally at ease with the classic rock, jazz, psychedelic pop and rock styles. Judging by his live shows, which are littered with meaningful jokes and throw-away philosophical comments, this could be but the tip of the iceberg. He first entered the halls of fame in the mid 1960s with his band the Mothers of Invention (the name speaks for itself) and has since delighted audiences with his own particular blend of humour, political critique and innovative, musical sound.

We're Only in it for the Money (Verve, 1968) is most representative of his work.

Everything
Zappa composed a burlesque rock opera (*Joe's Garage, 1, 2 & 3*, CBS), has made films (including *200 Motels*), conducted the Royal Philharmonic orchestra, produced a cartoon, played with John Lennon and composed a score for Pierre Boulez . . .

1970–1977

The curse on rock music

On the whole, the 1970s were distinctive for a visible loss of creative momentum caused by an organized ideological and commercial take-over bid by American and European show-business. After almost a full decade of cultural and artistic protest, after such explosive high points as Woodstock, the rock world was struck by a series of tragic deaths, destroying its creative core in a macabre repetition of the fate which totally debilitated the first rock generation in the 1950s.

In the first instance, a long series of 'accidental' deaths, this time mainly due to drug abuse and sheer carelessness, deprived the rock world of some of its major musicians: the most sorely felt was, of course, that of Jimi Hendrix, who died of asphyxiation (and not of an overdose) in 1971 after having taken too many sleeping pills. Brian Jones, founder of the Rolling Stones, with his musical curiosity and adventurous spirit, drowned in July 1969, forever depriving the band of an innovative and fantastic touch. Janis Joplin, that extraordinary white blues singer with the truly black voice, died of an overdose of loneliness and heroin in October 1970. Otis Redding, the undisputed idol of soul music at the end of the 1960s, whose international audience was half black, half white, went missing while piloting his private plane in December 1967. Jim Morrison, the thought-provoking singer for the Doors, with his tortured lyrics and angelic looks, overdosed in Paris in July 1971. Alan Wilson, singer and harmonica-player with Canned Heat, died of hypothermia in Canada as a result of a stupid bet; the blues lost one of their most original voices when King Curtis, legendary sax player to whom some of the masterpieces of soul music are credited, was stabbed to death in Harlem in August 1971. Syd Barrett went mad: committed in 1969, he was released to the care of his mother and has not made a recovery; prolonged contemplation of 'another world' turned the inventor of the Pink Floyd sound into a profound schizophrenic. Duane Allman died in October 1971, and was followed one year later by his bassist, Berry Oakley.

This is not the complete list of casualties –

to those who physically disappeared from this world should be added those who lost themselves, or more often sold (and, it has to be admitted, at a good price) themselves out. First place in the ranks of these weary heroes has to go to Bob Dylan, who did not even appear at Woodstock, and wrote not one song on the Vietnam War. Mick Jagger dragged the Rolling Stones into commercial rock and was content to manage the massive Stones 'industry'.

The Beatles, now broken up (this was the most dramatic event of 1970, although it was both symbolic and expected), attempted solo careers that, in the main, were not very striking, despite Lennon's *Imagine* and George Harrison's 'My Sweet Lord'. Ringo Starr made films (what films?) and Paul McCartney fulfilled his dream of becoming a singer-songwriter whose appeal extended to music-lovers of all ages, a kind of younger Elvis without the peanut butter and banana sandwiches; McCartney, at least, kept his figure.

The start of the 1970s, then, saw the

Pub rock, 1970–1980

Deliberately shunning big concerts and well-known labels, the last rock purists spent the 1970s playing the pub circuit. A fundamental part of the British music tradition, the fact that groups like Dr Feelgood, Rockpile and the Inmates played in front of limited pub audiences helped preserve the country and blues roots and British rock.

Some of the biggest names in what was to become new wave music owe much of this purist movement: Nick Lowe, that versatile musician who had played with both Dave Edmunds (Rockpile) and Graham Parker (the Rumour), produced many of Elvis Costello's records. Other important figures in the pre-punk movement, including Ian Dury, inventor of the famous punk slogan 'Sex and drugs and rock'n'roll', started out in the pub circuit.

Pub rock, musically close to early rock, was therefore a precursor of the punk movement, with which it shared a dislike of progressive rock and massive concerts.

death of what had been the very essence of Sixties' rock – regeneration of the true rock'n'roll spirit through the search for new sounds and the creation of an alternative teen culture through the protest movement. Until 1977, when punk music first reared its wild head (once again the tidal wave that was punk came from Great Britain), rock became a hackneyed music form, relying on tried and tested styles and becoming what can only be described as light music. Rebel rock fans went into mourning for the apparent demise of their beloved music. These were dark days for an art that claimed to be new.

The 'supergroups'

Backed by the creation of a veritable music media empire (*Rolling Stone* in the States, and *Rock and Folk*, *Melody Maker* and *Best* in Europe) and made rich by all the highly publicized festivals, the rock establishment quickly found a way to get a return on its sometimes considerable investments; the first really big recording studios date from this time (the end of the 1960s). Equipment became increasingly sophisticated and massive concerts meant that rapid advances were made in live sound; computerized light shows and then giant video screens emerged and soon became an indispensable part of every concert.

High-tech concerts were financed by tours on such a scale that stars rarely had any contact with their adoring public. Whole stadiums were filled in the twinkling of an eye, some groups even stayed on the road for as long as a year. At the same time teenagers' growing buying power meant that they could purchase more new releases than before, with the result that many bands broke the million-copies-sold barrier with unprecedented speed, the aim of these massive tours being to promote the new album sandwiched between 'classic', older tracks which the audiences could easily recognize.

From the start of the 1970s, all tours were announced weeks in advance by the rock-establishment-controlled radio and TV, in the press and on posters. These years saw the growing importance of a 'look', not only in terms of the stars' stage costumes, but also in carefully marketed range of products like badges, T-shirts, car stickers and photo albums designed specially for fans.

Slowly but surely, the visual dimension became more important than actual sound: the Rolling Stones who, despite the tragedy

at Altamont, had continued their live performances, were the first to re-vamp the technical and commercial aspects of their shows. The Stones have their private plane, dozens of lorries, a portable recording studio and their own label. Between his two brushes with the law and a number of publicity-seeking scandals, shrewd businessman Mick Jagger has run R S Records far better than the Beatles (the first to own their own company) managed Apple. In the 1970s, a number of other supergroups smashed records previously held by such artists as Elvis, the Beach Boys and Dylan: with their diverse styles, Fleetwood Mac, Grateful Dead, Pink Floyd, Rod Stewart, Supertramp, Deep Purple, the Eagles, Crosby, Stills, Nash and Young, Elton John, Kiss, Status Quo, Roxy Music, Wings and Led Zeppelin attracted immense crowds, sold millions of albums, and played in front of audiences of 100 000 during their commercially successful but musically mundane, exhausting tours.

However, some bands did try to avoid the traps created by the rules of supply and demand in music: unfortunately one, Creedence Clearwater Revival, was but a shooting star, ruined by a series of unscrupulous and dishonest managers. The band Hot Tuna, with its purist tendencies, earned more respect than money, as did the indefinable King Crimson and the elusive J J Cale.

Between 1970 and 1977, it is no exaggeration to say that rock had a close brush with death. Artistic exploration having given way to a 'get rich quick' attitude, rock in turn became an institution with its own powers, conspiracies and rules and regulations. Not since the first wave of rock had been snuffed out had this whole music form come so close to complete ruin.

And yet, the musicians are not to blame; most of them were carried along on the crest of a wave of unexpected success, and had looked sincerely for new modes of expression. And even if most artists eventually sold out to commercialism, this is partially because the Seventies' teen-audience was less demanding musically and more open to media pressure.

The birth of mainstream rock

During the 1970s, it became usual to refer to the kind of music produced by the supergroups (despite their obvious stylistic differences) as 'mainstream'. At the time, the Stones' sound was close to blues rock and heavy metal, and had little in common with Fleetwood Mac's more polished sound or the Bee Gees' overtly light music, yet they were all within the rock mainstream.

They do, however, have certain points in common: they all share the same kind of international audience, are extremely professional and technically accomplished. Little by little, FM radio stations and the rock media were to hard-sell these groups to bring them a wider audience. In the 1970s, experimental groups like early Pink Floyd sold the most rock albums, and managed to attract a fair number of classical music-lovers. Progressive rock musicians (King Crimson, Al DiMeola, John MacLaughlin, Chick Corea and Herbie Hancock) took part in the fusion of jazz and rock, with the unexpected and unhoped-for help of the great Miles Davis.

While the boundaries between simple rock (from the blues) and the symphonic orchestrations typical of 'spacey' rock were gradually being broken down by popular demand for easy listening, the rock 'species' slowly entered the list of 'acceptable' music. In 1971, the first chairs of rock were created in a number of Californian universities, while the jazz rock produced by certain outsider artists impressed and influenced some of rock's best musicians.

Having become a citizen of the music world, a 'culture', a thesis topic and an accepted music form, mainstream rock legitimized musicians who had formerly been labelled 'drug addicts' and 'delinquents'.

Heavy sound

One of the most marked tendencies in the 1970s was for a heavy electric guitar sound and rhythmic simplicity. This was the era of heavy metal and hard rock which, to the uneducated ear, sound remarkably similar.

It is true that today, these two sub-genres are difficult to distinguish. Hard rock is generally defined as having a marked early blues influence but, due to advances in sound technology the rhythms and individual instruments are highlighted. Therefore, some of the biggest names in early rock, including Cream, the Yardbirds and Hendrix, but occasionally Rory Gallagher and Ten Years After and of course the recognized founders of the genre, Steppenwolf, Led Zeppelin, Black Sabbath and Deep Purple, actually produced a hard rock sound. Heavy metal can be distinguished from the above by the

particular care taken by both performers and fans to obtain the right look: this was a combination of leather, studded jackets, canvas patches embroidered with either a picture of the band or its emblem, tight jeans or bellbottoms, boots and long hair.

Musically speaking, these two genres have much in common: an extremely noisy and steady double-time drum beat, screaming vocals blasted out by unkempt vocalists, and guitarists whose climactic ultra-fast solos exceed, at least in terms of speed, those of the best musicians in previous decades. The bassist, never a front man (except in the cases of Thin Lizzy and Motörhead) generally does his best to add to the racket produced by fellow band members: the American band Grand Funk Railway reached the 120-decibel mark in concert (the same sound-level as Concorde taking off). All Motörhead concerts are a major trial to the ears, and when Jimmy Page of Led Zeppelin got out his bow to scrape it across the guitar strings, the ear-splitting result was enough to try the strongest of constitutions.

Besides these hard rock groups, certain other individuals created a look that was so eccentric that it could not fail to catch the attention of fans and soon became an intrinsic part of the hard and heavy rock image: flashy clothes, platform boots, spangles and glitter, permed hair and a stage act that was both vulgar and primitive, using live snakes, puppets, planes, flying pigs, giant inflatable phalluses, ghost train decors, exhausting light shows and flashing stroboscopes.

Inevitably, faced with the unleashed savagery of certain heavy metal groups and the sophistication of the 'decadent' element in glam rock (Elton John with his hats, scarves and multicoloured trousers; Bryan Ferry of Roxy Music looking as if he had just stepped off the cat-walk; Bowie, then Jagger, with their gender-bending look; Marc Bolan of T Rex with his outrageous make-up) it was ironically the genuine players, with their rough, simple music and dress style, who tended to appear ridiculous: Mick Taylor, lead guitarist with the Rolling Stones, often played sitting down, as did J J Cale, and to many, Rory Gallagher's old Stratocaster (which is idolized today) seemed old-fashioned. The height of bad taste was reached with the American heavy metal group Kiss, who not only used the Nazi SS logo on their album covers, but drew most of their inspiration from superhero comic books. Some time

*Guitarist **Keith Richards**, inventor of the Stones' sound, has used a great many different makes of guitar. Here we see him playing a Gibson 'Les Paul', which was ideally suited to the blues rock the band was producing at the time this photograph was taken (during the making of Godard's film* One Plus One*). The rise of the harder punk rock sound encouraged him to give up all other makes in favour of the Fender Stratocaster, of which he owns several models which he always uses in concert.*

later, Iron Maiden and Iggy Pop were to carry on in this absurd and distasteful vein, which really had nothing to do with the actual music they were producing.

Outwith the mainstream

Very few rock artists survived this difficult 'anything goes' period; aware of the threat, Bob Dylan himself directed his energies in to his 'Rolling Thunder Review', which was initially intended to be an incognito pub tour but ended up in crowded stadiums . . . For a long time, King Crimson was the spearhead of the progressive rock movement, but the band had to separate after a number of years of commercial failure. Genesis, Yes and Pink Floyd were

engulfed by a success that was so sudden and unexpected that it disturbed the mental balance of more than one of their members, who had started out as musical purists.

Unlike Clapton, certain avant-garde guitarists were left stranded in the intellectual jazz rock ghetto (John MacLaughlin, Chick Corea, Larry Coryell as well as some talented bassists such as Stanley Clarke, who is credited by modern funk musicians at being the inventor of bass-slapping). Like Gallagher, Ten Years After and Alvin Lee, Johnny Winter kept on with blues rock which he gradually brought closer to hard rock, but the audiences shrank. For a time, it looked as though Neil Young was going to take over from

Custom-built for **Jimmy Page**, lead guitarist with **Led Zeppelin**, the double-necked Gibson S G shows both an excessive concern for image, and a true desire to explore virgin territory.

Dylan, but he remained outside the mainstream. Lynyrd Skynyrd defined Southern rock, but their following was basically confined to a hard core of true blues rock fans in the south. Lou Reed and Bowie were the forerunners of the punk wave. With Foreigner, the father of 'FM rock', the Bee Gees and the Rolling Stones (*Emotional Rescue*) disco hits, the sterile rock produced by Supertramp, Queen and Roxy Music, it was obviously time for another revolution: it came in the form of the Sex Pistols. Rock was saved once again, this time by music produced by punks.

AC/DC

Australian hard rock group

Making the blues work for hard rock

Hard rock's distorted sound and pounding rhythms were tempered by Angus Young's feeling for the blues.

An Australian band, they became famous in the second half of the 1960s. They were particularly successful in Britain and France. Their non-conformist style, coupled with guitarist Angus Young's skills and the hoarse voice of their first singer, Bon Scott, with his simple, untamed look, were also a hit in the States.

After Bon Scott's accidental death (he was replaced by Brian Johnson), AC/DC's music became more commercial and run-of-the-mill. The blues rock, wild riffs and general overall feeling of the music, gave way to conventional, lacklustre hard rock.

High Voltage (Atlantic, 1976), **If You Want Blood, You've Got It** (Atlantic, 1978) and **Dirty Deeds Done Dirt Cheap** (Atlantic, 1981) were released at the height of the band's popularity.

Schoolboy
To an even greater extent than the previous decade, in the 1970s it was essential for bands to have a particular, instantly recognizable look. The AC/DC look was based on the wearing of schoolboy shorts on stage, intended to represent the adolescent nature of their music.

Aerosmith

American heavy metal group

Aggressive, but at the same time, commercial rock

They were perhaps America's most popular heavy metal band in the 1970s.

Formed in Boston, the band produced highly original hard rock, easily recognizable for its jumpy rhythms (which owe much to classic rock) and master guitarist Joe Perry's blazing solos and intros. In 1975, after years of limited tours that were not very lucrative, the group had a smash hit with the album *Toys In The Attic*, which contains their best tracks.

After four years of sell-out tours and a number of hit records (10 million albums sold), especially in the States, the group separated (1980) then got back together in 1982, at the instigation of singer Steven Tyler, to cut *Rock In A Hard Place* (CBS), but this time without guitarist Joe Perry. Perry rejoined the band in 1985 for the album *Done With Mirrors*.

Aerosmith, Toys in the Attic and **Rocks** are their best albums (CBS, 1973, 1976).

Cover version
Aerosmith recorded perhaps the best cover of the Beatles' 'Come Together', which is on the soundtrack for the *Sergeant Pepper* film.

Alice Cooper
Glam-rock group

Exhibitionism and bad taste

Because of their deliberate provocation, on-stage antics and outrageous look, the band is seen as a distant ancestor of punk.

It would be untrue to say that Alice Cooper had a lasting musical effect on rock. On the other hand, from the start of the 1970s the band drew attention to themselves with their outrageous shows, obscene suggestions and apocalyptic views on the end of the Western world. It was thanks to the efforts of Frank Zappa, who shared their views on Western morality, and producer Bob Ezrin that Alice Cooper became famous. The group's style was simplistic, but little by little, they set more ambitious lyrics to typical heavy metal tunes.

Along with certain other popular artists (Bowie, Lou Reed, the New York Dolls, Iggy Pop), Alice Cooper parodied the role of social critics adopted by Sixties' musicians and heralded the coming punk explosion.

Love it to Death (Warner, 1971) was released at the height of their popularity.

Accessories

Vincent Fournier appeared on stage with a range of props including snakes, revolting masks and costumes that would have been appropriate to the set of a horror movie. . . .

Black Sabbath
English heavy metal group

Pioneers

Cultivating a satanic look and a style which owed much to blues rock, they were never able to shrug off their heavy metal image.

The group has always been heavily influenced by the strong character of singer Ozzy Osbourne, who directed the band towards hard, extremist rock with a thick, fuzzy sound, simple riffs ('Paranoid', 1971) and a stage-act that was based on weird make-up and decors taken from the medieval imagery surrounding witchcraft and black sabbaths (whence the band's name). The departure of the lead singer for an uninspired solo career threw the rest of the band into confusion, although they tried (unsuccessfully) to keep going in the same musical direction.

With over 12 million albums sold, this small-time Birmingham heavy metal band had nevertheless managed to penetrate the American market, taking advantage of the hard rock wave. Today, Black Sabbath is recognized as one of the foremost and genuine hard rocks bands.

Paranoid (Phonogram, 1971) helped popularize heavy metal.

Horror

Ozzy Osbourne was one of the musicians who depicted Satan as a hard rock personality, following on from the Stones who had launched the movement only to give it up shortly afterwards. Black Sabbath remained faithful to that primitive and somewhat superficial image, without ever trying to develop it further.

Blue Oyster Cult
American hard rock group

Forgotten pioneers

Blue Oyster Cult evolved through psychedelic music to 'high tech' music.

Initially, Blue Oyster Cult bore the names 'Cows', 'Oaxaca', 'Soft White Underbelly' and 'Stalk Forest', names which give an indication of their hesitation between the hard rock and psychedelic music forms.

However, in 1972, having fixed on a name, the band produced its first eponymous album, which placed it firmly within the hard rock main stream. With their clear guitar riffs, pounding rhythms and topical lyrics, the group had no difficulty finding an international audience for its music: Blue Oyster Cult began to be considered as possible successors to Led Zeppelin and as serious rivals of Deep Purple.

Their continuous Seventies' tours kept them very much in the public eye, but since the start of the 1980s and the demise of the fashion for hard rock, they had become more legendary than real.

Blue Oyster Cult (CBS, 1972) is an important record. Highly recommended.

Debatable
In order to harden their image, the Cult brought certain controversial emblems back into fashion: there were frequent reports of photos of German army tanks and planes, Iron Crosses and drawings reminiscent of swastikas being seen backstage.

J J Cale
1939– American country rock guitarist

The soft touch

The delicacy and refinement of Cale's playing remains unmatched to this day. He was one of Dire Straits' most formative influences.

Cale is a multi-talented musician, for not only is he a superlative guitarist, but he also arranges scores, composes, produces and sings. Since he became famous, he has influenced a whole generation of rock musicians, with a remarkable absence of fuss and sordid scandal. By the end of the 1960s, he had already been spotted by some of the stars, notably Eric Clapton, who immortalized his 'After Midnight'. Lynyrd Skynyrd's version of 'Call Me the Breeze' and Santana's of 'Sensitive Kind' earned him the respect of the professionals, but it was Clapton's cover of 'Cocaine' that made him known to rock audiences.

However, despite his musical genius, Cale is still firmly attached to his quiet family life, only leaving his midwest ranch for the occasional tour.

Special Edition (Mercury, 1984) is an excellent compilation of all his best tracks. A unique sound: irreplacable.

Secret
According to his wife, J J Cale plays his guitar every evening facing the setting sun. She believes that he sounds better then than on any of his records.

Phil Collins

1951–   Rock drummer and singer

British Pop's 'Mr Nice'

He steered Genesis from progressive rock to massive popular success and is a superstar in his own right.

Born in Hounslow in London, Phil Collins is the son of a theatrical agent and his introduction to show business was as a child actor. He played the Artful Dodger on stage in *Oliver!* in 1964 and had a cameo role in the Beatles's film *A Hard Day's Night* the same year. His real passion however was the drums, and he made his first public appearance playing amateur nights at his parents's yacht club.

After a spell with art rock band Flaming Youth he joined Genesis as a drummer and took over on vocals when Peter Gabriel left the band in 1975. He gradually emerged as the band's central figure and moved them away from art rock towards a more commercial pop sound.

Always a prolific performer he recorded two albums with the jazz-influenced Genesis offshoot Brand X in 1975 and 1976 and then launched his solo career with the album *Face Value* in 1981. Despite instant commercial success (that first album included the massive hit singles 'In The Air Tonight' and 'I Missed Again') he continued to play with Genesis (who released *Abacab* in 1981) while pursuing his solo career.

His second solo project *Hello, I Must Be Going* (1982) included another hit in his version of the Supremes' 'You Can't Hurry Love'. Subsequent albums have included *No Jacket Required* (1985) and *But Seriously . . .* (1989).

Diversity

Collins has also undertaken production work for acts as diverse as Adam Ant, Howard Jones and John Martyn, recorded the Oscar-nominated theme to *Against All Odds*, he has drummed with Eric Clapton, Band Aid and Midge Ure's Mandela All-Stars and he has recorded successful duets with Marilyn Martin ('Separate Lives') and Philip Bailey ('Easy Lover'). Confirming his reputation as one of music's best all-round performers he returned to acting, after a gap of almost 20 years, in the mid-1980s. After playing a caricature Cockney in an episode of the American series *Miami Vice* he accepted the title role in *Buster* (1987), a film based on the life of the Great Train Robber Ronald 'Buster' Edwards.

One of rock's most self-effacing stars, he has nevertheless built a massive international following.

But Seriously . . . (Atlantic) is probably his best solo album.

Global Village

Renowned in the music business for his workaholic tendencies, Phil Collins was the only performer to appear live at both the American and British legs of Live Aid on 13 July 1985. Leaving the stage at London's Wembley Stadium at 15.46 London time he travelled by helicopter and Concorde to JFK stadium in Philadelphia, where he appeared on stage at 20.40 Eastern Standard Time.

Creedence Clearwater Revival

Swamp rock group

Hit factory

A product of the Sixties, this Californian band managed to keep on playing untarnished rock into the early Seventies.

Primitive style

At a time when the West Coast was spreading its psychedelic and experimental message to the rest of the late Sixties' rock world, Tom Fogerty and his Blue Velvets were more interested in producing simple, punchy rock music, characterized by catchy melodies and anti-intellectual lyrics. Swimming against the general tide, the band soon acquired, and lived up to, their primitive country rock reputation.

Using rhythms passed down from the

blues of the Old South and from the swamp areas of the Cajun country, Tom and John Fogerty, Stuart Cook and Ray Clifford recorded popular tunes which evoked daily life in rural areas. Their first album, *Creedence Clearwater Revival*, was released in 1968. These three words soon came to describe one of the most famous Seventies' groups. A whole series of rock gems followed: first, their cover version of 'Susie Q' went gold, followed closely by 'Proud Mary', 'Bad Moon Risin', 'Green River', 'Born on the Bayou', 'Down on the Corner' and a cover of 'I Heard It Through the Grapevine' which ended up outshining Marvin Gaye's excellent original. In 1971, barely three years after their first hits, CCR were ahead of the Rolling Stones in the American charts with 'Hey Tonight!'

The break-up

Exhausted by their endless tours, worn down by quarrels within the group and serious problems with their manager and their record company, the exceptionally talented musicians that were Creedence Clearwater Revival separated in 1972.

After an absence of almost ten years, John Fogerty made a comeback to the forefront of the rock scene with his amazingly masterful album, *Centerfield* (1985). However, despite fans' hopes, CCR will almost certainly never perform together again.

CCR, Bayou Country and **Cosmo Factory** (Fantasy, 1968, 69 and 70) are the classics to buy. An excellent compilation album **Creedence Gold** (Fantasy, 1972) is still available. Also available on CD are **Chronicle, vols 1 and 2, Greatest Hits** and **Complete Hit Album, vols 1 and 2** (Fantasy, 1978), depending on which selection of tracks the buyer prefers.

Record

In 1970, CCR reached number one in the American charts five times with: 'Down on the Corner', 'Fortunate Son', 'Poorboy Shuffle', 'Travellin' Band' and 'Up Around the Bend'. Totally without precedent.

Royalties

John Fogerty unwisely broke his contract with his record company. He also lost his case against the same company. Today he does not earn a penny in royalties from any of his Seventies' hits, and even has to pay when he wants to play them in public. He is one example (amongst many others) of an artist cheated out of what is rightfully his by the tangle of rules and regulations that govern all American show-business.

Crosby, Stills, Nash and Young

Country rock group

Legendary band with a turbulent past

A 'too many chiefs and not enough Indians' situation coupled with permanent quarrels prevented CSN&Y from forming a stable line-up.

The Neil Young period

David Crosby (guitar and vocals, one of the founding members of the Byrds), Stephen Stills (keyboards, guitar, vocals, formerly of Buffalo Springfield) and Graham Nash, the singer with the Hollies, founded 'Crosby, Stills and Nash' in 1968. Their first album, with its vocal harmonies and polished half-acoustic, half-electric guitar work, showed a strong Byrds influence. It was an immediate hit, but the band were still having difficulty in distinguishing themselves from other country rock line-ups.

The arrival of Neil Young, also of Buffalo Springfield, orientated the group towards rock. Young's guitar playing was harder, his keyboard work more spirited and his singing harsher. Crosby, Stills, Nash and Young reached the heights of fame with *Déjà Vu* (1970) and their double album, *Four Way Street* (1972).

Clashes

Despite their popularity, the group, one of the most original on the country rock scene at the start of the 1970s, was torn apart by personality clashes between the outstandingly talented members (Nash's 'Ohio' was a smash hit), parallel solo (Stills) and duet careers (Crosby and Nash) and the sudden deparature of Young in 1972.

Although the line-up reformed on numerous occasions, CSN & Y never fully regained their early, well-deserved, popularity.

Déjà Vu (Atlantic, 1970) is the album which best reflects CSN & Y's most productive period. Although the style is much the same, the overall sound on **Allies** (Atlantic, 1983) is more modern.

Crosby, Stills, Nash and Young

133

Deep Purple

English hard rock group

Still idolized by contemporary hard rock musicians

With a single track, 'Smoke on the Water', they entered the realms of rock legend.

Early days

Formed in 1968, Deep Purple were quick to find the key to fame; with a combination of steely tempo, simple, pounding rhythms, singer Ian Gillan's shrieking vocals and guitar hero Ritchie Blackmore's improvisations, the band is one of the acknowledged founders of a genre that had been vaguely explored by Hendrix and Led Zeppelin. Deep Purple's first album, *Shades of Deep Purple*, released in 1968, demonstrates their ability to play old tunes in a heavy metal manner, for example Neil Diamond's 'Kentucky Woman', and Ike and Tina Turner's 'River Deep, Mountain High'.

Released in 1970, 'Black Night' confirmed the growing celebrity of a band that was to dominate the whole hard rock genre in the 1970s.

The myth

Deep Purple in Rock had an impact on the genre as a whole and became a point of reference for all rock musicians, influenced the Stones' sound and brought the band into direct competition with Led Zeppelin. A string of Top Ten hits in both the European and American charts made Deep Purple the most famous hard rock band in the world. With the release in 1972 of 'Highway Star' and especially the unforgettable 'Smoke on the Water', the band became a legend.

The best moments of Deep Purple's world tour are recorded for posterity on *Made in Japan* (1973), the band's best live album to date.

Business

In the following years, they maintained their position at the head of the pack of prominent rock groups, but their albums of the time (*Burn, Stormbringer*), show that, as a band, they were musically burnt out, and indeed, they separated in 1976 for various members to pursue solo careers.

Reunited in the 1980s for a world tour, the members of Deep Purple showed that they had not lost their touch, only their songwriting abilities.

In Rock (Warner, 1970) and **Made in Japan** (Warner, 1973) are both musts.

An aside
'Smoke on the Water' is a description of the fire at the Montreux casino, on the shores of Lake Léman, which took place during Frank Zappa's 1971 concert.

Best of
It is rare for a compilation to reach the top of the charts, but this actually happened with *Deepest Purple* in 1980.

Ritchie Blackmore

The Eagles

Californian country rock group

Businessmen or musicians?

Hotel California gave them the keys to the élite supergroup club, and gave country rock a more modern sound.

The Eagles' first albums had a strong flavour of traditional country music. Although the line-up consisted of California-based musicians, with the exception of Glen Frey, who was born in Detroit (and friend of another Detroit or 'Motor City' native, Bob Seger), members of the band hailed from the Union's rural states, Nebraska, Florida and Texas.

The first album released by the Eagles (who had chosen this name for its 'street gang', 'country', 'Indian' and 'tough' associations) was an unqualified success (*Eagles*, 1972) as was *Desperado* the following year. *One of These Nights* (1975) easily broke the million barrier, and *Hotel California*, cut one year later, has sold more than 10 million copies to date. *The Long Run* (1979) was their last great album.

Fleetwood Mac

English blues group, then Californian rock supergroup

A success story based on beauty and savoir-faire

Once they had given up their early blues style, Fleetwood Mac became one of the most famous soft rock groups of the century.

The original line-up, led by guitarist Peter Green, Mick Fleetwood and John MacVie, had little success with its first overly purist, blues repertoire. Their move to the States brought them into contact with a range of new musical influences; the recruitment of truly talented (and physically attractive) female vocalists turned Fleetwood Mac into one of the 'sexiest' bands on the West Coast.

Carefully avoiding the growing fashion for heavy metal, 'Big Mac' exploited vocal harmony and skilfully crafted instrumental work, and with the relase of *Rumours*, became the best-selling band of the 1970s. They had no less than four hit singles from this album alone!

Rumours (Warner, 1977) is strikingly well-constructed.

Look

One of the contributing factors to the band's success has been the beauty of its female members, unmatched vocalist Stevie Nicks, and talented backing vocalist and songwriter, Christine MacVie.

135

Foreigner
FM rock group

Half-way house between hard and soft rock

With their eclectic attitude, they laid the foundations for a flourishing genre known as 'FM rock'.

Firstly labelling their music 'hard pop' in order to highlight the ambiguous nature of their style, the members of Foreigner earned the respect of both rock and FM radio station audiences in America and in Europe. As early as 1976, but mainly from 1978, Foreigner combined hard rock sounds, which were the height of fashion at the time, with an awareness that the musicians' act and look had to be toned down or they would attract the attention of the puritan associations which were conducting a relentless and merciless anti-rock campaign.

The Foreigner sound, which admittedly lacks originality, can nevertheless be considered as one of the best in FM rock, a musical genre which has dominated American TV and radio music stations for a number of years.

Their second album, *Double Vision* (Atlantic, 1978), is worth buying, as is the more recent *Records* (Atlantic, 1982).

> **Toto**
> Made up of top session players, this band took FM rock to the limits of instrumental and melodic perfection.
> *Toto IV* (CBS, 1982) is a masterpiece.

Rory Gallagher
1949– Irish blues rock singer and guitarist

Faithful to the blues

Guitar hero and showman extraordinaire, Gallagher now plays blues with a hard rock veneer.

Having left his band, Taste, in 1971, Gallagher embarked on a brilliant solo career that was punctuated by the release of some of the most authentic blues rock albums of the 1970s. Playing a mandolin, an acoustic guitar, a harmonica or his electric guitar with its full, solid sound, Gallagher aimed to highlight his two passions: to sing of the struggle in his native Ireland, and to keep the blues flag flying.

Today, with the fashion for hard sound a thing of the past, he has been more or less forgotten.

Irish Tour 74, **Tattoo** (Polydor, 1973), **Photofinish** (Chrysalis, 1975) and **Stage Struck** (Chrysalis, 1980) are all unforgettable albums.

> **Antique**
> Rory Gallagher plays a 1962 L series Stratocaster which, with its scratched paintwork, looks like a relic from a bygone age. A period piece, this guitar is famous throughout the rock world.

Genesis
English progressive rock group

Springboard

Thanks to Genesis, two prominent Eighties' rock musicians, Peter Gabriel and Phil Collins, made their débuts.

Their first important release was *Foxtrot* (1972). The group's style emerged from the combined talents of guitarist Anthony Phillips, keyboardist Tony Banks, singer Peter Gabriel and bassist Mike Rutherford, later including guitarist Steve Hackett and drummer Phil Collins. Their first songs have a strong psychedelic flavour, but the members of Genesis evolved together towards a preference for more technical music, rivalling the masters in that field,

Pink Floyd. They also developed their distinctive, theatrical live stage-act.

In 1975, Peter Gabriel left the group, allowing Phil Collins to unleash his creative energy. Collins took over on vocals and led the band towards the more commercial mainstream (*Abacab*, 1981).

The Lamb Lies Down on Broadway (Phonogram–Abkco, 1974) was released during Genesis's most fruitful period.

Political views
Peter Gabriel was the first rock singer to speak out against the apartheid régime in South Africa: 'Steven Biko' (1980) describes the death under torture of the black leader.

The Grateful Dead
Californian acid rock group

Pioneers of the hippy movement

The Grateful Dead are far from dead: they are still performing today.

That this Sixties' band of almost mythical proportions is still going strong comes as a surprise to many, for the Californian alternative 'flower power' culture is long dead and buried. It is perhaps the attitude of this group of 'musical ideologists' that has ensured their lasting popularity, particularly in the States, where not long ago they managed to pull as large a crowd as Bruce Springsteen! Even in Europe, they have a considerable following of faithful 'Family' fans. In the Grateful Dead, hippy philosophy lives on: their songs still

vindicate pacifism, ecology, life in communes, squatters and drugs (in more moderate terms, of course, than twenty years ago).

Jerry Garcia now graces stages worldwide with his magnificent, bushy white beard; against his will, he has become an institution.

Live Dead (Warner, 1970) and **Europe 72** (Warner, 1972) give a good idea of their style.

Reunion
For the recording of *Dylan and Dead* (1988), Bob Dylan, the king of protest song, got back together with his old comrades at arms.

George Harrison

1943– English pop singer and guitarist

Ex-Beatle who went on to have an erratic solo career

Influenced by the mystical philosophies of India, he tried to spread their message through his songs.

A friend of Ravi Shankar, the Indian sitarist who reached the height of his fame in the 1960s, Harrison added an original, oriental touch to the Beatles' music ('Within You, Without You' on *Sergeant Pepper*). After the group's split, over which he had no control, Harrison recorded a triple album (totally unheard of at the time) which groups together the best of his work, including the famous 'My Sweet Lord', a gentle, mystical number which is entirely representative of his style. In 1971, Harrison organized the famous 'Concert for Bangladesh', then withdrew to devote himself to composing film soundtracks, accomplishing most of his work in the studio.

Since the release of his tribute to John Lennon, 'All Those Years Ago' (1981), Harrison's work has lacked inspiration, despite a recent album which testifies to his undeniable talents as a musician.

All Things Must Pass (Apple, 1970) was produced by Phil Spector and boasts the collaboration of guitar hero Eric Clapton.

Second career

In 1979 Harrison helped Finance the Monty Python film *Life of Brian,* leading to the formation of his HandMade Films production company. Films produced by the company include *A Private Function* (1985) and the Madonna film *Shanghai Surprise* (1986).

Hot Tuna

American blues and country rock group

Partnership of virtuoso musicians

Their attempt to return to traditional musical roots was a commercial failure, perhaps because they refused to become part of the system.

Formed by Jefferson Airplane's guitar hero Jorma Kaukonen and Jack Casady Hot Tuna deliberately set out to produce acoustic blues. Their combined skills were such that their cover versions of the great rural blues classics are perfect: in terms of technique and general atmosphere, their reprises are as close to the originals as possible. However, little by little this kind of acoustic music went out of fashion and was replaced by 'bigger' sound. Hot Tuna then made the successful transition into the country rock mainstream.

Throughout the whole of the 1970s, Hot Tuna retained a healthy following. The band toured regularly, but deliberately limited the size of its concerts.

Hot Tuna, Burgers and **Double Dose** (RCA, 1970, 72 and 77) are superb albums.

Speed

Jorma Kaukonen is considered to be one of the best all-round guitarists in rock history. His perfect mastery of the blues picking technique and his speed on the electric guitar are legendary.

Elton John
1945– English singer and pianist

A blend of outrageous costumes and conventional music

Somewhere between rock and easy listening music, Elton John, singer and songwriter extraordinaire, earned the respect of the music establishment becaus of his unwavering professionalism.

Elton John cannot be called a true rock musician for his music appeals to an extremely wide and varied public. His catchy tunes and arrangements are more to the taste of music-hall and light music lovers than to contemporary rock fans. However, from his very first performances, in the framework of his partnership with lyricist Bernie Taupin, it was obvious that his intention was to bridge the gap between

rock and easy listening. 1969 saw the release of *Empty Sky*, 1970 that of *Elton John* and by 1971 he had reached number seven in the British charts with 'Your Song'.

A series of hits, his extravagant stage-act and costumes and fun style combined to make him one of the most popular stars in the Seventies and Eighties.

Don't Shoot Me, I'm Only The Piano Player (MCA, 1972) and **Goodbye Yellow Brick Road** (MCA, 1973) are his best albums.

Hits
Throughout 1970s, Elton John broke box-office records all over the world, even when he moved into disco music in 1976. He moved back into the rock mainstream with *Jump Up* in 1981.

Journey
American rock mainstream group

Typical commercial rock line-up

Influenced by a form of hard rock whch they were quick to tone down, the members of Journey are stars in the States.

Journey's idea, which didn't really come off in Europe, was to blend watered-down heavy metal and early hard rock with pop tunes. Although they kept a distorted heavy sound, they produced lacklustre lyrics and melodies that would have been rather basic had it not been for arrangements borrowed from 'spacey' rock.

From 1976 onwards, Journey became one of the biggest selling bands in the

States. With their TV commercials, giant tour with the Rolling Stones (1981) and regular, repetitive albums, the band's members exploited all the means put at their disposal by the rock establishment to their best advantage.

Infinity and **Evolution** (CBS, 1978, 1979) are most typical of their style.

Radio stations
Journey is one of those bands which gained a following through constant exposure on the radio and on MTV, the TV music channel. They are the perfect example of what is called mainstream or FM rock.

King Crimson
English progressive rock group

Mavericks

Unwilling to compromise its high principles, the technically brilliant King Crimson line-up was forced to break new ground in the field of rock music.

In 1969, the release of King Crimson's first album, with its disturbing cover design and difficult, inspired music, announced the arrival on the music scene of an important new group whose songwriting abilities have rarely been matched to this day.

Guitarist Robert Fripp's experimental tendencies, Pete Sinfield's wild poetic lyrics, Michael Giles's drum solos and the added cachet of their numerous guest artists made up an experimental rock cocktail, which was soon re-named 'progressive rock', an explosive blend of jazz, psychedelic rock, electronic sounds and unusual 'effects' (for example, playing recordings backwards). The recruitment of drummer Bill Bruford elevated the band to the status of idols for other more commercial groups (including Pink Floyd and Genesis). King Crimson split up in 1974 but Fripp reformed the group in 1981 for the album *Discipline*.

In the Court of the Crimson King (Atlantic, 1969) and **Lizard** (Atlantic, 1971) are musts.

Kiss
American heavy metal band

Rock for the seven to seventeen age group

Simplistic, outrageous, and deliberately commercial, Kiss had a devoted following.

Using adolescent fantasies, and deliberately playing on the violence implied by their logo (Nazi SS-style double 's'), Kiss took the fashion started by Alice Cooper to its extreme limit, particularly in terms of their stage presentation. The Kiss stage act was based on make-up and costumes based on superhero comic books, and was littered with explosions, smoke clouds, flying men, and giant dolls. This tacky ensemble, reminiscent of fairground ghost trains, made Kiss one of the best selling bands in the 1970s.

Double Platinum (Casablanca, 1978) gives a sufficient idea of the kind of conventional heavy metal produced by Kiss.

Hits
The Kiss numbers 'Rock and Roll Night', 'Naked City' and especially 'I Was Made For Lovin' You' all went platinum. The group's memory inspires more respect in the States than in Europe.

Led Zeppelin

English hard rock group

Founders of a genre

Singer Robert Plant and guitarist Jimmy Page popularized a style that has been copied by several generations of rock musicians.

At the end of the 1960s, while rock seemed to be heading inexorably towards either psychedelic music, the high-tech sounds produced by Pink Floyd or Simon and Garfunkel's folk rock, Led Zeppelin's first album, released in 1969, popularized the exploration of new sounds begun by Jimi Hendrix shortly before his death. Led Zeppelin set Hendrix's masterly guitar solos and thick, almost distorted sound to heavier, simpler rhythms. The 'hendrixian' innovations were made more accessible to the general rock public by the band's use of a steady blues-influenced beat, and the charismatic combination of ex-Yardbird Jimmy Page's improvisations and Robert Plant's screaming vocals.

In a short space of time, after the release of a few superb albums, Led Zeppelin virtually created heavy metal (there was already a pun in the band's name: Led-lead) which was soon to be called hard rock. Their most famous numbers became rock classics: 'I Can't Quit You Baby', a reprise of an old Chicago blues song, then their own compositions such as 'Dazed and Confused', 'Whole Lotta Love', 'That's the Way' and especially their theme song, 'Stairway to Heaven'.

Despite the decline in their popularity at the end of the 1970s and the tragic death of drummer John 'Bonzo' Bonham, the band are one of the most legendary in rock history.

Led Zeppelin I, II, III (Atlantic, 1969, 1970) and **Untitled** (Atlantic, 1971) are a must for all 'big' sound, blues rock and hard rock fans. For those who are merely curious, the compilations which draw together their best tracks will suffice.

Jimmy Page

A guitar hero, for many years he was idolized by all heavy metal guitarists. In some ways, he was a blend of two of his illustrious predecessors: from Hendrix, Page inherited his taste for new sounds and impossibly complex solos, and from Clapton, the smooth and disciplined elements in his style.

His career, which he had begun at the tender age of 16 as a session musician on other performers' records, took shape when he joined the Yardbirds and was consolidated when he left to found Led Zeppelin in 1968.

As songwriter, score-arranger and producer, he was responsible for all the band's creations. He is respected by the whole music profession not only for his inspired live performances, but also for his modesty. Today, his activity is limited to composing film scores.

Curiosities

Jimmy Page was the first guitarist to attempt to play his instrument with a violin bow. He also made famous the double-necked guitar which allowed him to use two different tunings during the same piece.

Lynyrd Skynyrd

Southern American rock band

The new sound of the South

The founders of Southern rock, the legendary band Lynyrd Skynyrd influenced an entire era and created a genre that is still popular in the United States today.

The accidental death of Duane Allman having shattered the Allman Brothers, it was Lynyrd Skynyrd who took their place as leaders of American blues rock, coupling the rhythmic simplicity of the rural blues with the sounds produced by all the experiments that were taking place on the West Coast. A new genre, 'Southern rock', was born. Characterized by boundless, frenetic musical energy, Lynyrd Skynyrd's songs were patriotic and reactionary (and also virulently anti-feminist, with racist overtones), a sort of salute to the

Confederate flag (black civil right organizations demanded the boycott of Lynyrd Skynrd concerts). In contrast with the English rock bands of the time (Led Zeppelin and Deep Purple), Southern rock, with its more straightforward, simplistic and anti-experimental outlook, only played a limited part in the formation of hard rock.

Crazy for an almost distorted sound and completely at ease with massive tours (they supported the Who and Clapton in concert, and played at the long Atlanta festivals), from 1973, Lynyrd Skynyrd was the most popular band in the South.

Ironically, although their fans were 'rednecks', truckers and Hell's Angels, the band led by Ronnie Van Zant and Ed King produced the most fundamentally black music of the period; Lynyrd Skynyrd used the same subject material as the early blues, making a cult of (Jack Daniels) whiskey, putting down women in general and glorifying the travelling life and fleeting love affairs.

With their ability to play souped-by classic blues numbers acoustic-style, Lynyrd Skynyrd gave rock such masterpieces as 'Sweethome Alabama', 'Freebird' and 'Whiskey Rock'n'Roller'.

Gold and Platinum (MCA, 1979) is an anthology. **Street Survivors** (MCA, 1977) is a must. **Legend** (MCA) is a reasonable compilation.

Lynyrd Skynyrd

> **Mockery?**
> The group's name is a deformation of the professor who had Ronnie Van Zant thrown out of college. His name was Leonard Skinner.
>
> **Deaths**
> In October, 1977, a plane crash deprived the group of singer Ronnie Van Zant and master guitarist Steve Gaines.

Motörhead
English heavy metal band

Decibel level record

Cultivating their rebel image, the members of Motörhead were able to survive the punk wave.

Although Lemmy Kilminster began his career at the very start of the 1970s, it was not until 1975 that Motörhead was born. They (Lemmy on bass, Eddie 'Fast Fingers' Clark on guitar and Phil Taylor on drums) found their definitive style not long after the release of their first album. *Overkill*'s violent lyrics and brutal arrangements won them fans from punk audiences. With their tough look, overtly sexist statements and songs glorifying a drug- and alcohol-orientated lifestyle, the band maintained its rebel

image. At their concerts, fans' eardrums have to be able to withstand the incredible decibel levels as the band turn their equipment up full. However, since the start of the 1980s, their heavy metal has become more conventional.

Overkill and **Ace of Spades** (Bronze, 1980) are heavy rock monuments.

Roadie
Lemmy started out as one of Jimi Hendrix's team of roadies, responsible for setting up, transporting and looking after the musician's equipment. He freely admits that it was at this time that he came to love 'big' sound.

Mountain
Hard rock group

Forgotten precursors

The West–Pappalardi due was one of the first to patent the hard rock formula.

In 1969, American guitarist Leslie West, with his impressive 120-kilo build, formed a partnership with bassist-producer Felix Pappalardi and released a début album called *Mountain*, a title which referred not only to West's colossal size, but also to its heavy rhythms, distorted improvisations and pounding drum beat.

Influenced by Cream, Mountain produced cover versions of several Jack Bruce numbers, and recruited organist

Steve Knight, whose playing toned down the band's initial heavy style. Without ever matching the popularity of their British counterparts, Mountain had four years of relative commercial success on the American market.

Since the break-up of the band in 1972, the members of Mountain have all pursued undistinguished careers.

Best of (Phonogram) gives a good idea of the kind of music they produced.

Cinema
Mountain's celebrity was based on the use of 'Mississippi Queen' in the sound track for *Easy Rider*, the famous Sixties' cult film.

Pink Floyd

English electronic rock group

Blend of rock and symphonic music

They introduced and developed synthesized sounds and became one of the most successful and popular bands in the history of rock.

The Barrett period

The group was founded in 1966 by bassist Roger Waters and his singer-guitarist friend Roger 'Syd' Barrett. With the recruitment of two other architecture students, Rick Wright and Nick Mason, Pink Floyd entered history as the first English psychedelic band, attracting huge audiences with their high quality sound, visionary lyrics and drug-orientated lifestyle; moreover, the visual aspect of their stagecraft (the use of remote controlled lights, slides, whirling colour patterns, smoke and fog effects and suspended objects seemingly caught in mid-flight, etc) was the brainchild of the Barrett-Waters partnership, and made use of the most sophisticated equipment available at the time.

From 1967, with their 'spacey' sound (produced by their use of synthesizers) and surrealist lyrics (LSD was the drug of the decade), Pink Floyd began to compete seriously with the big English rock bands, and were strikingly original. Barrett, who was already losing his grip on reality, composed some astonishing numbers; Waters, who was not exactly attracted to straight rock and despised pop, was looking for another form of musical expression, and Wright was a talented keyboard player, who helped design and perfect the very first synthesizers. Drummer Mason also refused to play simple rock.

Pink Floyd's first musical period came to an end when Barrett, exhausted by drugs and mentally ill-equipped to cope with the pressures created by the band's overnight international success, had a nervous breakdown and was replaced by Dave Gilmour. This first period was extremely fruitful: they broke away from dance and easy-listening music, defining a radically new sound. Released during this period, *The Piper at the Gates of Dawn* can therefore be termed an 'historic' album.

Differences of opinion

With the departure of Syd Barrett and the arrival of his replacement, guitarist and singer David Gilmour, Pink Floyd entered the second period of their career: while the newcomer's skills did not erase the memory of Syd Barrett's creative flights of fancy, the band nevertheless gained a reputation for technical excellence and partially shrugged off their wild image, without losing their position as leaders of the psychedelic movement.

Released in the autumn of 1969, *Ummagumma vols 1 and 2* confirmed the band's domination of the world rock scene and propelled them to the same commercial level as such early Sixties' greats as the Beatles and the Rolling Stones. Their music was a credible alternative to pop, which was fast losing momentum, and nascent hard rock. Their soundtrack for Barbet Schroeder's film *More*, and the use of some of their tracks in Antononi's *Zabriskie Point* (1970) guaranteed them a reputation as musical intellectuals. The following year, *Meddle* showed that the band had totally mastered the new instrumental style which, once the ghost of the legendary Syd ('acid') Barrett had been exorcized from their

> **Technique**
> It would appear that Pink Floyd used quadrophonic sound for the first time on stage at the Rainbow in London in February 1972. This performance, which was impressive for the time, was not spoilt by any unwanted sounds or feed-back. Little by little, Pink Floyd became reputed to have the best sound in rock.

creative consciousness (particularly in the case of anxiety-ridden Roger Waters), was to shape all their further musical work. At the same time, Adrian Maben's musical documentary, *Live at Pompeii*, confirmed the band as world rock leaders in the eyes of the intelligentsia and their ever-increasing following.

World fame came with the release of the extraordinary *Dark Side of the Moon* (1973) which is the best-selling and most popular album in rock history, only having been dropped from the American best-seller lists for two weeks since it first appeared on the market. Along with other tracks which later became classics ('Time', 'Us and Them' and 'Dark Side of the Moon'), Pink Floyd's first real hit, 'Money', is on this album.

Towards the crisis

September 1975. Rock appeared to be stylistically burned out. The supergroups were no longer producing anything of interest, routine was choking the life out of creativity. Pink Floyd seemed to be the only glimmer of hope; the long-awaited flash of light on that bleak musical landscape came in the shape of *Wish You Were Here*, which marked the beginning of Roger Waters's leadership of the band; through him, Syd Barrett's old demons began to reappear. A whole song was dedicated to him: 'Shine On, You Crazy Diamond' is a tribute to the madness of the genius who founded Pink Floyd, but who was now permanently locked in a terrifying state of schizophrenia. 'Wish You Were Here' is a beautiful love song, and an indication of Waters's feelings about his divorce. 'Welcome to the Machine' is another sign of Waters's (who, since *Dark Side*, had become the group's principal lyricist) disillusionment. The album was a huge success.

The concept album *Animals* reflects Waters's growing pessimism and the problems he was having in his personal life. The sales figures are breathtaking; after all these years, *Dark Side* is still listed in the album charts in Europe and the United States. *Animals* is certainly not their best album, but audiences at their massive concerts still clamour for 'Sheep', 'Dogs' and 'Pigs on the Wing'.

Madness

Madness seems to be one of the main themes in the history of Pink Floyd: after

the dramatic fate of Syd Barrett, Roger Waters entered a phase of megalomania which, after he refused to acknowledge his problem, turned to hatred of stardom and the star system. Obsessed by the stars' inability to really communicate with their fans, and haunted by his angry treatment of a young fan during a concert, Waters's behaviour became increasingly erratic. He began to consider Pink Floyd as his own creation, his property, and saw himself as the unique beneficiary of Barrett's philosophical and aesthetic heritage. Power-mad, he stopped Wright from playing and barred Gilmour from composing.

This paranoia contributed to the band's last great album and second hit, *The Wall*. A vision of Waters's sense of isolation, it was conceived together with an ambitious film of the same name; directed by Alan Parker, it is sometimes pretentious and over-ambitious, but was a smash box-office hit. *The Wall* expresses all the difficulties the group were experiencing in their attempts to stay together: as Gilmour later stated 'these are Waters's problems, not ours'.

Waters's obsession is omnipresent in both the record and the film. He believed that society was loathsome and that school was a machine designed to break spirits. 'We don't need no education. . . . Hey, teacher! Leave them kids alone' sing a choir of children on the most famous track from the record and film.

The split

The Final Cut (1983) had an especially sombre and despairing anti-military theme. Composed entirely by Waters, the other members only took part in it to present a united front. After Waters's inevitable departure, Pink Floyd, now grouped around David Gilmour, recovered some of the original sound typical of *Dark Side* and *Wish You Were Here* and went on mammoth, impressive world tours intended to boost sales of their album, *A Momentary Lapse of Reason* (1987). Each of the Floyd musicians later attempted a solo career.

The Piper at the Gates of Dawn (Tower, 1967) and **A Saucerful of Secrets** (Pathé, 1968) are both heavily influenced by the strong personalities of Barrett and Waters, who explored virgin territory in the field of sound.

Pink Floyd *in the 1970s*

Ummagumma (1969) was the band's long-term best-seller and shows astonishing mastery of the new synthesized sounds.

Meddle (1979) marked a turning-point in their musical direction and, with its astounding track 'One of These Days', is still a firm favourite with fans.

Dark Side of the Moon (Harvest, 1973) can only be described as a masterpiece, a rock monument; great stuff.

Wish You Were Here (Columbia, 1975) complements the above beautifully, as does **Animals** (1977).

The Wall (1979) is an impressive concept album.

A Momentary Lapse of Reason (EMI, 1987) is a good résumé of the band's work, but without the presence of Roger Waters . . .

A Delicate Sound of Thunder (EMI, 1988) sums up their 1988 world tour.

Gargantuan appetites
An official supplier confirms that for two 1988 concerts, he delivered 150 litres of milk, 300 litres of water, 600 litres of Coke, 100 litres of orange juice, 350 cans of beer, 50kg of meat, 25 chickens, 400 eggs, 10kg of fruit and 100kg of vegetables to the Pink Floyd outfit.

Rock movie
The hero of the film *The Wall*, Boomtown Rats vocalist Bob Geldof, became famous for his inspired interpretation of the more psychotic aspects of Roger Waters's personality.

Court case
In 1985, Waters went on a world tour with Eric Clapton and prevented Gilmour, Wright and Mason from using the band's name during their tour. After a well-publicized court case, and in exchange for 30% of the profits, Gilmour won the right to use the name to get the band back together (minus Waters) and to play Waters's songs, of which there are many in Floyd's concert repertoire, in public.

Queen
English hard/stadium rock band

Lucrative blend of styles

The Queen cocktail is made up of hard rock, easy listening and funk.

Formed at the start of the 1970s, Queen, unlike many contemporaries, avoided unrewarding pub and club dates, and instead embarked on impressive concert performances, leading to an early record contract. Their first album, *Queen*, released in 1973, earned critical hostility from the music press, but valuable exposure on UK and US tours with Mott the Hoople allowed Queen to begin to make a name for themselves in the middle of the decade. With their 1974 single 'Killer Queen', the band, led by vocalist Freddie Mercury, entered the British charts. Queen's contributions to rock helped to fill the void in the pre-punk UK pop scene, with Mercury as a charismatic frontman and Brian May on guitar, while Roger Taylor and John Deacon contributed hit songs.

Breakthrough

The album *A Night at the Ocean*, released in 1975, was believed to be the most expensive UK LP production since the Beatles' *Sergeant Pepper*. This album included the stunningly successful hit single 'Bohemian Rhapsody': this six-minute masterpiece with classical overtones, hard rock and heavy metal became the longest running UK no. 1 for 20 years, reaching no. 9 in the US charts. It also helped to initiate the beginnings of the video era. This was followed up well in 1976 by the hit singles 'We Are The Champions' and 'Somebody to Love', which were both highly placed in

the European and American charts.

The following albums continued to demonstrate their great versatility and maintained the band's popularity. In 1979, they appeared at charity concerts for Kampuchea, but later aroused controversy by appearing in South Africa's Sun City. Their next great successes were the funk-influenced 'Another One Bites the Dust', which reached no. 1 in the USA, and Mercury's 'Crazy Little Thing Called Love', a rockabilly-style single. Creating the soundtrack to *Flash Gordon* in 1980, they became the first band to achieve a major film.

Their next UK no. 1, 'Under Pressure', recorded in 1982 with David Bowie, revealed their great distance from their early days of hard rock. Their enduring success with further hit singles and albums brought 500 000 fans at a time to dates on their UK tour, during which the album *Live Magic* was recorded.

Although Mercury and Taylor also pursued solo careers, the band's line-up remained unchanged from 1971 until Freddie Mercury's well-publicized death from AIDS in November 1991.

Sheer Heart Attack (EMI Parlophone, 1974) is a good example of their early hard rock style, and includes the single 'Killer Queen'.

Queen: Greatest Hits (EMI Parlophone, 1981) contains their best known tracks.

The Works (EMI Parlophone, 1984) includes world-wide no. 1 'Radio Ga-Ga' and several other hits.

Idols

Two Queen albums bear titles borrowed from the Marx Brothers: A Night at the Opera and A Day at the Races.

Rhapsody revival

Soon after Freddie Mercury's death, 'Bohemian Rhapsody' was rereleased on 9 December 1991. It instantly shot to no. 1 in the UK charts where it remained for five weeks; after 11 weeks it was still highly placed.

Roxy Music

English art rock group

Sophisticated, well-groomed work

Cultivating eroticism and elegance, Roxy Music were the first to introduce an element of high fashion into rock.

After studying art and working in local R & B bands in Newcastle, Bryan Ferry moved to London in the late 1960s. Together with talented keyboards player Brian Eno and saxophonist Andy Mackay, he formed Roxy Music with the aim of creating an original musical and visual formula. Roxy Music's rise to fame was startling, their original style and glamorous image being widely welcomed in the music press: only David Bowie had as much influence on musical expression at this time. Eno's experimental approach and Ferry's interest in 1950s rock 'n' roll combined to produce one of the most creative and individual new albums of the 1970s, *Roxy Music*, in 1972.

It wasn't until after the release of an inventive follow-up album, *For Your Pleasure*, that disputes arose between Ferry and Eno over the band's future plans: Eno left in late 1973. Eno's departure and subsequent solo career forced Roxy Music to place greater emphasis on their image. The album *Stranded* introduced multi-instrumentalist Eddie Jobson and included the hit single 'Street Life'. Ferry's parallel solo career also began at this time with the release of albums in 1973 and 1974, confirming his reputation as a pioneer of the new sophisticated rock 'n' roll.

It was in 1975 with the release of *Siren*, often considered to be their weakest album, that the band's success appeared to be fading. The first four albums had been outstanding successes, but it did not seem that Roxy Music could maintain the same momentum. Ferry, Mackay and guitarist Paul Manzanera all became involved in solo projects. Ferry's *Let's Stick Together* was not well received, despite including a no. 4 hit single as the title track. *The Bride Stripped Bare* (1978) could have improved his credibility, but received little attention at the time.

Revival

Ferry worked once again with Manzanera and Mackay to produce *Manifesto* in 1979, which included two hit singles, and in 1980 Roxy Music released their only UK no. 1, a cover of John Lennon's 'Jealous Guy'. Roxy's last release was the live album *Musique/The High Road* in 1983. Bryan Ferry remains one of the distinctive voices of rock, and Roxy Music are remembered for their clever band of R & B, funk and pop, skilfully presented as a synthesis between rock music and easy listening.

Roxy Music (ATCO, 1972) contains many of the most original tracks.

Street Life (EG Records, 1986) is a compilation of Ferry's and Roxy Music's best known hits.

Hit

Bryan Ferry cut a fair number of big hits in the 1970s, either with Roxy Music ('Stranded', 'Love Is The Drug', 'My Only Love', 'Dance Away', 'Angel Eyes', 'Jealous Guy', and 'Avalon') or as a solo artist ('Tokyo Jo', 'The Price of Love' and 'More Than This').

Status Quo
English boogie rock band

Instantly recognizable, punchy rock

They soon ran through the range of styles offered by commercial boogie.

This band started in the early 1960s and performed under various different names until 1967, when they symbolically took the name Status Quo.

At that time, they were playing both pop and psychedelic rock, without ever really fixing on a truly personal style. From 1971, they adopted a nascent heavy metal sound and attempted to incorporate elements from Southern rock into their music. With their limited creative powers, they could only belt out simplistic, straightforward tunes at a fast and furious pace. However, they attracted a substantial following

'Down, Down' (1975) and especially 'Rockin' All Over the World' (1977) (written by Creedence Clearwater Revival) and 'What You're Proposing' (1980).

With 35 million albums sold, Status Quo are amongst the best-selling bands of the 1970s.

Rockin' All Over the World (Phonogram-Capital, 1978) and **Greatest Hits** are worth buying.

> **Fashion**
> In 1986, Status Quo decided to give their image a complete overhaul. The resultant single, 'You're in the Army Now' was a blend of catchy melody, synthesized sound and soft rock. It was a smash hit.

Rod Stewart
1944– English mainstream rock singer

One of the most famous voices in rock

He deliberately opted for commercial rock.

Inspired by R&B, Rod Stewart had two vital assets: a powerful, hoarse voice and an attractive physique; from his earliest performances, he sang the blues ('Good Morning Little Schoolgirl' in 1964) then worked with guitarist Jeff Beck (*Truth*, 1968). With his friend, the future Rolling Stones guitarist Ron Wood, he played with the Faces, and produced two excellent

albums, *First Step* (1970) and *Long Player* (1971).

After the departure of Ron Wood, he embarked on a solo career which was successful mainly due to his ability to adapt to changing fashions and his skills as a singer: *Blonds Have More Fun* (1978) and *Tonight I'm Yours* (1981) are his best albums.

Some of his tracks, including 'Sailing', 'Do Ya Think I'm Sexy?', 'Passion', 'Tonight I'm Yours' and 'Stay With Me' have since become dance classics.

A double-album, **Absolutely Live** (WEA, 1982) contains all his greatest hits and is an absolute must.

Supertramp
Progressive rock group, then stadium supergroup

Polished melodies and careful harmonies

Their various albums are still popular.

The music produced by Supertramp cannot really be called original. Although the members are undeniably skilled, the band has never attempted to stand out from the major musical trends that dominate the decades of its existence. It is precisely this ability to adapt to changing fashions that has allowed the band to survive with ease and commercial success. Initially, the band, with its Munich-based Anglo-American line-up founded by Rick Davies (vocals and keyboards) and Roger Hodgson (many-faceted musician and prolific composer) was part of the new progressive rock movement in the 1970s.

Little by little however, the band's output became clearly geared towards the easy listening market (FM radio stations, hit parades, supermarkets, airports, etc). Supertramp scored a number of hits during the decade, whose catchy lyrics and polished, sophisticated style had a wide appeal and were even popular in night clubs.

Crime of the Century (A and M, 1974) and **Breakfast in America** (A and M, 1979) are their best albums.

> **Europe**
> Although Supertramp are internationally famous, their biggest sales figures have been in Britain and France: over four million copies of *Crime of the Century* and *Breakfast in America* were sold in these two countries alone.

Wings
English pop group

Led by an ex-Beatle

Paul McCartney left his mark on Wings's music.

After the Beatles split up, Paul McCartney was not content to cut solo albums. Therefore, with his wife Linda, he recruited a number of skilled musicians and formed Wings. At first, the memory of the much-missed Beatles, still fresh in the minds of the public, worked against him, but McCartney gradually reminded fans of his extraordinary talents as a composer of popular tunes and sales took off. Throughout the 1970s, Wings popularized a 'post-Beatles' style in the soft rock movement, with such songs as 'Give Ireland Back to the Irish', 'Band on the Run' and 'Venus and Mars'.

After several successful international tours, McCartney dissolved Wings in 1980 to pursue a solo career.

Their first album **Wild Life** (EMI-Capitol, 1973) and **Wings Over America** (3d-EMI) are both indispensable.

> **Goody two-shoes?**
> Faced with John Lennon's overtly rebellious image, McCartney has often been depicted as apolitical and well-behaved. That this is an over-simplified and largely false version of the reality is proved by his song 'Give Ireland Back to the Irish' (1970) and his problems in Japan caused by his possession of hashish.

Yes

English progressive rock band

Pink Floyd and Genesis's serious rival

Incessant changes in the line-up prevented the group from establishing a stable musical identity.

It is impossible to list the countless changes in Yes's line-up in a few words. However, one thing is sure: drummer Bill Bruford's expertise definitely influenced the direction taken by Yes in its early days. The group's first four albums, released between 1969 and 1972, placed them fully within the progressive rock movement; it was no accident that Bruford subsequently left the group to join King Crimson, one of the leaders of the genre. The next series of albums had a strong 'classical' rock influence, a form of rock that had been made popular by Pink Floyd. The band's contact with Vangelis gave their music the synthesized overtones usually associated with soft rock and easy listening, but the guitar sound, supplied by master guitarists Steve Howe and Chris Squire (bass) was always highlighted.

All the members of Yes, which broke up in 1981, have attempted solo careers. In 1989 four of the band's most respected members reformed as Anderson, Bruford, Wakeman and Howe. The name Yes was kept by a separate band led by Yes's original bass player Chris Squire.

The Yes Album (Atlantic, 1971) and **Classic Yes** are good buys.

Springboard
The group Asia, which was hugely successful at the start of the 1980s, was made up of two former Yes members (Howe and Downes) and Carl Palmer (formerly of Emmerson, Lake and Palmer).

Neil Young

1945–   American folk rock singer and guitarist

Followed in Dylan's footsteps, then carried on where he left off

His lonely journey took him from folk song to hard rock.

Canadian-born Young is a demanding musician and remarkable guitarist. A former member of Buffalo Springfield, he began to move towards heavy rock at the start of the 1970s, as his work with the group Crazy Horse proves. His short-lived participation in the Crosby, Still and Nash line-up marked the band's most fruitful period, but he left due to personality clashes with the other members of the quartet. Neil Young's solo career is exemplary and completely lacking in compromise: he played what he wanted without conceding to current fashions and yet managed to retain a hard core of fans with such diverse albums as *After the Gold Rush* (1970), *Harvest* (1972), *Tonight's the Night* (1975), *Rust Never Sleeps* (1979), *Reactor* (1981) and *Freedom* (1989).

Harvest (Reprise, 1972) is a master-piece. The **Decade** compilation (Reprise, 1978) is well constructed.

Everywhere
Neil Young has recorded with Crazy Horse, The Band, Nils Lofgren, Joni Mitchell, Dylan, Crosby, Stills and Nash and many others, proving that he was able to adapt to all the styles of rock that were popular in the 1960s and 1970s.

The revolution within the revolution: the punk explosion (1977–1980)

Rock is dead

In 1976, the Western world was in the throes of a grave economic crisis provoked by a rapid rise in crude oil prices after the 1973 Israeli–Arabic conflict. The United States were less affected because of their own natural resources. France drowned the problem in endless political debates. Germany and Italy were already having to deal with an organized and powerful terrorist movement, represented by the Baader gang and the Red Brigade respectively.

Britain saw the last bastions of its foundering economy crumble: the car industry was close to bankruptcy, the textile industries were in a period of extreme difficulty, as were those associated with coal and steel. As international trade had come to a virtual standstill because of the economic recession, the Merchant Navy was permanently in dock.

Prices went up, salaries stayed the same, unemployment figures rose and the British nation, already traumatized by the spectacular and bloody tactics of the IRA, had to face up to growing collective despair.

There remained the leisure activities: football, always the national pastime, knew its hours of glory. The betting shops and casinos were full, as a large number of people, edged out of the job market by the economic crisis, tried to compensate for their enforced idleness with a date with Lady Luck.

For the younger generation, however, there was nothing: unemployment benefit, government grants to go to 'art school' and part-time jobs did not do much to cheer up teenagers who were bombarded by unemployment figures and lists of factories due to close down every night on television.

In another era, rock would have been there to help force awareness of the situation, to provide a legitimate expression of revolt, and some entertainment. But by this time, rock was dead. Dead, at least, for teenagers who could no longer identify with 30-year-old millionaires who, moreover, had elected to live abroad. In the mid-1970s, the rock industry (which made up an élitist society in its own right) was particularly isolated from the realities of life in Britain's grey suburban housing estates. And those who peopled the estates had little in common with the happy band of workers and employees who each owned their own little red-brick house in a row of other, disturbingly similar, little red-brick houses. Even the latter are not to be pitied and in their own way, perpetuate the old dreams of the British Empire, which aimed at making a world bourgeoisie of its subjects.

It was at the heart of the drifting, uneducated, violent and despairing generation spawned by the concrete jungles, those endless rabbit warrens hastily constructed after the war, that the new protest movement emerged. Because rock was dead, tightly controlled by a handful of world superstars who had turned it into a closed shop, the rock establishment had to be destroyed, and the rock establishment was all those who, after having fought and criticized the West's social structures and institutions in the past, had traded their rebellion for a villa on the Côte d'Azur or in California.

With the punks (whose name is self-

> **Eighties' humanitarian rock**
>
> When Bob Geldof, leader of a new wave band called the Boomtown Rats had the idea of calling on British rock musicians to raise funds for famine stricken Ethiopia, little did he know that he was creating a principle that was to be abused in the 1980s: the charity rock concert. Band Aid, Live Aid, the Amnesty International tour, and the Wembley anti-apartheid tour were all initially organized by new wave artists but other rock musicians later joined in (Jagger, McCartney, Springsteen, Jackson and Dylan).
>
> Fundraising events had been around much longer than rock, but by turning these concerts into single-minded, morally-aware gatherings, to some extent, Eighties' rock lost in intensity what it had gained in popularity, a clear conscience having replaced the healthy anger of its early days.

explanatory) and their brutal, sometimes obscene protest against the star system, beautiful music, the guitar heroes, quality sound and professionalism, rock revolution rose like a phoenix from the ashes.

The punk world vision

There was no thought in the punk movement. Punk philosophy can only be described in metaphors; however, in the first years of the revolution until 1979–80, there was definitely a punk ideology, a fantastic conception of the world which was more a complete refusal of, than a suggested replacement for, the system already in force. The punk revolt had no theoretician and was to disappear as soon as the dynamism of its first members had fizzled out, becoming in turn grist for the rock establishment mill.

Punk ideology presents the world as composed of children and parents; in this respect, it is reminiscent of the conceptions predominant in rock'n'roll, then the mod movement and American counter-culture. The Sex Pistols, leaders of the punk movement, confirmed that their aim was to accentuate the generation gap: 'The basic idea in punk is to turn children against their parents,' declared Sex Pistols vocalist, Johnny Rotten.

In the eyes of the punks, the world was a collection of social injustices: there are rich and poor, strong and weak and wolves and lambs; children of a social and economic crisis, the punks created, and deliberately flaunted, a distorted, parodied image of the results of that society; with their black coats and workers' boots, their cheap guitars and home hair-cuts, they cultivated a 'poor look'. Refusing education, whenever they could, they put state and family education on trial. The underlying aim of punks was to use their appearance and behaviour to humiliate society as a whole.

This cult of failure, despair and ugliness was to be fully expressed in punk 'fashion', which could turn any teenager into a scarecrow overnight. Seen as an aesthetic expression and the outward proof of a refusal to be part of society, punk fashion rapidly caught on in Britain and swept aside the dress norms previously promoted by rock stars.

Punk fashion

In 1976 the first teenagers kitted out like crows were spotted in London: creating an overall sombre and wild impression, young people of both sexes favoured old and patched overcoats, preferably in black, tight PVC trousers and Army and Navy Surplus Stores wear. These distinctive outfits, most often bought at second-hand stalls in suburban markets, underlined impecunious nature of their rebellion.

In order to complete the picture, and not be confused with simple down-and-outs, young punks shaved all or part of their heads (the famous 'Mohican' cut). Less extreme was the rough crew cut.

The famous safety-pin through the cheek was an 'accessory' reserved for the confirmed extremists, who copied this gesture made fashionable by Richard Hell of the group Television. The less hardy limited themselves to another (less painful) of Hell's innovations: the typical spikey hair held up by Vaseline®. They saw themselves as the doomed, animals condemned to live only at night, as parias. The punks claimed to be unable to bear daylight: thus they wore dark glasses.

The mods' mid-length hair held some shock value at the start of the 1960s. Then, the first shock over, society had absorbed the hippy look without difficulty. But the punks were striking for their aesthetic nihilism, their total disinterest in looking 'good'. It took all the genius of Zandra Rhodes to turn punk styles into high fashion.

Punk music

This basically apolitical, uneducated and idle (because of the economic climate) young generation was able to bring about the only truly white rock musical revolution; despite its links with the reggae produced in London's Jamaican ghettos, punk music stands independent from the black music forms which created rock. At the beginning, the punks' hatred of rock was so extreme that they refused to be called 'punk rockers'.

Punk melodies are not entirely ruled by the three-chord structure which rock had borrowed from the blues. Their tunes are closer to English ballads and Scottish airs; the most famous punk songs are parodies of already existing works, most of which had absolutely nothing to do with rock (the British national anthem, 'God Save the Queen' and 'My Way' from Frank Sinatra's repertoire; Bowie, punk's great uncle, did the same with Brel's 'Le Port d'Amsterdam').

When the punks 'really' sang, that is when they stopped shouting tuneless melodies or talking in a monotone, like Lou Reed, the Stranglers and the Buzzcocks in their early days, the profoundly English character of their inspiration is immediately evident: this is particularly obvious in the records cut by the Clash, the Damned and Joy Division. The whole new wave movement inherited punk's apparent rejection of the American-born three-chord system inherent in the blues and classic rock, exemplified in the work of such groups as Simple Minds, the Cure, the Boomtown Rats, Devo and XTC.

Punk rhythms are easily recognizable: unlike rock, where the first beat is strong, or reggae, which has a strong beat-off-beat pattern, in punk every beat is strong, which is tantamount to doing away with the beat entirely. Through ignorance, or just deliberate provocation, punk guitarists and drummers continuously maltreated their equipment, literally hammering on their instruments; punk guitarists, impressed by the Who's Pete Townshend and his wildly windmilling arm, adopted and adapted this gesture.

Bassist Sid Vicious, with his boundless energy, invented the 'pogo', the famous punk dance, jumping in the air at every beat like a puppet on springs.

Punk sound is very hard and distorted, close in nature to hard rock; this was their only concession to standard rock: the amps were turned up full, the instruments spewing out a veritable sound wall through which the singer's voice could only just be heard. Only a few bands evolved towards greater musical skills, but they (including the Clash, Joy Division and the Damned) only survived the first 1976 wave of punk by a few years.

Panic

The punk revolt, which was as much a protest against rock itself as against society, had immediate repercussions: feeling threatened at its very core, the rock establishment burst into feverish action. 'No Elvis, no Beatles, no Rolling Stones in 1977' said the Clash. The punks had a deep hatred of Mick Jagger, Eric Clapton and Pink Floyd. Bell-bottomed trousers and long hair were out. Standard rock rhythms and the guitar heroes' special effects were despised and mocked. The 3-year-long punk storm was enough to break classic rock's monopoly of the music trade. However, the next force to be reckoned with was new wave.

New wave: towards the lull (1980–1991)

The end of punk

None of the history-making groups which emerged in or around 1977 survived. All the original punks converted to new wave or gave up the fight altogether. The two leading bands in the movement, the anarchy-preaching Sex Pistols and politically-minded Clash, split up, the former in 1978, the latter in 1983. The Stranglers' original line-up lasted until 1990, though their musical direction had shed most of its punk origins by the mid-Eighties. The extremism of the early punks cost the lives of many of the movement's pioneers, but their brief, explosive careers totally changed the face of rock. The situation had totally changed from 1976: the rock establishment could no longer rely on a constant demand for the same kind of music, or on the reputations of complacent 'stars for life' such as the Stones, or bands that were packed with skill but lacked originality, such as Floyd.

Today's stars are the Cure, Simple Minds, U2 and Sting. At one time or another, all of them were involved in the punk movement: Robert Smith of the Cure played with Siouxsie; when he started out as a performer, Jim Kerr of Simple Minds came close to punk music; Sting, in his Police days, started the trend for close-cropped, bleached hair; and Edge of U2's guitar-playing is influenced by his knowledge of punk.

New wave took the place of punk rock; the new movement was a watered-down, acceptable version of the old: gone were the nihilism, the violence, the safety pins through cheeks and ears and the booming, distorted sound that characterised punk. In short, nothing remained that could shock the classic rock system which most now believed was here to stay.

The new wave style

New wave really took hold at the start of the 1980s.

Musically speaking, new wave was far more sophisticated than punk: the melodies are truly sung, very often in a high clear monotone (this is the most audible punk influence). The guitar sound is clear and heavily overlaid, principally with the spiralling effect produced by the chorus pedal, but also with other echo-producing gadgets such as the phaser and the flanger. New wave sound made a clean break with the distortion that pervaded punk; the sound is still forceful and becomes harder when bands perform live, but on the whole, the guitarists specialize in bare, enthereal solos. The guitars are backed up by synthesizers, which would have been anathema to any early punk band (the synthesizer being, at that time, central to the art rock the punks so despised). The drum sound is clear and dry, filled out by the synthetic percussion provided by programmable drum boxes; the bass is precise and sometimes slapped.

These principal characteristics have emerged afte 10 years of new wave. The early star cluster (Dexy's Midnight Runners, XTC, B52's, Devo, Orchestral Manoeuvres in the Dark, Joy Division, Joe Jackson, Elvis Costello, Ian Dury, Blondie and Magazine) only produced a few big names, which today are superstars: the Cure, Simple Minds, U2 and the Police (who, despite their split, have continued to exercise a fascination over all existing bands).

The storm is certainly over: the punks have either disappeared or have become well-behaved rock musicians. Even if new wave fashions (led by the Cure and the Police) originally stemmed from punk fashions, the element of revolt has been erased from their lyrics: humanitarian issues and social awareness (ecology, pacifism and human rights) have replaced the punks' 'No future'.

The old rock musicians' last stand (1977–1990)

Mainstream rock

In the United States, 'mainstream' has become the accepted term used to describe all those kinds of rock music which, by their underlying ethic, their melodic structure and their sound, are united in their rejection of punk rock and new wave.

This mainstream principally consists of the older rock musicians from the 1960s and 1970s and others whose nostalgia for the good old days led them to move back into the most classic forms of rock music (sometimes at the cost of a much needed visit to the fountain of youth, aka the plastic surgeon!).

Although Britain supplied rock history with an enormous corps of rock musicians, and indeed is known as rock's second home, the expression 'mainstream' is seldom used, for the biggest British bands at the end of the 1980s were either a product of new wave (U2, Simple Minds, the Cure) or had heralded that movement, like Bowie. In the States however, the charts were flooded with the 'big' sound of classic rock.

The rock establishment is not dead

The best-selling songwriters in the States are those who have direct link with their rock predecessors: Tom Petty, Bob Seger and Bruce Springsteen stormed the American music market with their jaunty, predictable rock numbers. The Eurythmics 'made it' in the States as soon as they abandoned synthesizers for an aggressive sound and soul-inspired vocals. Springsteen had his biggest hit with 'Born In the USA' (which could also be read as 'Rock Was Born in the USA'), a number which affirms loud and clear his emotional ties with post-Vietnam America.

The American establishment could not sit back and do nothing in the face of the massive creative orgy provoked by the English punk and new wave movements.

The American bands claiming to be transatlantic branches of these movements have disappeared, but the States has accepted U2, mainly because of their on-going flirtation with classic rock. Simple Minds, who have all but abandoned the outward signs of new wave, are starting to bite into the American market. The Cure, who, in terms of behaviour, lyrics and sound, have remained more faithful to early new wave, have a very limited following in the States.

The Americans accept the English when they look American or adopt blues structures to create à l'American. Thus the Rolling Stones's 1981 tour was the largest the country had ever experienced. Since then, Springsteen and Michael Jackson have done even better. Dire Straits were received with open arms, as were the new English (Def Leppard, Iron Maiden, Saxon) and German (Scorpions) heavy metal bands, which were the result of nostalgia for hard rock's hour of glory which come to an end in Europe.

The rock museum

None of these hard rock groups broke new ground in the years that preceded punk: they continued with their childish imagery, pounding rhythms, distorted sound and technical skills. Watered down, this trend produced squeaky-clean hard FM, which was much appreciated in the States (Pat Benatar, Toto, Foreigner).

The last group of nostalgia-ridden bands, such as the Stray Cats, took refuge in the worship of sounds from a bygone age. George Thorogood, Stevie Ray Vaughan and the whole of Southern rock (especially ZZ Top) continue to blast out Elmore James's basic chords, Hendrix's solos and John Lee Hooker-style rhythms . . . As for Lou Reed and Iggy Pop who, with Bowie, were the last to break free from glam rock, they became their own idols . . .

158

The Bangles
Californian pop group

Beatles sound-alikes

These four Americans recreated the musical ambiance of the Fab Four with talent and professionalism.

The Bangles' authenticity made a welcome change from the hundreds of pale imitations which had appeared as bands tried to recreate the Liverpool four's sound. At the end of an unusual musical journey, the Bangles accomplished what no other band had been able to do. An all-female line-up, and thus constantly under threat of their look being taken more seriously than their music and by over-exposure on the FM radio network, the Bangles patiently imbued their songs and performances with the Beatles 'touch' (perfect vocal harmonies, sophisticated melodies, power-

ful rhythms and light, floating solos). And to recreate the magical sound of their idols, they even got the equipment right (Epiphone and Rickenbaker guitars, Hoffner bass and Ludgwig drum kit).

All Over the Place (CBS, 1984) and **Different Light** (CBS, 1985) are their best work.

Everything (CBS) shows various influences, but is interesting all the same.

> **Cult**
> 'All the Sixties' groups are a gold mine. All four of us really appreciate the Sixties' myth. I think that it was a great era' (interview for *Sounds Magazine*, November, 1988).

Blondie
New wave band

The Marilyn Monroe of rock music

Beauty, originality and popularity: Debbie Harry had all the ingredients for lasting success. However, she was but a shooting star.

She began her career as a member of the legendary underground band, The Wind In The Willows, then joined the Stilettoes. In 1975, she founded Blondie with Chris Stein. An avant-garde mélange of disco and pop, the band was to become one of the most popular precursors of the new wave movement. Gifted with a superb physique and a voice which she controls perfectly, Debbie Harry entered the charts with such excellent numbers as 'Denis' (1978) and, with her leopard skin outfits and pro-

vocative stage-act, moved closer to punk. 'Heart of Glass' and 'Union City Blue' demonstrated the range of the band which, with 'Call Me', became internationally famous. Despite their success, the band broke up in 1981, because of personality clashes. Harry subsequently pursued a moderately successful solo career as a singer and actress.

Blondie, Plastic Letters (Chrysalis, 1979) and **Blondie's Hits** (Chrysalis, 1981) are their best work.

> **The Blondie fashion**
> Debbie Harry's success popularized the fashion for leopard skin trousers and outsized T-shirts, as well as ruffled blond hair, a style inherited from the punks who, in 1978, had not yet hit America.

David Bowie

1947–   Glam-rock singer and guitarist

The 'Duke': suave and sophisticated

Although he was once one of the most individualistic performers in the business, Bowie has gradually become an institution, a living legend associated with punk.

In the 1960s, Davy Jones (he changed his name in 1966 to avoid confusion with the Monkees' singer Davy Jones) cut a number of tracks that lacked originality and owed much to the black American music and English rock which were popular at the time. *Space Oddity*, released in 1969, and *The Man Who Sold the World*, released the following year, demonstrated his increasing willingness to break new ground.

'Ziggy'

Two years later, Bowie as Ziggy bought out his first, enormously successful, concept album, *Ziggy Stardust*, playing the first of a series of characters which have peopled his long career; in the course of the tour which followed the album's release, Bowie appeared on stage in female clothing or pretending to be a transsexual; he also dressed as an alien, with outrageous make-up and spiky bright orange hair. The band, which called itself 'The Spiders From Mars', gave ambiguous concerts in an alternatively science fiction and medieval stage-setting, combining aggres-sive music and lyrics that expressed a pessimistic view of the world. The intell-ectual nature of Bowie's preoccupations led him to create 'doubles', imaginary and inventive characters which Bowie played in his rock-theatre style shows (including the Thin White Duke, Diamond Dog, Ziggy Stardust and the Glass Spider).

The 'Duke'

Bowie's career developed without any one major influence, along the same lines as those of his friends, Iggy Pop and Lou Reed. That he is so famous today is in part due to the new movements his style helped form: both punk rock and new wave owe much to his deliberately provocative stage-act.

Ziggy Stardust and **Diamond Dogs** (RCA, 1972 and 1974) are typical of his first period.

Scary Monsters and **Let's Dance** (RCA, 1980 and 1983) were hugely successful.

> **Cinema**
> Throughout his career, Bowie has appeared to the public in the guise of a whole range of personae. Cynical and romantic, the Duke's personality has always been ambiguous: he has been outrageous and sober, homosexual and husband and father, singer and actor, and leader and loner at the same time. The opportunity for him to act out his fantasies was presented to him by the cinema, which also gave him the chance to write film soundtracks.

David Bowie

The Clash

English punk rock group

Four real musicians in the punk camp

Less nihilist and more politically motivated than other punk bands, the Clash were the only 'thinkers' of the movement.

In the wake of the Pistols

Joe Strummer, Mick Jones, Paul Simonon and Topper Headon were fans of the Sex Pistols and actually supported the band on one of their first tours (the famous 'Anarchy' tour). However, the Clash had soon gathered a substantial following and were able to give their own concerts.

All of their lyrics express the initial energy that characterized the punk movement: 'White Riot' calls on whites to rise against the system, like the black Notting Hill riots; '1977' proclaims the definitive break with rock past: 'No Elivs, no Beatles, no Rolling Stones . . .'

Autonomy

Little by little, the Clash proved that, as a punk band, they were second only to the Sex Pistols. They subscribed less to the anarchy proposed by punk ideology than to a more concrete, politically motivated attitude (hence their tours against the National Front, Thatcher and apartheid). Until the group's demise, their lyrics were a constant, vitriolic condemnation of Western institutions, giving the punk movement a semblance of coherence, a sort of theoretical basis. At the same time, 'Career Opportunities', 'Tommy Gun', 'Spanish Bombs' and 'London Calling' showed a genuine desire to work on their musical arrangements. Their sound is less distorted than that of other punk bands, the vocals more audible and the guitar solos better worked-out. The double album *London Calling*, followed by the triple album set *Sandinista!* and *Combat Rock* won them the admiration of punks worldwide, but this did not prevent the band from splitting up in 1983.

The Clash (Epic, 1977) and **London Calling** (Virgin, 1979) are musts.

'Combat Rock'

Frequently assaulted by militant members of neo-nazi organizations, the Clash were also persecuted by the police, who cut off the electricity during their concerts, used tear gas and truncheons on the audience and took in members of the band for questioning.

The Clash

Elvis Costello
English pop rock singer and guitarist

Nostalgia, avant-gardism and megalomania

Steering a delicate course between rockabilly, pop and new wave, Elvis Costello claims to be the last genius in rock music.

Elvis Costello's success is more due to his genuine talent as an agent-provocateur than to any musical originality. His stage name brings to mind the great Presley, and his guitars (Fender Jaguars and Gretschs), Fifties' rock and country and western. His own compositions, which range from the openly plagiaristic, through social commentary to the distinctly avant-garde, have attracted a very mixed following, including 'rockabilly kids', Springsteen fans and even neo-punks.

His albums are as varied as his moods and have lost none of their popularity.

My Aim Is True and **This Year's Model** (Columbia, 1977 and 1978) are very much in the rock'n'roll tradition.

Trust and **Punch the Clock** (F-Beat-Columbia, 1981) show a wider range of influences.

Unpleasant
For some unknown reason, Elvis Costello is always unpleasant to journalists who, in revenge, have often voted him the most unsporting artist of the year because of his arrogant, aggressive attitude.

The Cramps
American punk rock band

Strange music and provocative behaviour

Somewhere between psychedelic music, glam rock and punk, the Cramps were particularly noted for their crazy stage-act.

The brutality of the Cramps shows is famous in the rock world: inspired mainly by the decadents (Alice Cooper, Iggy Pop and Bowie) and by a number of punk artists (The Sex Pistols and Siouxsie and the Banshees), their stage-act relied heavily on overt provocation and was a blend of erotic strip-tease, outrageous make-up and suggestive gestures.

However, the band's genuine claim to originality was their clever fusion of two distinct musical trends: American music, which is more professional and in which improvisation plays a lesser role (rockabilly and hard FM) on the one hand, and imaginative European punk on the other. Together, 'Poison Ivy Rorsach', Lux 'Interior', Bryan Gregory and Nick Knox formed a shock line-up which helped initiate the United States to punk rock.

Psychedelic Jungle (CBS, 1981) and **Smell of Female** (CBS) give an idea of their interesting musical voyage.

Tours
Better known in Britain than in their own country, the Cramps supported a number of big bands (the Clash, the Police) in concert before becoming famous in their own right.

The Cure
English new wave band

New wave sounds

After having been paid-up members of the post-punk wave, The Cure went on to become one of the modern supergroups.

The Cure musicians come from Crawley, a small town in Sussex. Robert Smith, undisputed leader of the band, is the son of a Blackpool miner. As a young musician, he soon fell under the spell of the punk movement, but his involvement was brief as he was more demanding in terms of musical quality.

London

Once they had moved to the capital, the band's chance to become famous came in 1980 when they cut a number of promising records: *Three Imaginary Boys* and *Boys Don't Cry* placed them firmly in the post-punk current. Their fourth album, *Faith* (1981), sold even better, but differences of opinion within the group undermined its continuing existence. In spite of all this, their fifth album, *Pornography*, is well crafted, with an overall gloomy, tormented and depressed atmosphere. The sound is entirely characteristic of new wave, with the use of echo and chorus guitar effects, a smooth drum beat, monotonous, toneless vocals and high melodies. The sound seems to come from far off and is almost disembodied, while the despairing and anguished lyrics add to the aura of menace and panic. *The Head on the Door* is somewhat lighter in tone and produced two smash hits, 'Close to Me' and 'Standing on the Beach'.

The world

With their concert at Orange, France, in 1986, The Cure confirmed their position as the world's leading new wave band. The band's sombre clothes, sound (which became harder live) and spiky dark hair, emphasized their link with the punk movement, whose look, in a more acceptable form, they helped popularize.

Boys Don't Cry (1979) and **Pornography** (1982) are musts. **Concert Live** (1987) gives a good idea of the crude and austere live sound typical of new wave bands. **Disintegration** (1989) is reminiscent of the disturbing atmosphere of **Faith** (all these albums are on the Fiction Records label).

Early new wave

Not all the bands which emerged at the end of the 1970s reached the same heights of fame as U2, the Cure and Simple Minds, and yet most of them followed a truly new wave pattern. The biggest of these now almost forgotten bands helped define the genre: Joy Division, Devo, the Undertones, the Smiths, the Specials and Wire created a sound which was sometimes close in nature to punk, then almost imperceptibly became more sophisticated and ended up producing high quality vocal and instrumental arrangements. The Human League, Depeche Mode, the B52's and the Buzzcocks all refused to commmpromise their musical integrity.

Moderate

Having learned a lesson from the fall of the Sex Pistols and the Clash, The Cure's members carefully avoid taking an overtly political stance. Robert Smith has made public his distrust of political parties and his sympathy for Greenpeace. He has also stated that he sees no difference between Thatcher's stubbornness and that of the striking British miners. We have definitely came a long way from the first punks. . . .

Robert Smith *of the Cure*

The Damned
English punk rock band

First punk rock band with a cult following

Constant modification of the line-up explains their many changes in direction.

There were too many strong personalities in the Damned's initial line up for the band to stay together for any length of time. By 1976–77, they were definitely producing punk music and had become part of that movement. Their style was an aggressive combination of irony-laden lyrics, staccato bursts of notes pounded out on the guitar and forceful solos inherited from heavy metal ('Feel All Right'). In 1979, Brian James left the band and formed Lords of the New Church with Steve Bators, formerly of The Dead Boys, Steve Jones of the Sex Pistols and Terry Chimes of the Clash. Captain Sensible also left the band. A few

Top Ten hits watered down the aggressive tone of their punk rock. They went on to experiment with neo-pop, new wave, psychedelic music and rap, straying further and further from their musical roots.

Their double album, **The Light At the End of the Tunnel** (MCA), is an absolute must as it traces the various stages of their career.

The Black Album (IRS, 1981) is excellent.

> **Respect**
> Originally conceived as an ironic nod in the direction of the Beatles' *White Album*, the Damned's *Black Album* is actually punk rock's tribute to the 1960s. *Strawberries* (another reference to the Beatles) is also interesting.

Def Leppard
English hard rock group

Five teenagers out to conquer the rock world

With their polished hard rock, sophisticated choral work and a lively stage-act that has general appeal, Def Leppard are one of the most popular hard rock bands today.

Def Leppard's celebrity can in part be attributed to the boost the band were given by the British music press, who in 1980 promoted them as the only truly British answer to the increasingly popular imported American heavy metal music. Five teenage musicians, a shrewd business manager and an eye-catching album cover later, and Def Leppard were on the road to stardom: *On Through the Night, High and Dry* and especially *Pyromania* earmarked them as

the successors of such hard rock greats as Led Zeppelin and Deep Purple.

Their complete mastery of both vocals and instruments make Def Leppard one of the most interesting hard rock bands today, especially as, unlike many other hard rock bands, they owe their fame more to their musical abilities and style than to their look.

Pyromania (Vertigo-Phonogram, 1983) is a good album.

> **Prodigies**
> At the start of their career in 1979, the average age of Def Leppard's members was 15. They were 16 when their first album was released. This is a kind of hard rock record, as it usually takes many years to master the guitar.

Dire Straits
English mainstream rock band

Inimicably clear guitar sound

Strongly influenced by J J Cale, the Everly Brothers and the Shadows, Mark Knopfler is one of the last guitar heroes.

The apprenticeship

After spending most of his teens studying (he later taught English literature) and improving his guitar playing (he used to accompany his sister when she sang in pubs), Mark Knopfler decided to become a professional musician. He formed the band Dire Straits and played country rock tempered with pop and folk. His laid-back guitar style and the inimicable purity of his sound were particularly striking when compared with the rising tide of early punk. The band had their first concert in July 1977, signed to Phonogram in the same year and released their first album in June 1978. The ball was set rolling for Dire Straits, the most famous British band of the 1980s.

Overnight fame

'Sultans of Swing' is the band's theme tune and took the album to the number five spot in the American charts. Britain, still recovering from the shock created by punk rock and increasingly preoccupied with nascent new wave, paid scant attention to a band who were producing such 'American' music. With album after album, Dire Straits became firmly rooted in a cool and sophisticated rock form, composing suave, symphonic pieces studded with fast-flowing guitar solos. Several world tours, coupled with phenomenal success in Germany, France and the United States confirmed them as the best-selling band of the 1980s (the compilation *Money for Nothing* broke all 1988 sales records).

Now officially acclaimed as the last of the guitar heroes, Knopfler was free to indulge in his favourite pastimes as session guitarist (on Bob Dylan's *Slow Train Coming*) and soundtrack composer (for Bill Forsyth's *Local Hero*).

Money for Nothing (Phonogram, 1988) is an excellent introduction to Dire Straits' own particular brand of atmospheric rock.

Discography
Instantly recognizable for Mark Knopfler's rough Dylan-style vocals and pure guitar sound, each Dire Straits album has its own particular flavour. By 1991, they had released *Dire Straits*, *Communiqué*, *Making Movies*, *Love Over Gold*, *Alchemy*, *Brothers in Arms*, *Money for Nothing* and *On Every Street* (all on Phonogram).

Mark Knopfler, the last guitar hero, pictured here with his Fender Stratocaster. Knopfler joins the list of talented guitarists who have preferred this particular model (including Hank Marvin of the Shadows, Buddy Holly, Jimi Hendrix and Eric Clapton).

Eurythmics
British techno-pop then mainstream rock duet

The perfect duo: absolutely complementary

Although heavily synthesized music was originally their speciality, Eurythmics evolved towards less avant-gardist, more commercial rock.

Changes

The duo's first release in 1983 contained the seeds of their future success. Eurythmics was born of a collaboration between two completely different personalities, who had formerly been members of the new wave band the Tourists. On the one hand was Annie Lennox, an exceptionally talented vocalist with post-modern top-model looks and a penchant for eccentric clothes (she has appeared on stage wearing tulle tutus, classy dresses or black leather), and on the other was Dave Stewart who, with his dark glasses and long hair, is more influenced by the 1960s. A genius with his hands and a prolific composer, Stewart is as much at home on the keyboards during techno-pop purple passages ('Sweet Dreams' and 'Sex Crime') as he is on guitar for their R & B and Seventies' hard rock inspired hits.

From their very earliest days, Eurythmics seem to have hesitated between traditional and electronic rock, which accounts for the changes in tone from album to album, which alternate between these two tendencies: while *Sweet Dreams are Made of This* and *Savage* helped define a new wave sub-genre called 'techno-pop', *Be Yourself Tonight*, *Revenge* and *We Too Are One*, showed the duo's fondness for more classic rock with a wide appeal.

Unity

The Eurythmics duo are perhaps most impressive for the number of diverse musical elements they fused together: for various different tracks, they blended new wave with FM rock, R & B with synthesizers, aggressive solos with operatic vocals and pop ditties with thoughtful lyrics. As a result, the distance between these elements has been reduced.

Technique

Dave Stewart is a respected producer and arranger: most of the great contemporary rock songwriters have called on him for help: from Bob Dylan to Ray Charles, not forgetting ZZ Top, Liza Minnelli and Mick Jagger, the list is endless. It would be difficult to find one artist who was not in some way indebted to him.

Be Yourself Tonight (RCA, 1985) and **Revenge** (RCA, 1986) are their most technically accomplished albums.

Sweet Dreams Are Made of This (RCA) was the album which launched their career.

We Too Are One (RCA, 1989) shows a return to the band's twin preferences: a blend of synthesized music/techno-pop and classic rock.

Sexy
Annie Lennox, the disturbingly attractive Ice Queen of Eighties' rock, has made clever use of Hollywood vamp-style gimmicks to get her audiences going: during the 1987 tour, her skilful, slow striptease down to a lacy red brassiere, became one of the highspots of every concert.

Successful reject
Asked to compose the soundtrack for the film adaptation of Orwell's *1984*, Eurythmics produced 'Sex Crime'. The violently modern single, with its synthesized vocals and electronic effects, did not feature on the soundtrack, but was a huge hit in the European charts.

Iggy Pop and the Stooges
Decadent rock group

Pioneers of punk rebellion

At the end of the 1960s, Iggy Pop's nihilist lyrics and provocative behaviour heralded the storm to come.

Detroit, 'Motor City', gave rock not only Madonna and Bob Seger, but also MC5 and Iggy Pop and the Stooges, the most indomitable rebels of the lost, post-Woodstock generation. With their predilection for progressive hard rock and their political ideals, despite the brevity of their careers, these two legendary line-ups influenced nascent hard rock and the punk movement, which instinctively adopted their outrageous behaviour.

Separated from The Stooges, Iggy carried on in the same vein. He was influenced by David Bowie, with whom he wrote the 1983 hit, 'China Girl'.

The Stooges (Electra, 1969) and **Raw Power** (CBS, 1973) are rock monuments.

Lust For Life (CBS, 1977) is his best solo album.

Longevity
Despite two spells in drug and alcohol detoxification centres and a turbulent personal life, Iggy Pop retained his vital energy. He even found the timme to write an autobiography, entitled *I Need More*.

Iron Maiden
English heavy metal band

Distinct lack of imagination

The second-generation heavy metal bands used all the same ingredients as their earlier counterparts.

Iron Maiden invented modern heavy metal by setting a precedent which forced other bands to create a particular image, an instantly recongizable disguise, whose originality would be commercially exploitable. By using a grotesque monster in their stage-act, a sort of giant skeletal doll, Iron Maiden invented a new way of appearing on the music market. From then on, groups were recognized more by their logos than by their names or (even less) by their sound (it would be difficult to distinguish a heavy metal band by its sound, for they are all equally noisy).

As the visual concept took precedence over actual musical quality, the whole of contemporary heavy metal slipped into mediocrity. Iron Maiden, whose albums always sell well, are the perfect example of this phenomenon.

Iron Maiden (Harvest, 1980) and **The Number of the Beast** (EMI) are quite sufficient.

Facile
Iron Maiden took their name from the medieval instrument of torture, and each of their album covers depicts the machine in a different situation. As the same artist designs all the sleeves, it would be impossible to confuse Iron Maiden with any other band.

The Jam

English new wave band

They explored early punk rock together

Equally attracted to the music produced by the Who and the Kinks, the Jam were incapable of choosing between the old and the new.

The Jam's début coincided with the punk wave of 1977, with which the group is mistakenly associated. In fact, Paul Weller's role models were mainly Sixties' artists such as Pete Townshend of the Who and Ray Davies of the Kinks. The Jam and these mod bands have in common their on-stage violence and the uncompromisingly gloomy picture of suburban city life presented in their songs' lyrics. Caught up in the new fashion, the Jam, with their Sixties' style guitars and lyrics, did their best to adapt to new wave music. Their many hits, including 'Going Underground' (1981). 'A Town Called Malice' and 'Beat Surrender' (1982), justified their particular blend of old and new, which served as a link between new wave and Sixties' rock.

This is the Modern World (Polydor, 1977) is the best of their eight albums.

> **Follow-up**
> After The Jam split up, Paul Weller formed Style Council, which became famous within the framework of new wave.

Jean-Michel Jarre

1948– French electronic rock keyboards player

An original mixture of classical music and rock

In his hands, the computer became a rock instrument.

Jean-Michel Jarre is in a league of his own in the music world: his compositions are experimental in nature but sell well; he has a penchant for rock but uses instruments symphonically; he claims to prefer an intimate atmosphere but gives massive open-air concerts like any other rock gathering. Over the years, he has become expert at controlling several synthesizers and pre-programmable drum machines at the same time.

His electronic music is an interesting development for rock music as a whole, and is a blend of 'spacey' rock and classical music.

Oxygène and **Equinox** (Polydor, 1977 and 1978) are best-sellers.

> **Hereditary**
> Jean-Michel's father is Maurice Jarre, famous Hollywood film music composer.

Kraftwerk
German techno-rock band

The cool sound of computerized music

One of the first bands to produce a totally electronic sound and to pre-programme their instruments, Kraftwerk inspired many new wave performers.

Formed in 1970, Kraftwerk were among the most talented players to experiment with the new synthesizer-keyboards which had just appeared on the market. Pushing their experiments further than the limits defined by bands such as Pink Floyd and Genesis, Kraftwerk became famous with their astonishing first album, the chilling and spellbinding *Autobahn*.

The next albums served to reinforce the progressive aspects of their music, which, moreover, was increasingly reliant on synthesizers. Their live show was a feat of mechanical inventiveness, demonstrating their absolute mastery of computer techniques and their associated gadgetry.

All new wave keyboards players esteem Kraftwerk as a major source of inspiration.

Autobahn (Mercury, 1975) and **Computer World** (Warner, 1981) are astonishing.

Obscure
Despite the rather abstract nature of their music, Kraftwerk had a worldwide hit with 'Radio Activity', which was highly placed in the charts.

Madonna
1958–   Pop rock singer

The biggest sex symbol in the history of rock

Her stunning figure and piercing voice are carefully marketed products, which make her blend of rock, easy listening, soul and electro-funk absolutely irresistible.

A self-made woman

She is the living embodiment of the American Dream, which dictates that, with courage and talent, anyone can 'make it'. Like Sinatra, Stallone and Dean Martin, she was the product of a poor Italian suburb.

Her father barely spoke English; when her mother died leaving six children, her father re-married. She did not get on with her new stepmother and was sent to a convent school. She left at the age of 17 and got a job as a waitress in New York. To earn some extra cash, she posed for 'artistic' photos and took a role in a porn movie. With her savings, she took dance lessons and was spotted by producers when touring France with disco crooner Patrick Hernandez. On her return to New York, she took part in small-time concerts given by second-rate new wave bands.

Thanks to her friendship with a disc jockey who played the demo tape of her first

Confusion
Certain tracks on Madonna's first album were so heavily influenced by funk music that they were played on black radio stations ('Lucky Star' and 'Burning Up'). Many listeners were surprised to find out that the singer was white.

170

(very funky) track, 'Everybody', she was signed to Sire Records. She entered the charts with 'Burning Up' and then her first album, *Madonna*. A star was born. The daring video for 'Borderline' not only confirmed her sexy half-punk, half shop-girl image, but turned her into one of the biggest sex symbols in the history of rock overnight. It was the start of a blazing career, founded on the continual search for the right look and careful scrutiny of the ever-changing fashions in music.

The Madonna phenomenon

Madonna's second album, *Like A Virgin*, backed up by a number of 'sexy' videos (such as 'Material Girl' in which she appears as Marilyn Monroe, or 'Like a Virgin' for which she is dressed as a bride) was a huge success, with over nine million copies sold. The singles from the album went gold, then platinum in a matter of weeks (eight million copies for 'Like a Virgin', 'Material Girl' and 'Into the Groove'). With three hit singles on one album alone, Madonna was now truly a star.

Madonna's style

She went on to compound her new status with a third album and a world tour. Her physical appearance had changed: a stringent diet and work-out plan had helped slim and tone her body, and although she had had her hair cut short and bleached new wave style, she had refused to part with the heavy earrings, necklaces and crucifixes which had caused such an outcry at the start of her career. Madonna deliberately set out to seduce with her sexy fishnet stockings, skimpy black leotards and flouncy skirts. The audiences loved it; the tour was an unqualified success. Musically, with her black and disco influences, she is close to electro-funk. With her shrewd ear for commercially viable music, she is one of the powerhouses of contemporary American rock.

Initially dismissed as a simple hit parade phenomenon, Madonna totally dominated the mid-1980s music scene with a well-crafted, catchy sound ideally suited to the dance floor and a sometimes controversial, half sex-kitten, half businesswoman image.

Like a Virgin (Sire, 1984) is a must.

Madonna and **True Blue** (Sire, 1983 and 1986) are interesting.

Who's That Girl and **Like a Prayer** (Sire, 1987 and 1989) are perhaps more conventional.

Actress

An all-round artist, she refused to accept the sexy dumb blonde image bestowed on her by the media. Her role in Susan Seidelman's film *Desperately Seeking Susan* (1983), an insight into New York's alternative milieu, was received with critical acclaim. On the other hand, her next film, *Shanghai Surprise*, in which she played opposite her then husband Sean Penn, was a flop. She also starred in *Dick Tracey* (1990) and has recently been treading the boards of a Broadway theatre. Critics describe her performance as adequate.

Madonna

The New York Dolls
Glam-rock band

Deliberately shocking

Self-styled agents-provocateurs, they heralded the punk movement.

From 1973, the complacent American rock industry was shaken to its very core by the meteoric rise of an innovative band called the New York Dolls. Cultivating a gender-bending, rather threatening image, the band's lyrics on love, city life and modern society in general were imbued with a dark cynicism and an atmosphere of despair. In the United States, with their outrageous make-up and excessive alcohol and drug intake, they were hailed as the appointed successors to the Doors and MC5. In fact, with their tense numbers, sharp guitar sound and skin-bashing drumbeat, the Dolls were closer to hard rock. To their unadorned and bitter rock music, they added nihilist lyrics which became a favourite with punks a few years later.

After the accidental death of the drummer and constant quarrels between the other members of the band, the Dolls split up in 1975.

New York Dolls (Mercury, 1973) and **Too Much Too Soon** (Mercury, 1974) are interesting.

Johnny Thunders, the leader of the band had a chequered solo career in France and in London, where he performed in punk pubs and clubs. The quality of his outrageous shows was very erratic. He died in 1991.

Tom Petty and the Heartbreakers
Mainstream rock band

Brought up on folk rock

The ghosts of Dylan, the Byrds and the Rolling Stones haunt their compositions, which already show a strong Springsteen influence.

Tom Petty and his band are very well known in the States and Australia, where their particular brand of dynamic folk rock with its distorted sound, is still popular. Their lyrics are rather bland, but Tom Petty's earnestness made him an ideal successor to the Band: like the Canadian group which backed Dylan for many years, Tom Petty and the Heartbreakers discreetly supported Dylan on numerous American, Australian and world tours.

Tom Petty never fully broke away from his idols, and if all his albums resemble both their work and each other, they at least show just how difficult it is for contemporary American rock artists to emerge from the shadow of their great ancestors.

Damn the Torpedoes (Backstreet, 1979) and **Pack up the Plantation** (double album, MCA, 1985) are worth a look.

The Police

English reggae-rock group

The meeting point of many different influences

The Police trod an original and exemplary path between reggae, jazz and pop.

Début

The band was formed in 1977 by a Corsican guitarist living in London called Henri Padovani. He recruited an American drummer, Stewart Copeland and an English bass-player, Gordon Sumner, more commonly known as 'Sting', aiming to produce music with a strong punk and new wave bias. Invited to the 1977 Mont-de-Marsan rock festival, at Sting's insistence the Police took on an English guitarist, Andy Summers, whose original approach was to orientate the band's music towards reggae. Padovani, who was much more interested in 'hard' rock, left the band, and the Police as we know them were born.

The way up

One year later, national radio stations were playing a strange kind of music, close to reggae but sung by what was unquestionably a white voice. Although Sting's voice lacks strength, the tone is instantly recognizable and his range is impressive. The guitar sound was still somewhat distorted, but the band's use of chorus pedals (preferred by new wave bands) marked their move away from the sounds of punk.

The single 'I Can't Stand Losing You' from *Outlandos d'Amour*, which was recorded under the most basic studio conditions, took them into the American and British charts for the first time. This was how matters stood at the start of 1979; The following decade was to see their meteoric rise to the pinnacle of fame.

Confirmation

After their first triumphant world tour, the three musicians, who, by this time, had fixed on a decidedly modern look (the dark clothes and short, bleached hair, inherited from punk fashion) went back into the studio. The album, released at the end of 1979, was revolutionary: *Reggatta de Blanc* contained four hit singles which were to propel the album to the top of the charts within a matter of weeks. The sound of *Reggatta de Blanc* came as a surprise to everyone: polished and lively, the music was overlaid with poetic lyrics energetically sung by Sting; the drum beat provided by Stewart Copeland, another pupil of the hard school of jazz, was technically accomplished. The melodic structure was more overtly reggae than on the first album. 'Message in a Bottle', 'The Bed's Too Big Without You', 'Bring on the Night' and 'Walking on the Moon' demonstrated

Sting

After the Police split up, bassist Sting embarked on a world tour to promote his ambitious solo album *Dream of the Blue Turtles*; heavily influenced by jazz and drawn towards topical lyrics ('Russians' and 'They Dance Alone'), Sting gradually moved in to a league of his own in the rock world: he has shown his willingness to take part in the charity and politically orientated concerts that abounded in the 1980s (Amnesty International, the 'Free Mandela' concert). Having changed his look (he has grown his hair and now plays an acoustic guitar), had a number of screen roles and written a book on ecology intended to defend the Amazonian Indians, he has created a link with the Sixties' generation. His polished compositions and seductive voice have attracted a wide following.

their now absolute mastery of their art. Having become the biggest stars in British rock overnight, the Police embarked on a triumphant world tour in 1980.

Fame

Their third album, *Zenyatta Mondatta* (1980) was a smash hit with fans who were now used to the sound of reggae-rock, but the critics found it repetitive. The Police then gravitated towards more complex and esoteric music, expressing their new direction in *Ghost In The Machine* (1981). However, this sudden change in style disorientated their fans. The band was quick to react and returned to the familiar style of their early days. *Synchronicity* (1983) topped charts worldwide thanks to 'Every Breath You Take', a classic pop rock track with was a discotheque favourite.

Worn out by personal differences and commitment to solo projects, the band split up at the height of their fame.

Outlandos d'Amour (1978), **Reggatta de Blanc** (1979) and **Synchronicity** (1983) are absolute masterpieces and should not be missed.

The Singles (Virgin, 1988) is an extremely interesting compilation which covers the band's whole career.

Blond

That the three members of the Police all had blond hair came about by chance: Sting had been asked to bleach his hair for a commercial and the other two decided to do the same. Therefore, when the Police were first discovered, it was wrongly thought that they were part of the punk movement.

Leisure activities

After the band split up, the three members of the Police were able to indulge in their favourite pastimes: drummer Stewart Copeland devoted himself to polo and was selected for a local team. He also worked on a film documentary about the Sex Pistols. Guitarist Andy Summers published a book of photographs and has had exhibitions in London galleries. Following in the footsteps of David Bowie, but with less success, Sting has had various screen roles.

The Police

The Pretenders
Anglo-American pop rock group

A rocky blend of old and new

Influenced by the Kinks and the Rolling Stones, Chrissie Hynde was most successful as a minimalist rock singer.

The Pretenders had a British number one with 'Brass in Pocket', taken from their first album. The line-up had already been working together for some time and were used to performing live, which to some extent explains the incredible energy that dominates the album.

The crude nature of the arrangements and the tension that pervades the Pretenders' music meant that they were classed as a new wave band, although their sound is closer to Seventies' rock than to new wave, which calls for the use of synthesizers.

With their dry rhythms, well-crafted solos and Chrissie Hynde's stage presence and sensual vocals, the Pretenders became one of the most influential bands of the early 1980s. Their hits include 'Talk of the Town', 'Message of Love', 'Back on the Chain Gang', 'I Got You Babe' and 'Middle of the Road'.

Pretenders (Real Records-Sire, 1979) is a must.

Single Records is a compilation (WEA, 1987).

'I Got You, Babe!'
Chrissie Hynde lived with Ray Davies, leader of the Kinks. After the birth of their daughter, she left him for Jim Kerr of the Simple Minds. With UB40 she recorded 'I Got You, Babe'. Ray Davies wrote 'You Really Got Me' . . . Ironic! Hynde and Kerr have subsequently separated.

Lou Reed
1942–   Glam-rock singer and guitarist

The poet of taboo subjects

With Bowie, he heralded the punk movement, but he remained faithful to the blues influence.

After having founded the Velvet Underground in 1965, and experienced many ups and downs, Lou Reed met David Bowie and accentuated his ambiguous, depressive style. With the relase of *Transformer* in 1972, he became world-famous. His poisonous poet reputation was confirmed by tracks on life in the city ('Walk on the Wild Side') and on homosexuality ('Vicous' and 'Make Up'). The extremely gloom *Berlin* (1973) and the experimental tone of *Metal Machine Music* (1975) heralded a long period spent in an artistic wilderness, punctuated only by a series of lacklustre releases. Back to the forefront of the music scene thanks to *New York* (which included the hits 'Dirty Boulevard' and 'Romeo Had Juliette'), Lou Reed has returned to the unadorned style typical of his early releases.

Transformer, Rock'n'Roll Animal and **New York** (RCA, 1989) are his best albums.

Forerunner
'Sweet Jane', which features on one of the albums released during his Velvet Underground days (*Loaded*, 1970) was adopted as the anthem of the first punk movement.

The Runaways

American hard rock group

The first 'metal queens'

This all-female line-up was a breeding ground for talent.

By 1976, the traditionally macho heavy metal milieu was having to face up to the fact that woman wanted to play too. The Runaways, launched on the West Coast at a time when the early hard rock players seemed to be losing momentum, benefitted from the critics' curiosity. Four girls, aged between 17 and 24, following in the footsteps of Led Zeppelin! Nevertheless, they kept their promise: their albums and concerts more than matched the standards laid down by their male counterparts. *Live in Japan* is a nostalgic tribute to Deep Purple; the two guitarists, Joan Jett and Lita Ford, skilfully recreated the musical atmosphere associated with the early hard rock players.

After this ground-breaking group split up, each of the members embarked on a solo career.

Runaways (Mercury, 1976) and **Queens of Noise** (Mercury, 1977) are worthwhile buys.

> **Rivals**
> Girlschool and Rock Goddess come from Britain. As the supporting act for various male groups (Motörhead, Def Leppard and Iron Maiden), these bands surprised everyone.

Saxon

English hard rock group

Second-generation hard rock

Following in the footsteps of Led Zeppelin and Deep Purple.

After the Australian invasion led by AC/DC and Rose Tattoo and the lack of inspiration to which the genre's major songwriters had fallen prey, British hard rock began to look around for new home-grown talent.

In the very middle of the punk explosion, while show-business's traditional structures were on the brink of crumbling totally, Saxon attempted to answer the revolt popularized by the Sex Pistols with a rather conventional image.

It was not until three years after the line-up was formed, in 1980, when the punk movement was gradually losing popularity and new wave was emerging, that Saxon had their first entry in the British Top Ten. Saxon use the same tried and tested recipe: leather, motorbikes, apocalyptic concerts and eyecatching record sleeves with a strong 'Conan the Barbarian' style, medieval, sci-fi influence.

Wheels of Steel (1980) is their second and best album.

> **Image**
> Today, every hard rock group has to have its gimmick: Judas Priest has bondage, Motley Crue, leather and chains, Iron Maiden, blood and gore, ZZ Top, their beards, Twisted Sister, androgyny, Saxon, the Middle Ages, Motörhead, a bomber, etc.

176

The Scorpions
German hard rock band

From psychedelia to hard rock

Formed at the start of the 1970s, this band took a long time to show its true colours.

At the start of their career, the Scorpions were strongly impressed by art rock's electronic tendencies, which were prominent in Germany at that time. There were also grave problems within the band, and the line-up was changed several times. It was not until their Japanese tour in 1977, that the Scorpions became known on an international scale.

From then on, the group's following expanded with amazing speed: the 1979 and 1982 American (with an audience of 30 000 at Los Angeles) tours crowned them the kings of hard rock, if only for a short while. Their album *Love at First Sting* entered the Top Ten, and was a smash hit in the United States. Scorpions' polished hard rock had conquered the world.

Love at First Sting (Harvest–EMI, 1984) is an excellent example of hard rock.

Decor
Forced by heavy metal public image tradition to find a distinctive trademark, the band appeared on stage mounted on a huge motorized scorpion. What a surprise!

Bob Seger and the Silver Bullet Band
Mainstream rock band

Populism, energy and business

When serious-mindedness and sincerity replace originality . . .

Bob Seger is one of those untiring performers whose love for his job can never be questioned. Born in Michigan, singer-guitarist Seger gradually and painstakingly worked his way up through the ranks to join his role models: it was only after six years of small-time tours that he finally released a successful album, *Live Bullet* which was the vinyl event of 1976 in the United States. Reminiscent of Creedence Clearwater Revival, Seger produced his own particular blend of R & B-style arrangements (Tina Turner's 'Nutbush City Limits') and Rolling Stones/ classic rock influenced melody lines ('Bo Diddley' and 'Katmandu').

The group's dynamism and musical ability ensured their international success. The Silver Bullet Band are one of the best-selling rock bands in the United States today.

Live and **Night Moves** (Capitol) are both well-crafted albums.

Prudence
The Silver Bullet Band produces catchy, mainstream rock with a discreetly distorted sound which is ideally suited to American FM radio stations. As a rock musician, Bob Seger cultivates a well-balanced image, and has never tried to hide his hatred of communism and drugs.

177

The Sex Pistols

English punk rock band

The Attila of rock

In the space of three years, the Sex Pistols exploded rock's traditional musical and commercial structures.

Pioneers

Owner of a fashion boutique on London's King's Road since the 1960s, Malcolm McLaren branched into the music business and promoted himself as a manager for alternative bands. The first to benefit from his sense of timing and his feeling for publicity stunts were the legendary New York Dolls. On McLaren's advice, they accentuated their provocative and debauched, sexually ambiguous image and began to produce more aggressive music. Despite the efforts of their manager and manipulator, the Dolls split up.

Back in London, McLaren took on the Swankers, adapting their line-up to create a more balanced team: Glen Matlock, the only 'real' musician of the four, on bass, Steve Jones on guitar and Paul Cook on drums. The addition of frenzied and magnetic vocalist John Lydon completed this almost entirely amateur line up.

Obsessed with sex and thriving on deliberate provocation, McLaren found a new name for the band: the Sex Pistols, John Lydon was henceforth called Johnny 'Rotten' and, when Matlock left the Pistols in 1977, his replacement was called Sid Vicious.

November 1975: the band's first live concert was far from perfect musically, but they really couldn't care less. The idea was to compensate for their musical ignorance with an irreverent, boundless and particularly destructive energy.

During a now infamous televized interview on 1 December 1976, the Pistols replied to the interviewer's rather sarcastic, aggressive questions with incredible vulgarity, verbally attacking the established order. The overall impression was one of organized terrorism.

Leaders of a radical, extremist rebellion overnight, the Pistols began to arouse much curiousity, especially in the eyes of the media which did not yet take the punk movement seriously. However, the ball had been set rolling. In three blazing years, the punk movement (which the Sex Pistols had founded) was to wipe out the most deeply rooted traditions of the rock world.

The white riot

November 1976: barely a year after their first live performance together, the band, which had signed to EMI the month before, released their first single. It was immediately obvious that, in terms of fashion, outlook and music, black was the colour of punk: the lyrics of 'Anarchy in the UK' were so violent and insurrectional that the single was immediately banned. EMI cancelled the contract, offering to pay £10 000 compensation. McLaren

---

Derision

The Sex Pistols made fun of the classic rock 'guitar heroes'. They expressed their contempt by playing in the simplest and most violent manner possible. Their sound, characterized by a veritable guitar 'wall' broken only by the vocalist's screams, was still quite close to hard rock. However, the ultrafast, tense punk beat is instantly recognizable.

Argument

It was because of the film produced by McLaren and directed by Julien Temple called *The Great Rock'n'Roll Swindle* that Johnny Rotten left the Pistols in 1978 to form PIL. Rotten, who was calming down somewhat, could no longer bear the extremism of McLaren and Sid Vicious. The latter died of an overdose in 1979, after murdering his girlfriend of the time.

accepted. He had just finalized arrangements for an 'Anarchy tour' consisting of 20 British gigs. Fifteen of the concerts were banned. New punk bands, which had emerged after the Pistol's earlier appearances, supported their idols for the remaining five gigs, but with the obvious presence of the police, the atmosphere was one of tension.

Despite these setbacks, McLaren was sure that the scandal surrounding the band would eventually work in their (and his) favour and had noticed that they had the unconditional support of the country's disillusioned teenagers. In March 1977, through the medium of the Sex Pistols, he dropped another bombshell on the British rock establishment, which was still complacently resting on the laurels won in the glorious past (by such bands as the Beatles, the Rolling Stones, Pink Floyd, Deep Purple, Led Zeppelin and Genesis): their gross parody of the British national anthem, 'God Save the Queen' was a vitriolic attack on Queen and country. Released to coincide with the celebrations for the Queen's silver jubilee (25 years on the throne), the Pistols' second single consolidated their 'outcasts from society' status. Despite a general ban, it reached number two in the charts. Prior to the single's release the band's record contract had again been cancelled, but McLaren saw this as another break for the band.

Once more he was proved right. Sid Vicious boosted the band's morale; his extremism and hatred of the whole of society was far greater than Johnny Rotten's. With their spiky hair, ripped T-shirts and dark, gloomy clothes, the Pistols carried on insulting the rock establishment and society, which was now on their side. In the end, a young, up-and-coming record label, Virgin, agreed to sign the lepers of rock. Despite the break-up of the band in 1978, the Pistols were to remain the most important influence of the decade.

Never Mind the Bollocks (Virgin, 1977) is a must.

The Great Rock'n'Roll Swindle, Some Product and **Flogging a Dead Horse** (Virgin, 1980, 1978 and 1979) are all posthumous compilations.

Sid Vicious

Simple Minds

Scottish new wave band

One of the three big bands to survive the new wave

More 'futurist' than U2 and less depressing than the Cure, Simple Minds tried to hold on to the social awareness that marked their early work.

Similarities

Simple Minds and U2 evolved along parallel lines attaining, like the Cure, supergroup status. The sheer power of these three bands destroyed what was left of new wave. Simple Minds and U2 played on their commitment to humanist, left of centre causes (Christian pacifism for the Irish-born members of U2 and moderate social issues for Simple Minds). The Cure admit to being influenced by New Order and Echo and the Bunnymen. Simple Minds obviously owe a great deal to Joy Division, Talking Heads, Magazine and, of course, Bowie.

Differences

Simple Minds have no intention of playing rock'n'roll or appearing with B B King. The members of U2, being Irish, exert a certain amount of fascination over the United States. But Simple Minds, like the Cure, have an all-European following. On the other hand, Simple Minds concerts are sumptuous affairs, with impressive light shows and acoustics. The Cure appear in dark suits on a stage bathed in white light.

Prospects

Simple Minds have already been together for a number of years. The band has survived all manner of setbacks and changes in the line-up. They have released some of the major albums in rock history, including the excellent *Once Upon a Time*. However, their earliest releases (*Life in a Day, Celebration* and *Sons and Fascinations*) are also worth noting.

Once Upon a Time (Virgin, 1985) is a must.

New Gold Dream (Virgin, 1983) and **Live in the City of Light** (Virgin, 1987) are both remarkable for their original atmosphere and the talent of the band members.

Jim Kerr

> **Stance**
> When questioned on the problem of the band's political stance, Jim Kerr replied 'For me, *Sun City* is the perfect example of what rock should be today: great rhythm and meaningful lyrics'.

Siouxsie and the Banshees

English punk rock band

The enchantress of the British punk movement

A former Sex Pistols groupie, she was later recognized as a singer in her own right.

Originally one of the infamous 'Bromley contingent' of Sex Pistols fans, Siouxsie appeared at the first punk festival in September 1976 in a band that included Sid Vicious, who joined the Pistols shortly afterwards.

Siouxsie's style is first and foremost her elaborate, instantly recogizable make up, which accounts for her brooding, avant-garde look. Apart from her cover-girl looks, Siouxsie has demonstrated her ample talents as a musician, giving British punk her taste for polished arrangements. Close to the new-romantics and art rock,

she also uses afro-rock rhythms. Despite various changes in the line-up (former members include the Cure's Robert Smith and Magazine's John McGeoch), fifteen years after it was formed in 1975, the band is still active.

The Scream (Polydor, 1978), **Kaleidoscope** (Polydor, 1980) and **Once Upon a Time** give an idea of the wide scope of their talents.

Culture

Since her very first performances, Siouxsie has shown her knowledge of 'primitive' music forms: 'Juju' refers to Nigerian 'juju' music; 'Feast' uses Amerindian and Hawaiian melodies and percussion instruments.

Patti Smith

1946– Underground singer-poet

An intellectual using her talents for rock music

With her blend of Rimbaud-style symbolism and Springsteen-like energy, she influenced all punk rock.

Her feeling for literature and training in that field drew her close to Rimbaud, her favourite author. The collections of poems she published from 1972 onwards were striking for their audacious metaphors and the Baudelairian despair of the subject matter. Surrounded as she was by rock music and avant-garde culture, she decided to put her poetry to music. In 1976, *Horses* was incredibly successful, and was linked to the emerging punk movement in Britain.

Closer to Bob Dylan than to the Sex

Pistols, Patti Smith worked with Bruce Springsteen (bringing out a version of his 'Because the Night') then got married to one of the survivors of the revolutionary band, MC5.

After a fifth and last album, Patti Smith retired from the music scene to start a family.

Horses (Arista, 1975) is a must.

Easter (Arista, 1978) was also very successful.

Neighbours

While she was living in Woodstock with a rock critic who had become her guitarist, Patti Smith had Bob Dylan for a neighbour. They were on friendly terms and shared a love of Rimbaud and Baudelaire.

Bruce Springsteen and the E Street Band

Mainstream rock band

The 'Boss'

His perfectionism saved 'classic' rock from total disaster.

The 'new Dylan'

This was his first nickname; John Hammond, who signed him to the Columbia label was convinced that this young musician from New Jersey could be a credible successor to the mastermind of the protest movement.

And yet, to his great disappointment, Springsteen cut a rock record, *Greetings from Asbury Park*, which contained strong reminders of his pub- and bar-playing days. Even on his first album, it was evident that Springsteen differed from Dylan: Springsteen uses none of the typical poetic devices, no images, no metaphors, no powerful or complicated symbols, preferring street language, lachrymose stories about girls, lost loves, high-ways, loneliness, unemployment and injustice. Springsteen might well play guitar and harmonica, but he would never be the new Dylan.

The future of rock'n'roll

For many years, he was dogged by this expression coined by Jon Landau in 1974, but the future of rock'n'roll could not be the too original *Born to Run*, nor the too modern *Darkness on the Edge of Town*, nor the too pretentious *The River*. Springsteen was neither the 'future of' a genre, nor the 'next' anybody. Slowly but surely he created an impressive body of music, which gave classic rock a new stylistic wealth.

The 'Boss'

Stubborn, authoritarian and perfectionist, he shut himself away with a four-track and recorded *Nebraska*, a powerful masterpiece of simplicity, single-handedly. Having done that, he returned to good old rock, which he enriched with the use of synthesizers. The long-awaited album *Born in the USA* exploded on the music scene in 1987. With his usual energy, simplicity and skill, Springsteen brought the whole of American rock to the forefront of the music scene during the world tour organised to promote the album.

Born to Run, Nebraska and **Born in the USA** (CBS, 1975, 1982 and 1987) are his best albums.

Bruce Springsteen

> **Fame**
> The Boss's best tracks are well on their way to becoming rock classics: 'Rosalita', 'Jungleland', 'Darkness on the Edge of Town', 'Hungry Heart', 'The River', 'Johnny 99', 'Reason to Believe' and 'Born in the USA' are poems written with the romanticism of a typical American which baldly depict his hopes and fears for the future of his country.

The Stranglers
English punk rock then new wave band

From outsiders to firm public favourites

They were the only punk group who really knew how to write melodies. This tendency distanced them from their musical roots.

That the Stranglers were different from the rest of the bands in the punk movement was patently obvious from their very first album released in 1977; without sacrificing the characteristic rebellious energy of the punk movement, they placed greater emphasis on the quality of their musical arrangements. *Rattus Norvegicus* and *No More Heroes* indicated that their music could possibly evolve towards concept albums and psychedelia.

The Stranglers' later releases show that the band had, to some extent, sobered down: their early anarchism had given way to a more moderate political stance; punk rhythms and ear-splitting solos had been replaced by new wave ballads. In 1982, 'Golden Brown' reached the top of the charts. After a number of increasingly eclectic albums, they entered the European Top Fifty with 'Always the Sun' in 1986.

The Raven (UA, 1979), **Feline** (Epic, 1982) and **The Collection** (UA, 1977–82; Liberty, 1982) show the breadth of the Stranglers range.

Stranglers: The Singles (CD-EMI, 1989).

Men in black
As a nod in the direction of their punk roots, the Stranglers always appear on stage dressed in black.

Talking Heads
American new wave band

Intellectual, almost cerebral rock

They tread a delicate path between synthesized rock and black African music.

The group was formed in 1974 by David Byrne and Tina Weymouth. With the release of their first album, *1977*, Talking Heads were an instant hit. Their next releases are characterized by a heavily synthesized, precise and well-crafted sound influenced by Brian Eno, which heralded a new kind of rock. *Fear of Music* (1979) and *Remain in Light* (1980) contributed to their alternative, underground image (there are many references to the Velvet Underground members, Lou Reed and Nico, and to Andy Warhol) and to their reputation for progressive rock: the African folk rhythms mixed with new wave sounds resulted in a 'chic', original atmosphere which is still Talking Heads' trademark today. After their long love-affair with the sounds of Africa, the group returned to more classic new wave music.

The Name of the Band is . . . (Sire, 1981) is a live double album which gives an excellent idea of the band's style.

Modern
Talking Heads have often experimented with blends of different types of music and instruments. *Remain in Light* has a distinct Middle Eastern flavour; *The Name of the Band is* . . . is distinctive for the use of African instruments against a background of electronic music . . .

U2

Irish new wave band

New wave's conscience

Intensity, lyricism, commitment to worthy causes and a sharp-edged sound have made U2 one of the giants of contemporary rock.

The new wave influence

U2's early work was profoundly marked by the new English sounds which had emerged from the punk explosion. With their strong Christian commitment and humanitarian beliefs, U2 could not sanction the punk movement's call for violence, nor its deliberately chaotic, irreligious anarchism. With the release of their first single 'I Will Follow', it was obvious that they were drawn to the more moderate sounds of new wave, adopting its typically clear and well-crafted sound, clever guitar work and high-pitched vocals.

The punks' provocative anti-authoritarianism gave way to passionate calls for peace, love and solidarity between fellow men ('Sunday, Bloody Sunday', 'The Refugee' and 'In the Name of Love').

The American influence

After having grafted the main themes of the American Sixties' protest movement (pacifism and the overt condemnation of racism and social injustice) on to a barrage of English new wave sounds, the band took the plunge and decided to record a truly American record in the Memphis studio where Elvis had cut his first hits. As a further tribute to American rock, the band performed with B B King and recorded a cover version of a Dylan track.

War and **Rattle and Hum** (Island, 1982 and 1988) are their best albums.

Recorded live in 1983, **Under a Blood Red Sky** is excellent.

The Unforgettable Fire and **The Joshua Tree** show the extent of their talents.

U2 in Los Angeles, 1987.
From left to right, 'The Edge' (guitar), 'Bono' (vocals), Adam Clayton (bass) and Larry Mullen Jnr. (drums).

Van Halen
Heavy metal band

Blend of original numbers and cover versions of rock standards

A popular heavy metal band of the 1980s, the Van Halen line-up was centered on vocalist Dave Lee Roth and guitarist Eddie Van Halen

Formed in 1974, Van Halen's progression up the ladder of fame was slow; however, their break came with a cover version of the Kinks' 'You Really Got Me'. The band (whose name was taken from the surname of its two founding members, brothers Eddie and Alex Van Halen) played on the vocal power of singer David Lee Roth, whose male chauvinist attitudes and outrageous, lively stage-act attracted much attention. Eddie, who has been voted guitarist of the year on more than one occasion, has a penchant for the blues, rock'n'roll and soul. Incidentally, he played the guitar solo on Michael Jackson's 'Thriller'.

Dissolved in 1986, the line-up was re-formed without David Lee Roth, but their popularity is on the wane.

Van Halen and **Van Halen II** (Warner, 1978 and 1979) are their best albums.

Entertainment
Singer David Lee Roth sees himself as a simple entertainer, which is why he joined a TV station after leaving the group. His pop video for 'Just a Gigolo' was an international hit.

ZZ Top
Southern rock group

Long-awaited fame

They kept on producing heavy boogie-style blues, but bettered the quality of their sound with every new release.

ZZ Top's two major influences were the Sixties' southern bands (Lynyrd Skynyrd and the Allman Brothers) and the ever popular English rock band Status Quo. As the Southern rock formula never really made it commercially, the Texan trio gradually distanced themselves from their early blues rock sound (*First Album*, 1970; *Tres Hombres*, 1973) to follow in the footsteps of the successful Seventies' commercial rock bands.

It was not until the 1980s and the release of *Deguello* that they became more widely known. Gradually moving closer to a hard rock sound, the band had an international hit with *Eliminator* in 1983. The better known tracks of their more recent repertoire are backed up by eye-catching videos ('Got Me Under Pressure', 'Legs' and 'Sleeping Bag').

Tres Hombres and **Deguello** (Warner, 1973 and 1979) are typical of their first period.

Eliminator (Warner, 1983) is the album which propelled them to international fame.

Roots
'La Grange', their first national hit, owes its lively riff to John Lee Hooker and Canned Heat ('Boogie Chillen' and 'On the Road Again'). ZZ Top guitarist Bill Gibbons has never attempted to deny this debt.

James Brown

Black pop music,
from 1960 to the present day

Return to the roots

From the early blues to the electro-funk produced by Prince and Michael Jackson, black music has demonstrated its ability to develop along parallel lines to the white music industry. Initially confined to the 'race record' ghetto, through Southern and Chicago blues, black music had a major impact on the melodic and rhythmic definition of early rock'n'roll.

From 1960, as rock had become an almost exclusively white phenomenon, black music found itself back where it started, in the ghetto. It was in the ghettos that soul music burst into life; having provided the anthems for the whole black civil rights movement, soul music spread far beyond the boundaries of its 'natural' habitat (this was partially due to media coverage of civil rights but also because of its sheer stylistic originality). Born in the most underprivileged areas in America's great cities, soul invaded the music charts and exerted a powerful influence over a good number of American and British rock musicians, then gradually evolved towards a new, less overtly political form (explained by the triumph of the civil rights movements), which was mainly dance orientated: funk music first appeared at the dawn of the 1970s and slowly grew in popularity until it finally dominated the music scene in the 1980s and was adopted by many white rock musicians.

Much to the astonishment of the West, the Third World also emerged as a musical force to be reckoned with, producing both crude and sophisticated music, topical lyrics and lively rhythms, perfect dance (and even trance-inducing) music. Ska and reggae from poverty-stricken Jamaica, and afro-rock born in conditions of extreme privation caused by an endless series of natural and man-made disasters, came as an injection of fresh blood to all the most modern forms of rock. Thus, the future of rock'n'roll was to be found in its roots, which were deeply planted in the black soul and continent.

The reggae composed by Jimmy Cliff, Toots and Bob Marley was not merely a collection of spirited revolutionary songs, or an affirmation of their faith in the black race's imminent liberation from oppression, it was also truly original in terms of melodic, instrumental and rhythmic structures, and was incorporated into the work of the biggest contemporary rock bands: could the Police ever have become famous without reggae?

The afro-rock created by such artists as Pierre Akendengué, Xalam, Fela, Mory Kanté, Salif Keita, Touré Kounda, Alpha Blondy, Sunny Adé, and Youssou n'Dour, after their forerunners, Manu Dibango and Bembeya Jazz, and before the newcomers Johnny Clegg and Savuka, impressed black and white contemporary rock with its own blend of traditional-style chanting, sophisticated harmonies and skilful arrangements. The hit parades were overrun with white, black and multiracial bands who literally pirated contemporary African music.

Therefore, just as rock'n'roll was the result of the meeting between two popular music forms, whose major source was definitely black (Thirties' and Forties' rural blues), so contemporary rock would have been unable to break out of its deadly torpor (if we discount the punk movement, the 1970s were very poor in terms of creativity) had it not been for this absorbtion of African elements. Whether it was from the hypnotic, swaying rhythms of Jamaican reggae, Cuban and West Indian calypso rock or, more directly, from Mandingo (Western African) country rock and Zulu (South Africa, Namibia, Zimbabwe) rock, rock music as a whole drew its energy from the black continent. Rock music, which is still controlled by the white show-biz industry, cannot ignore the fact that, for the past 50 years, its stylistic automony from black music forms has been distinctly weak. The evolution of rock, even since 1960, is linked to that of black popular music.

Soul music

Soul music or R & B?

The distinction made between these two sub-genres today is distinctly artificial if we examine the way the terms were used in the past.

First fact: the black rock produced by Chuck Berry and Little Richard was qualified by blacks and whites alike as R & B. Ten years later, the separation between them and the artists termed 'soul singers' was indistinct and tenuous: James Brown, Otis Redding and Ben E King incessantly talked of soul, but Ray Charles and the Stax company sold compilations under the R & B heading that today are called soul. Moreover, at the same time, certain singers labelled soul and R & B declared that they were writing funk music (Wilson Pickett, James Brown and Arthur Conley, to name but a few). Therefore, at that time, neither critics, nor record labels, nor the performers themselves distinguished between R & B and soul music. It follows that black audiences and white buyers did not either.

Second fact: the term 'rhythm and blues' (R & B) is older and purely stylistic; the term 'soul' dates from the 1960s and contains an ideological connotation absent from R & B: for blacks, soul music indicated light music produced in support of the black civil rights struggle, with ambiguous lyrics whose political meaning was patently obvious to any listener.

Third fact: from the 1970s, the word 'soul', which indicated a whole, typically black, music movement (there were no white soul singers, while the Stones and the Animals started out playing what they called R & B), became the definitive term and totally replaced the older expression, R & B. This was to avoid any confusion with the music, both black and white, which for historical or geographical reasons had nothing to do with the black civil rights struggle between 1955 and 1970.

In the following chapter therefore, we have listed various different artists under the heading 'soul music' in order to simplify classification, but also because we have taken into account their own statements on the nature of their music, as well as the relationship between their output and white music. In any case, most of the great black artists have extremely varied repertoires: Ray Charles, James Brown and Otis Redding were constantly producing music referred to as both R & B and soul. Any firm categorization could thus only be artificial.

Civil rights music

By the end of the 1950s, soul music had become a means of expression for a whole miserable and disillusioned people trapped in America's massive industrial cities. The songs had a very strong social criticism element and were sung on the many protest marches, the 'sit-ins' and antisegreg-

---

Between soul, funk and light music: disco

Sly Stone, a black Texan, already had several years of a professional career behind him when he decided to orientate his band (who had an American number one in 1971 with 'There's a Riot Goin' On') towards dance music that would be attractive to both black and white audiences. Disco, with its steady dance beat, was the result of this idea which brought the main impulse of soul and nascent funk into white rock.

However, it was the Bee Gees, a white band, who with 'Saturday Night Fever' (35 million albums sold in 10 years) and 'Stayin' Alive' exploited Sly Stone's idea to its fullest potential. They were followed by Rod Stewart ('Do You Think I'm Sexy?'), the Rolling Stones ('Miss You' and 'Emotional Rescue') and even Bowie ('Fame').

Seen as an antidote to the savagery of punk rock, disco was all the rage in the charts and nightclubs until the start of the 1980s. Tight trousers, spangles, roller skates, acrobatic dance steps and a clean look swamped what was originally a credible musical genre, but quickly slipped into mediocrity, despite the efforts of excellent songwriters such as Sergio Moroder and talented singers (Donna Summer, Bonnie Tyler, etc).

Since 1982, Jackson, Prince, rap and then house music have restored black musicians as the leaders of dance music.

---

rationalist boycotts of which Martin Luther King was the political and moral symbol. Sam Cooke's 'A Change is Gonna Come', Otis Redding's 'Respect', James Brown's 'I'm Black and I'm Proud' Aretha Franklin's 'Think' and 'Dancing in the Streets' which was also sung by Martha and The Vandellas, Dony Hathaway's 'The Ghetto' and Marvin Gaye's 'What's Goin' On?' were the anthems of a period during which black people became fully aware of their fate, their struggle and their identity. The soul movement was accom-panied by the publication of a number of major literary works, in which certain black authors (who are considered classic writers today) used the novel or essay form to highlight the injustices of the black con-dition: James Baldwin, Richard Wright, then Stokeley Carmichael, Elridge Cleaver, Bobby Seale, George Jackson and Angela Davis all earned well-deserved fame, despite the vast differences in their politcal stances. The black political milieu was also divided between the moderate (Martin Luther King) and more violent (Malcolm X and the Black Panthers) approach to the civil rights question. In all the black suburbs and ghettos, soul songs accompanied marchers and rioters alike. Soul music was the cement of their struggle.

From gospel to soul

While it is true that the main theme of soul music was the fight against racial segregation in the United States, it is nonetheless also true that soul, especially in terms of the vocals, is a direct descendant of the Pentecostal and Baptist religious traditions, which were particularly active in Southern towns and rural areas: with the exception of Sam Cooke and Stevie Wonder, born in the state of Michigan, of Solomon Burke, born in Philadelphia and of Marvin Gaye, born in Washington, all the great black soul songwriters and performers are from the Deep South: Wilson Pickett, Eddie Floyd and Percy Sledge were born in Alabama, Joe Tex and Esther Phillips in Texas, Don Covay in South Carolina, Otis Redding, Ray Charles and Arthur Conley in Georgia, and James Brown, Aretha Franklin, Tina Turner and Rufus Thomas in Tennessee. It was in church that they received their first musical training, that their vocal technique took shape, and when they went on, often with grave misgivings, to commercial music, they carried with them a fervour

that the big swing bands and jazz ensembles could never communicate to their audiences. They also brought an emotion that was present in the very early blues, which was totally new to whites, and of which early rock'n'roll had only given a distorted image.

A decade of soul music

In actual fact, this musical genre, of which English Sixties' and Seventies' rock, Jamaican reggae and American funk were the direct result, only dominated the American music scene for a short period of time, which roughly corresponds to a decade, from the first civil rights marches in 1960, to the assassinations of Martin Luther King and Bobby Kennedy in 1968, the year in which the Southern States finally recognised black Americans as full citizens.

Of course, Luther King had organized the first boycott of segregated buses (in Montgomery, Alabama) in 1955, and the first soul hit, Sam Cooke's 'You Send Me' (if we discount Ray Charles, who brought out 'I Got a Woman' in 1954) was released in 1957. But soul's boom period, its hour of glory, was between 1965 and 1970. 1965 saw the release of Sam Cooke's famous 'Shake', Wilson Pickett's 'In the Midnight Hour'. Otis Redding's 'Respect' and James Brown's 'It's a Man's Man's World'. Two years previously, the first march on Washington had taken place in response to two deaths during the Oxford Town riots (which Dylan immortalized in song); 1963 was the year in which the soul movement was launched: the release of Sam Cooke's 'A Change is Gonna Come' and Martha and the Vandellas' rendition of 'Dancing in the Streets' coincided with the two month-long riots in Birmingham, Alabama. The first real uprising, it was put down by truncheons, police dogs and flame throwers. The end of soul music's politico-musical movement coincided with two series of important events: between 1968 and 1970, the civil rights movement lost its leaders (Martin Luther King, Malcolm X and Bobby Kennedy, brother of the assassinated president, who was standing for presidency in 1968 on an integrationalist ticket) in a series of bloody murders, throwing the 'brothers' and 'sisters' into despair. Then, with amazing speed, all the remaining barriers constructed by the Southern States to prevent blacks from exercising their rights as full American citizens fell within the space of the two years between 1968 and 1970.

The two 'majors' of soul

Musically, we owe the soul movement to the wisdom and professionalism of a few talent-spotters concentrated in two record companies run by a team of gifted musicians, but also to arrangers and songwriters, without whom the greatest performers of the genre would never have been able to express themselves fully. These two companies are called Tamla Motown and Stax-Atlantic. Without these studios, the one based in Detroit in the North, and the other in Memphis in the middle of the black ghetto, soul music would be totally different.

The manager of Tamla Motown, an ex-car worker, gave more than one star of soul his or her lucky break: thanks to his studio and the work of talented songwriters such as Smokey Robinson, Marvin Gaye, Lamont Dozier, the Holland brothers and Jo Hunter, who were also producers and arrangers, many major soul artists became famous. The backing of Phil Spector accelerated the studio's rise, with all-girl groups (the Supremes and Diana Ross, and Martha and the Vandellas), all-male line-ups (the Temptations), solo artists (Marvin Gaye and Stevie Wonder) then the Jackson Five (already starring Michael Jackson!). The polished 'Tamla sound', which was well suited to white show-biz tastes, completely took over the charts and earned millions for the studio's performers, who have gone down in history as the soul artists par excellence.

Stax and Atlantic were more geared towards Southern soul, and Memphis was their capital. Otis Redding, Rufus Thomas, Wilson Pickett, Aretha Franklin, Ray Charles, the Drifters, the Coasters, Sam and Dave, Arthur Conley and Percy Sledge, backed up by reputable songwriters such as Leiber and Stoller, and exceptionally talented session musicians such as Steve Cropper, Donald 'Duck' Dunn or Booker T stormed the international music scene with their authentic, raw soul.

The extended funk family

In black American slang, the word 'funk' suggests a wriggling or jiggling movement, or more precisely, the body odour that hangs over a crowded dance floor. Like the expressions 'boogie' and 'rock'n'roll', also of black origin, but older, the word 'funk' and the adjective 'funky' have strong sexual connotations. From the late 1960s, in musical terminology, funk music indicated a kind of dance music that had its roots in R & B (Arthur Conley's 'Funky Street', 1969), then was influenced by disco (James Brown's 'The Original Disco Man', 1977) and electronic music (Prince, Michael Jackson). However, other black music forms can be linked to funk, whether merely because they claim to be related or in more concrete terms of harmonic and rhythmic structure: early Eighties' rap, late Eighties' house and certain recent afro-West Indian and North West African (including *rai*) forms are funk derivatives.

And yet, despite its obviously predominantly black roots, funk is definitely not an ethnic music form. Since the start of the 1980s, funk has been the most commercial form of contemporary rock on the music scene; it dominates the charts, has taken over nightclubs and adapts with amazing speed to changing fashions. In fact, of all rock music's sub-genres, funk is the closest to light music and easy listening. Funk was not designed as music to be listened to, it is dance music, pure and simple; in the majority of cases, its claims are modest, although certain major songwriters have made a name for themselves in this genre, popularizing sophisticated sounds and rhythms, polished arrangements and technically complex (smurf and break dancing) and suggestive dances (house music).

'Classic' funk

The first musicians termed funk were those who, within the framework of soul and R & B, gave the most 'physical' shows, belting out lively up-tempo rhythms. The king of funk was, of couse, James Brown, with his on-stage skipping, hopping and leaping, and his famous face-twisting grimaces ('Sex Machine', 1970, 'Hot Pants', 1971). Otis Redding, mike in hand, moving across the stage on his knees during tear-jerking slow ballads ('I've Been Loving You Too Long') or jumping about for up-tempo numbers ('Shake' and 'Respect') was also one of the instigators of all that was visual, physical and new in funk. Wilson Pickett ('Land of a Thousand Dances', 1965; 'Funky Broadway', 1967) was perhaps the first real funk singer.

However, none of the Stax and Atlanta artists (Tamla Motown remaining deliberately soul-orientated at this point) was able to break away from the religious (gospel) and secular (the blues) musical backgrounds of their people. Despite efforts to quicken the pace of their R & B numbers, their music could never match modern funk's clever orchestrations and ornate rhythm patterns.

Electro-funk

Stevie Wonder was the first black artist to change over successfully from soul music (dominated by classic instruments such as the organ, the electric guitar and brass section) to modern funk, whose more electronic sound depends on the use of keyboards and an electronic percussion section. He integrated synthesizers into his music as well as the programmable drum machines which were the trademark of Eighties' electro-funk. He also cleverly used the fashion for disco to give it a diversity it had previously lacked, and inspired two grand masters of contemporary funk, Michael Jackson and Prince.

With 'Soft And Wet', Prince defined his particular brand of raw, animal funk stripped bare of all soul trappings. With his raunchy, forceful sound and provocative lyrics, Prince's shows were much more sexually suggestive than those of his predecessors, excepting Jim Morrison of the Doors and Jimi Hendrix. *1999* was the album of the 'funky kids' generation, an honour it shared with Michael Jackson's *Thriller*, which was less overtly sexual, but just as exciting on a musical level, and much more commercially viable. Jackson's talents as a dancer (he is an unsurpassed break dancer) and singer are far greater than those of Prince. The lyrics, without being too suggestive, remain faithful to traditional funk's most 'sexy' aspects ('Beat It', 'Thriller', 'Bad', 'Dirty Diana', etc).

Electro-funk, with its drum machines, its variably rasping or smooth vocals and clear or hard sound, its acrobatic shows and sexual imagery (Jackson's deliberate androgyny, gesticulations and hip thrusts, Prince's harem, outrageous theatrical antics and suggestive proposals) was to have a major impact on all rock (including English new wave, Bowie, Iggy Pop and Siouxsie) and easy listening music (INXS, Duran Duran and all the hit parade 'regulars').

Rap

Rap is a musical style intimately linked with the nightclub milieu. Born in the Bronx and Harlem at the start of the 1980s, rap is basically the art of churning out rhyming lines on love, music and daily life at high speed. It was initially started by disc-jockeys who voiced-over existing funk tunes, which they had adapted with the intention of surprising dancers; the DJ can mix two records, change from one record to another and back again with amazing speed, and manually turn the turntables anti-clockwise or back and forward in time to the beat ('scratch'), producing sound effects which they complete with the addition of remixed jingles, and re-recorded catch phrases played back at high speed ('repeat'), etc. Since the first rap hit entered the charts (Sugarhill Gang's 'Rapper's Delight'), some disc jockeys, such as Africa Bambaataa have become famous. Certain American and British groups have become internationally famous, popularizing not only an original form of funk, but a whole range of rap fashions: baseball caps and boots, multicoloured sweatshirts, and roller-skates. It was rap which also made

fashionable the portable radio-cassette recorders, which rappers called 'sound systems', as well as graffiti and 'tags' (logos sprayed on to subway cars . . .).

House music

Initially, house music was a form of rap particularly popular in Chicago. A pulsating, doctored music form, perfect for the sensual 'dirty dancing' style, house was the late Eighties' equivalent to disco.

Technically, house music is based on the remix principle, by which a whole new song can be made from exerpts taken from other songs; thus extracts from Beatles and James Brown songs were re-recorded and mixed with other sounds. More suited to a sound engineer than to a musician, this kind of work requires considerable synthesizer skills and, above all, the back-up of excellent 'samplers' who can turn everyday sounds into music. With all the technical means at their disposal, house musicians incorporated gasps, repeated catch phrases and lyrics played backwards into their music. Mixed with a steady drum machine beat, the early tracks served as the foundation for an electronic dance music.

House music had its chart-topping but short-lived bands (Beat Masters with 'Rock da House' and Marrs with 'Pump Up the Volume') and specialized production companies (Rhythm King in London). House music is also associated with the consumption of a superamphetamine known as 'ecstasy', sometimes mistakenly called acid (it has nothing to with the LSD so liberally consumed in the 1960s). House has remained faithful to the spirit of early funk: dance, trance and the pleasure of sweating out difficult rhythms on the dance floor.

Reggae

Ghetto music

It was not until the 1970s that reggae, a tribal, ethnic, but truly Jamaican form of music was discovered by a handful of white rock musicians. Reggae took the music scene by storm, fulfilling the rasta prophecy whereby the modern day Babylon, ie the Western industrialized countries, would be invaded.

Reggae became a full citizen of the rock world after Eric Clapton released a cover version of Bob Marley's 'I Shot the Sheriff' and Jimmy Cliff appeared in the half-documentary, half-musical, *The Harder They Come* in 1972. Jimmy Cliff, acknowledged leader of ska and then reggae until the arrival of Bob Marley, subsequently cut all his albums on the Rolling Stones' own label, and Keith Richards himself played on a number of tracks.

Reggae rapidly swamped white and black radio stations, replacing the stylistically burnt out R & B and competing with nascent funk. In a matter of years, Jimmy Cliff, Bob Marley and the Wailers, Toots and the Maytals and Burning Spear won the hearts of blacks in ghettos the world over, in the States, in Europe and in Africa.

The importance of reggae in recent rock history is considerable: reggae shocked the complacent and increasingly conservative rock world with socially aware lyrics highlighting the plight of the Third World and calling for peace, that were chanted by rioters in Kingston, Jamaica, Brixton, England and Soweto, South Africa.

Reggae gave rock back its feeling for socio-political messages that years of commercial exploitation had all but wiped out. Lastly, and perhaps most importantly, it was responsible for a thorough reform of Western rock's melodic and rhythmic structures, of which groups such as the Police are the prime example.

Reggae also provoked the rise of multiracial bands (UB40 and the Beat) which bridged the gap between two culturally and racially different audiences.

The beating of the rasta drums

Xaymaca (the 'Land of Springs' of the Arawak Indians exterminated by the Spanish and British) Jamaica, whose independence solved none of its problems, is a large Caribbean island mainly inhabited by descendants of black slaves. Impoverished by an endless series of agricultural crises and confined to squalid shanty towns (Trenchtown, Tivoli Gardens, etc), the majority of Jamaica's black inhabitants are unemployed and culturally underprivileged. Economically, the island continues to be exploited by both Britain and the United States, and the only true source of local income, which is monopolized by the privileged (basically white) few, is tourism: luxurious hotels hidden in coconut groves beside endless sandy beaches.

In both the rural areas and the slums, the songs that break the night are based on African models. The Rasta drums (two incessantly repeated beats, like a heartbeat), the bass guitar amplifying the thud of the 'burra', a three-drum set made of empty rum barrels stretched with goat skins, the cane flutes, and the African rhythms and off-beat chords strummed on the electric guitar combine together to blast out the music of a poverty-stricken people who can only hope that Jah, the god of Marcus Garvey (Jamaican prophet and founder of the Rastafarian religion) will grant them their wish, and let them rediscover the purity of life on the lost continent, the Africa of the immortals.

Starting from calypso and *mento*, and thanks to the ska created by such great songwriters as Don Drummond, Desmond Dekker and Jimmy Cliff, Jamaica produced her own reggae in the form of Bob Marley and Toots, but was also responsible for British bands like Steel Pulse and UB40 and the African Alpha Blondy. White rock musicians were obliged to start producing West Indian rhythms (the Rolling Stones' 'Emotional Rescue', and Dylan's 'Man Gave Name to Animals').

All British new wave was influenced by the Police's hybrid rock, whose most successful tracks are out and out reggae numbers (*Reggatta de Blanc, Outlandos d'Amour*). By the 1960s, ska had already crossed the ocean and invaded London's black Caribbean communities. Jimmy Cliff had many followers: the Cimmarrons and the Greyhounds were the first ska bands to be formed with the West Indian immigrant community. Then the term 'reggae' emerged with the release of Toots's 'Do the Reggay'. Toots's explanation of the origin of the term is that 'reggay' stands for 'regular people', the ordinary people.

As much as a hypnotic rhythm, a versatile, catchy and trance-inducing kind of music, reggae was a politico-religious shock to the rock scene, an uncompromising reminder of the existence of a Third, and even a Fourth World.

Reggae's political stance

In exactly the same way, but a few years or decades earlier, the slaves' and cotton-pickers' blues songs, the black Southern baptists' spirituals and the civil rights activists' soul music were all reminders that rock was essentially a form of resistance to misery and oppression. Even whites had caught on to this idea when they began to protest against the Vietnam war and moral codes through protest song, folk rock and the psychedelic 'flower power' movement.

However, in reggae the operative word is not flowers, but 'grass'. The Rasta religion advocates the use of 'ganja' (cannabis) to help generate mystical revelation, music, faith and even, if necessary, the energy needed for an uprising against injustice. Not since Dylan, the Doors and the punk movement had rock reached the levels of rebelliousness contained in a Bob Marley or Jimmy Cliff, or Peter Tosh song, or in the music produced by Alpha Blondy and Burning Spear. And not since the hippy movement had there been such an outcry for a return to a simple and natural way of life, symbolized by the Rastas' dreadlocks.

Reggae was a breath of fresh air in stylistic and thematic terms: it shook established rock stars out of their complacency. It was the poor man's rock. Thanks to reggae, rock became what it originally had been: music by the people for the people emotionally and socially close to those who actually created and consumed it. Thanks to reggae and afro-rock, thanks to the blues and soul, white rock could no longer ignore the fact that it was basically a black music form. Despite the efforts of history and the music industry, nothing could erase rock's proud 'Made in Africa' label.

Jimmy Cliff

Afro-rock

The sound of poverty

Around 1960, most black African countries gained their independence, which in most cases, except Algeria, was a case of a bloodless transfer of power from the colonial government to the Africans themselves. However, despite the problem of independence being solved, the worst was yet to be faced: once they had lost the large majority of their white managerial staff (who returned to their home countries) these African countries were totally incapable of self-rule. The sudden departure of the Belgians left what was later to become Zaire in a state close to anarchy. Some countries managed to install less corrupt and economically ineffectual régimes than others (Ivory Coast, Senegal), but the others were stifled by the weight of dictatorships (Guinea) or faced complete economic ruin (Mali, Chad, Nigeria, Gambia, etc). Some spent years fighting the colonial occupants (Angola, Mozambique) or struggled against local segregationalist régimes (Rhodesia, South Africa). East Africa, with its predominantly Islamic population, foundered in bloody civil wars (Ethiopia, Sudan), and tribal wars aggravated the situation in countries that were already suffering under the yoke of poverty (Tanzania, Uganda).

On the whole, it was a disaster. Economies that were already foundering under the double weight of gross mismanagement and corruption, were dealt a death blow by the cost of war. A large proportion of the gross national product was swallowed by the African armies in countries that were already desperately poor. The situation was scarcely propitious to a cultural expansion; no scientific or technical advances were made. Agriculture and, even worse, medicine stagnated or regressed.

And yet, cliché or not, the African people still sought entertainment (and many eye-witness accounts prove this). This carefree attitude and good humour, which acts as a panacea for all the ills caused by the direst poverty, is a palpable fact which can be measured by the amazingly frequent dances and festivals held in villages and towns. In view of their terrible living conditions, an extraordinary proportion of time and energy is spent on African music.

At the time of the mass white exodus, in terms of musical technology, Africa was extremely backward: in the whole of the formerly European African territories, there was virtually no sound or recording equipment at all. There were a few electric guitars, no basses, very few drum kits and only a handful of pianos and saxophones. According to the accounts given by afro-rock pioneers Fela, Manu Dibango, Salif Keita, and Mory Kante, the majority of their electric equipment was home made, old radio sets were turned into amps and the few saxophones they had were in a bad state of repair. The pioneers of the new African music form, with its first European then American and Jamaican influence, had none of the comforts provided for their white counterparts. The only bands which were able to perform under 'normal' conditions were those which had government backing. The traditional folk groups which played for the tourists in the big hotels were much better provided for than the jazz and rock bands which performed in city nightclubs.

This is why the great afro-rock songwriters had to choose between two strategies: either they could enter the corridors of power and become close enough to the government or dictator to be entitled to the technical and financial backing necessary for artistic creation, or they could leave for Europe, the West Indies or the United States. Some, like Fela, chose to protest against the established military powers, at great personal risk, but most supported the government. Salif Keita, Bembeya Jazz, Miriam Makéba and Alpha Blondy were all personal friends of Guinea's bloody dictator Sékou Touré, who, ironically, was the only official African financial backer of afro-rock.

A blend of music forms

It is possible that Africa's paucity in terms of musical equipment was to some extent behind afro-rock's high levels of creativity: the lack of means and electronic equipment may have pushed musicians to develop further the existing instruments at their disposal, namely the many kinds of acoustic percussion instruments native to the vast Mandingo country, and the plethora of varieties of *balafon* and *kora*, (types of xylophone and many-stringed guitar-harp); a more modern, Western flavour to the music was achieved with the addition of jazz-influenced trumpet and sax sounds.

Cuban aid given to the independent African countries also had a considerable effect on the development of afro-rock: Castro had thousands of salsa and calypso records sent to Guinea (and the the rest of West Africa), and these were one of the early afro-rock songwriters' formative influences. Thus in 1961, Bambeya Jazz, Guinea's national band (who were as much at ease describing the benefits of milk-drinking as they were singing the praises of Sékou Touré's policies), defined the hybrid Afro-Cuban music form, a blend of West Indian calypso and folk tunes, with a guitar accompaniment added by jazz-lovers, guitarist Sékou Diabate and trumpet player Sékou Legrow Camara. Born in the heart of Mandingo country, Salif Keita rounded off *peul* and *malinke* folk tunes, using electric guitars, a Westernized brass section and folk drums and vocals. Keletigui Traore followed the same pattern, using the Cuban *chaonda* rhythm, combined with American soul and

Manu Dibango

Guinean folk arrangments. Created in 1971 by Boubakar Traore, the Silyphone record company gave afro-rock artists the chance to record under quasi-professional conditions in their home country for the first time. The records, however, were still pressed in Europe . . .

This lack of technological and financial means therefore had a twofold effect: it opened a door onto the West, upon which Africa was still dependent for its records (pressed in Europe, the United States and Jamaica) and forced African musicians to exploit the full potential of their traditional folk music and instruments (percussion instruments, choral work, tunes, dialects, etc).

Fifteen years later, Fleetwood Mac's drummer did a six-month 'course' with black African drummers, Dizzy Gillespie went to Zaire to find inspiration, Paul Simon recorded with South African musicians and blues guitarists such as Arthur Collins and Johnny Copeland considered their African tours to be the experience of a lifetime. And, of course, Stewart Copeland, drummer with the Police, also spent some time learning from the black drummers.

Today, the African rock musicians are rarely out of the European charts: Mory Kanté, who spent 20 years playing for tourists in luxury hotels in Bamako, Abidjan and other cities, without ever

losing his taste for village dances, has finally been rewarded for his perseverance and originality. Salif Keita's fame has spread to the United States. Alpha Blondy is recognized as the best reggae musician in Africa. Fela has been released from the prison into which he was thrown by a Nigerian dictator for his part in an international protest movement (which numbers many other famous rock musicians in its ranks). King Sunny Adé played 'juju' music, the first form of African rock to be introduced into the West. Manu Dibango is an internationally respected artist. Xalam, Toure Kunda, Youssou n'Dour and Mamadou Konte are available on compact disc. At the present time, afro-rock is one of the major influences in contemporary rock music. Born in dramatic circumstances, it survived and spread thanks to the courage and perseverance of a handful of talented songwriters, and also thanks to the obvious love of rhythm and music that can be found in even the most miserable of African villages and shanty towns. The music created by Johnny Clegg and Savuka, indeed all the Zulu rock which emerged in South Africa, led by brilliant musicians (including Splash, Lucky Dube, Mahlatini and Juluka), has invaded the charts, captivating the hearts of a wide and varied audience with its catchy rhythms and the generosity of its humanitarian message.

The emergence of afro-rock marked the start of a movement that was to shift the centre of rock from its more recent base (Britain and the United States) back to its true birthplace, Africa. Afro-rock and reggae are by far the most innovative music forms to his the music scene since British pop, American protest song and the punk movement: to a greater extent than Michael Jackson and Prince's electro-funk, afro-rock has forced the whole rock genre out of a rut created by almost 30 years of white domination.

Alpha Blondy
Afro-rock/reggae singer from the Ivory Coast

A blend of three continents

Influenced by African music, reggae and Western rock, Alpha Blondy writes raw, original music.

A foundling, Alpha claims to be the son of a *griot* (a sort of travelling witchdoctor cum artist). His formative influences are to be found in the lengendary African band, Bembeya Jazz and Bob Marley, as well as in the rock produced by Presley and Johnny Hallyday. The time he spent in New York in 1975 allowed him to form a reggae band with Jamaicans from the Bronx. On his return to the Ivory Coast, he became a hit with nightclubbers and was idolized by the country's disaffected youth. Now based in Paris, he has entered the charts on numerous occasions with well-crafted albums. Alpha cleverly synthesizes the music and culture of several continents (for example 'Opération coup de poing' which is partially sung in the *dioula* dialect).

Jah Glory (WEA), **Jerusalem** (WEA-EMI, 1986) and **Revolution** (EMI, 1987) are excellent, but **Cocody Rock** (Pathé, 1984) is undoubtedly the best truly African reggae album on the market.

Abuse

His 'tough' reputation pushed his step-father to have him certified. Alpha Blondy was therefore wrongfully confined to a mental hospital for several months before he managed to escape.

The Beat
Multi-racial ska band

The combined influences of Africa and the West Indies

They were the first ska band to make it big.

Founded in Birmingham, England in 1978 by musicians of different racial and musical backgrounds (pop, reggae, rock, jazz), from 1980 the Beat were mainly popular as a live and dance band; a few numbers, propelled to the top of the charts by their success with nightclub-goers, helped launch the ska fashion or 'two-tone', as it was known in Britain.

The syncopated, staccato (from whence 'ska') guitar lines inspired by R & B rhythms and African drum beats, per-vaded their first albums and were an original musical development of early Sixties' reggae.

I Just Can't Stop It (WEA, 1980) and **Wh'appen** (WEA) are their best albums ('Mirror in the Bathroom', 'Best Friend', 'Too Nice to Talk to', etc).

What is Beat? (Arista, double album) is also very interesting, being a compilation of the band's greatest hits, together with a number of extended re-mixes.

Age gap

In 1978, the Beat's sax-player Saxa was 50 years old; the youngest member of the band could have been his son . . .

Bembeya Jazz National

Guinean afro-jazz and folk band

The root of all African rock

Formed in 1961, Bembeya Jazz had an impact on the music of the whole African continent and are still very popular there.

Début

The initial six-man jazz-orientated line-up was strongly influenced by South American and Cuban rhythms, and aimed to incorporate traditional African music into their work. Led by Sékou Diabaté, an extremely talented and versatile guitarist with an easy, flowing style, and made immensely popular by their inimitable singer Abudakar Demba Camara, soon found themselves at the head of a national movement to define a properly African musical idiom. Their rather embarrassing friendship with dictator Sékou Touré made it easy for them to record and to maintain a relationship with Cuban musicians. Between 1964 and 1968, Bembeya kept up a furious pace of touring and recording, but the accidental death of singer Demba, 'The Dragon', deprived the group of their most popular element in 1973.

The Bembeya style

Demba generally sang in the *dioula* dialect, but the incorporation of French choruses into his songs meant that the band's music appealed to the whole of French West Africa. Demba's singing was offset by a group of backing vocalists, while guitarist Diabaté poured out jazz riffs or variations on a Cuban calypso theme. An up-tempo beat was provided by bassist Mory Kouaté and the percussion section's blend of Western drums and African tom-toms. By 1965, the basic elements of afro-rock had already been defined.

Bembeya Jazz National (Syliphone Konakry), and **Bembeya Jazz National** (Sonodisc) are the best of their many albums.

The Guinean breeding-ground

In 1960, Sékou Touré had ordered over 60 complete PA systems. With this vast technical advantage, Guinea suddenly found itself at the head of the African musical movement. Many artists (including folk musicians, jazz players, singers, drummers and dancers) joined line-ups that were more or less financed by the Guinean government. Besides Bembeya, a number of other performers were important: the Amazones de Guinée (an all-female group led by Sana Diabat, sister of Bembeya's Sékou Diabaté); Xalam, with his afro-Cuban influence and a selection of unique musicians such as sax-player Honoré Copé, or topical singer and political refugee Miriam Makéba. After the success of the Konakry festival in 1964, afro-rock mushroomed. The first big African recording studio, owned by the Silyphone company, was also Guinean. Unfortunately, after the 1985 coup d'état, the company's entire stock of master-tapes was destroyed. In one fell swoop, 15 years' worth of truly African music was wiped out.

Research

Thanks to recent re-releases, it is easy to find Bembeya Jazz records in Europe. However, not all the records have a specific title, some being stamped simply with the band's name. To be sure of a quality album, check the date of its original release and make sure that the three 'big men' (Diabaté, Demba Camara and Mory Kouaté) actually played on it.

Black Uhuru
Jamaican reggae band

Ghetto born

Two reggae 'hard liners' used the talents of a singer to mellow their image.

Catchy rhythms and repetitive lyrics that range from the overtly rebellious to the obscurely mystical made up an explosive cocktail whose originality lay mainly in the vocal work. Thanks to two musicians who were later to become internationally respected, bassist Robbie Shakespeare and drummer Sly Dunbar, the Black Uhuru trio gave their extremist reggae a more commercial image which at one point indicated them as possible successors to Bob Marley and his Wailers. Less active today, at the height of their popularity Black Uhuru wrote afro-Jamaican music that, in terms of beat, was ideally suited to the dance floor, and, in terms of lyrics, supported the world-wide struggle for black emancipation.

Red (Island, 1981) and **Tear It Up** (Island, 1982) are both musts.

Unexpected
Bob Dylan himself recruited Dunbar and Shakespeare for one of his tours in the 1980s. Their musical association was extremely productive.

Booker T and the MGs
American instrumental R & B band

In the shadow of the stars

They virtually created the 'Stax' sound, then finally became famous in their own right.

Organist Booker T Jones and white lovers of black music guitarist Steve Cropper and bassist Donald 'Duck' Dunn formed the Booker T and the MGs (Memphis Group) line-up; these three musicians were responsible for most of the session work accomplished at the Stax studios, backing major artists such as Otis Redding, then were even employed by Atlantic, Stax's foremost rival, where they played with Sam and Dave, Wilson Pickett and many others.

Fed up of working as Stax's house band, Booker T and the MGs decided to cut a totally instrumental album, whose title track, a simple 'boogie' number, was an international hit; taking their cue from Booker T and the MGs' success, other insturmentalists tried out the same idea, with varying degrees of success (the Mar Keys, a soul ensemble, sax-player King Curtis and flautist Herbie Mann).

Green Onions (Stax, 1962) is definitely worth buying.

Dance
The MGs' instrumental style gave numbers that were already known in the 1960s a new lease of life (Ray Charles's 'I Got a Woman' and 'Lonely Avenue', Gershwin's 'Summer Time' and 'Twist and Shout' to name but a few).

James Brown

1928–   R & B and soul singer

'Mister Dynamite'

For many years he was the uncontested leader of soul and, with his punchy, topical lyrics, a star of the black civil rights movement.

Poverty

Raised in a poor black area in Augusta, Georgia, where the Southern law of segregation was strictly enforced, James Brown started his working life at the tender age of eight, as a pimp. He boosted his income by polishing shoes in the town's centre.

Sports-mad, he attempted a career in baseball, then as a boxer while he was still in his teens. A cash prize won at a talent contest allowed him to glimpse the possibility of a way of escaping the miserable life of Southern blacks and spurred him into choosing music.

Début

He began performing in the 1950s, firstly with the Three Swanees, then with the Famous Flames. Even at this stage, Brown's stage-act was frenetic and his costumes eccentric.

Fame

Gradually shrugging off his initial gospel style, James Brown moved closer to the more sophisticated music produced by the Drifters and Hank Ballard, while developing a taste for punchier, Bo Diddley-style rhythms. In 1958, 'Try Me' made him a household name, and was followed by a string of international hits ('Think', 'Night Train', 'Out of Sight' and 'Please Please Me') which made him the leader of the kind of music called both R & B and soul. The extraordinary show at Harlem's Apollo in 1967 won him the respect of both British and American rock fans and musicians. 'It's a Man's Man's World', a slow sensual number, opened the doors of the white rock industry (the Madison Square Garden concert in 1966), while 'Say It Loud – I'm Black and I'm Proud' placed him firmly at the head of the struggle for civil rights.

At the same time, Brown cultivated an outrageous sexy and macho image, which inspired and encouraged many other rock musicians: the daring 'Sex Machine' (1970) was also a smash hit. At the end of the 1970s, he moved into disco (*The Original Disco Man*, 1979) then took part in the rap movement ('Rap Pay Back') in 1981.

Live at the Apollo (Polydor, 1967) is an absolute masterpiece and should not be missed.

James Brown 16 Greatest Hits (Polydor, 1986) is an excellent compilation.

James Brown: Great Hits – Great Performances (CD, Duchesse, 1989) contains both studio pieces and the best parts of the Apollo concert.

Rebel

James Brown had numerous brushes with the American law, which he frequently criticised during his activist period. He has been involved in several fights, has been charged with speeding on numerous occasions and was recently sentenced for assaulting a police officer. He was in prison from 1989 to 1991.

Boxing

James Brown perhaps owes his incredible on-stage footwork to his training as a boxer. That he has lost none of his energy over the years is proved by his role in John Landis's film *The Blues Brothers* and by his more recent concerts.

Solomon Burke

1936–   R & B singer

The King of rock and soul

He successfully changed over from gospel to soul.

His training as a preacher allowed him to incorporate the communicative fervour of 'spirituals' and gospel music into his songs, while using modern sound equipment; with his repetitive lyrics and moral ('Everybody Needs Somebody To Love') or political messages ('I Wish I knew How To Be Free') Solomon Burke was one of the first to find a way of bridging the gap between black religious music and commercial necessity. His instant success encouraged him to add love songs to his repertoire ('Cry to Me', 'If You Need Me' and especially 'Got to Get You Out of My Mind', 'Down in the Valley' and 'A Change is Gonna Come', which have ambiguous lyrics).

The Best of Solomon Burke (Atlantic, 1965) is a good buy.

> **Pun**
> While he was working as a radio disc-jockey, Burke called his program *The Solomon Temple*, a biblical reference that was ideally suited to his singing preacher image.

Ray Charles

1930–   black rock and soul singer and piano player

The 'Genius', in a league of his own

He is behind so many changes in contemporary music that it is still impossible to judge the extent of his influence.

Ray Charles has cut so many hits that it is no exaggeration to state that, after Presley, he is the best known American musician in the world. Moreover, he is still active today, and several generations of fans rub shoulders at his concerts which, despite the artist's occasionally perceptible fatigue (understandable, in view of his age), have lost none of their original magic.

Born in 1930 in Albany, Georgia, Ray Charles Robinson was brought up in a squalid black quarter. Due to unsanitary living conditions, he contracted glaucoma. Therefore, not only was he born poor and black in a rich and segregationist country, he was also blind. Sent to a school for the blind, he learnt music in a cruel, repressed atmosphere which he grippingly describes in his autobiography. After he left Saint Augustine, he toured the bars of Florida, Georgia, Mississippi, Louisiana and Texas, not only as a singer and piano player, but also as a clarinettist and sax-player. This extremely difficult period nevertheless allowed him to perfect a range of repertoires that were adapted to his various different audiences: for old black workers, he sang old blues numbers, for the younger, unemployed inhabitants of urban ghettos, he was the first to blast out black rock songs ('What'd I Say?'), and he attracted the attention of whites with his clever blend of big band jazz and gospel. He also recruited a sexy backing group, 'the Rayettes', and a talented guitarist, Mickey Baker, for his line-up.

For Ray Charles, the 1950s were a slow progression towards international fame, with such releases as 'I Got A Woman',

'Hallelujah I Love Her' and 'Lonely Avenue'. In the following decade, he had reached his goal: he had series of hits, often with songs written by both black and white artists (the Beatles' 'Eleanor Rigby' and 'Yesterday'). He continued to flirt with rock music ('Hit the Road Jack', 'Rock House' and 'It Should Have Been Me') but held on to his highly personal R & B-influenced style. His distinctive, heart-rending, soul-baring voice (the expression 'soul music' was invented for his music) can also become honied for love songs like 'Georgia on My Mind' and 'I Can't Stop Lovin' You'.

Ray Charles, whose career continued to influence the Sixties' generation of rock musicians, launched the R & B and soul movements. The debt owed by the whole of the rock world to the 'Genius' is enormous.

20 Hits of the Genius (Commander) is one of the best CD Ray Charles anthologies.

Definition
'Soul music', he says, 'is when you take a song and you make it a part of yourself, a part that is so real and so true that people think it's really happened to you. I'm not satisfied until I've made them feel what I feel.'

Cruel
Ray Charles tells of how, at the start of his career, he played in a white bar whose owner delighted in paying him in tins and bottles, which he hid in various rooms, forcing Ray to grope around for them to the jeers and insults of the white audience, who were only too ready to have a laugh at a black person's expense.

Ray Charles

Johnny Clegg and Savuka
South African multi-racial Zulu-rock band

Bush and black township-produced rock against apartheid

A colourful blend of race and musical traditions, the Clegg-Savuka partnership has produced a string of original hits.

At the age of 13, white South African Clegg was already playing with Zulu musicians, learning their language and traditional dances. Little by little, he grafted the lyrics and feeling of American socio-political protest song onto African-style vocal work and drum beats. Then, with Savuka, he took advantage of the precedent set by Paul Simon's international hit *Graceland* and recorded with South African musicians.

Invited to France by the singer Renaud, the Clegg-Savuka group entered the charts with two astonishingly well-crafted albums in 1988. The untamed beauty of their lyrics and score arrangements, backed by creative and innovative musicians, surprised the whole of the Western world.

Third World Child (EMI, 1987) and **Shadow Man** (1988) are the true sound of Africa today.

Absurd
Johnny Clegg has given numerous anti-apartheid concerts in his native South Africa. Because of his nationality, he was banned from playing at the 1988 'Free Nelson Mandela' concert at Wembley.

Jimmy Cliff
1948– Jamaican reggae singer

Long before Bob Marley . . .

A pioneer of ska and reggae, Cliff is still active today and has never strayed from his musical roots.

From 1963 to 1964, he was part of the 'ska' music movement, which was later to be called 'reggae music': 'Miss Jamaica' was his first real hit and allowed him to move to Britain. However, he was disappointed by the fashion for soul, a form he found incompatible with his own tastes. Back in Jamaica, he continued with his initial style, releasing an album that was to become a yardstick for all the later reggae artists and which made an impact on Bob Marley and Toots: 'Many Rivers to Cross', 'Vietnam' and 'Wonderful World, Beautiful People', with their catchy, mellow rhythms and

topical, socially aware lyrics laid down the ground rules fo the reggae genre. Lasting, international fame came with the film *The Harder They Come*.

Somewhat eclipsed by the meteoric rise of Bob Marley in the 1970s, he has been reinstated since the death of the latter as the leader of the reggae movement.

Jimmy Cliff (Trojan, 1969), **The Power and the Glory** (CBS) and **Reggae Greats** (Island-Mango, 1986) are his best albums.

Revolutionary
Give the People What They Want (WEA, 1981) and *The Harder They Come* (Phonogram, 1973) contain Jimmy Cliff's most topical songs.

Sam Cooke

1935–64 Soul Singer

Sweet soul singer

The first pop star to emerge from the gospel scene, his 1957 hit 'You Send Me' launched the soul era.

Born in Mississippi and raised in Chicago, Cook (the 'e' was added to his name later) started singing gospel with his siblings at the age of nine as part of the Singing Children. After a spell with the Highway QCs in 1950 he joined the Soul Stirrers, one of the most established but also one of the most innovative gospel quartets of the time. With his smooth tenor voice and his good looks he quickly attracted a young female following for the group, and began to consider a secular pop career.

Because Speciality label boss Art Rupe was afraid of endangering the sales of Soul Stirrers records, and of invoking the wrath of gospel fans, Sam's first hit, 'Lovable' (1956) was released under the name Dale Cook. The following year he switched to the Keen record label for the release of 'You Send Me' (1957), which was to become one of the most successful records of the 1950s.

Jeans
Although he was not known for wearing denim, Sam Cooke's 'Wonderful World' (originally released in 1960) was used as the soundtrack to a British television advertisement for blue jeans in 1985. Reissued to coincide with the campaign, the single charted higher than it had the first time round.

Signed to RCA Records in 1960, many of Cooke's subsequent recordings were of trivial easy listening numbers chosen by the record company. His natural talent and gospel training still shone through, however, and many great records were made.

While many gospel singers of the time faced a deep personal conflict over the pursuit of pop success, Cooke had no such problem, recognizing as he did the common roots of gospel, R & B and soul music. Throughout his brief recording career he continued to attend gospel shows and although he flirted with many different musical styles, including such passing fads as the 'twist' ('Twistin' The Night Away'), he also made strong personal statements – most notably with 'A Change Is Gonna Come'. Cooke's final hit (which reached the Top Ten after his death), it is a song laden with religious and political meaning, inextricably linked to the emerging civil rights movement.

In December 1964, Cooke was shot to death by a woman managing a Los Angeles motel. In just eight years he had had 30 Top Ten singles in America, proving enormously popular with both black and white audiences: his music was to be an important influence on virtually every black artist to emerge in the 1960s: and yet he died before he could reap the benefits of the soul explosion which took place in 1965 and 1966.

Feel It! Live At The Harlem Square Club, (RCA) released in 1985, features material recorded live in a Miami Club in 1983.

Sam Cooke – The Man and His Music (RCA) is a digitally remastered double album which includes who tracks recorded with the Soul Stirrers.

Manu Dibango
c. 1933–   Afro-rock sax-player from the Cameroon

'Big Brother'

Seen as a pioneer by African rock musicians since the 1960s, his professionalism and exemplary career have inspired many others.

At the start of the 1960s, the newly independent African countries had absolutely no technical equipment whatever. This problem was even worse in black Africa which, torn apart be endless coups d'état and exhausted by poverty and civil wars, seemed unlikely to produce an autonomous music form. In 1963, there was not one properly equipped recording studio in the whole of West Africa. Manu Dibango spent many years trying to convince fellow-musicians and government officials of the gravity of the situation, then emigrated to France and then the United States. Back in the Cameroon, his native country, in 1975, he gave the whole of Africa the benefit of his experience. He is still working today, especially in France, where he is regarded as one of the foremost pioneers of Afro-rock.

Soul Makossa (Musidisc) and **Home Made** (Sonodisc) are both typical of his style.

Manu Dibango (Decca, 1979, CD, Afrovision 1984) is an excellent introduction to the master's work.

> **Experience**
> Until 1969, Manu Dibango worked with Dick Rivers, Eddie Mitchell and Nino Ferrer, both on tour and in the studio. At the same time, he played jazz-rock in Paris's piano-bars.

Earth, Wind and Fire
Jazz funk band

An original combination

Their blend of sophisticated jazz harmonies and dynamic funk rhythms made them one of the most popular bands in the 1970s.

Since the band first appeared in 1969, the sales figures clocked up by Earth, Wind and Fire have always been considerable, because their brand of music, later called jazz-funk, is catchy and easy to listen to; it appeals to a wide variety of audiences, from rock-lovers to nightclubbers, and from Harlem dwellers to tourists in the lounges of luxury, international hotels.

With its basic line-up of the three White brothers and such best-selling albums as *That's the Way of the World* (1975), *Gratitude* (1975), *All'n'All* (1977), *Raise* (1981) and *Powerlight* (1982), Earth, Wind and Fire prepared the way for the phenomenal success of Prince and Michael Jackson.

Best of EWF (Columbia, 1978) draws together their greatest hits.

> **Platinum**
> Some EWF hits sold over three million copies within three months of their release ('Shining Star', 'Serpentine Fire', 'Fantasy', 'Boogie Wonderland', 'Let's Groove' and 'Fall in Love With Me').

'King' Fela Anipulapo Kuti

1938– Nigerian Afro-rock singer and sax-player

Legendary leader of African rock

One of the most politically outspoken performers in Africa, Fela was also perhaps the first to face the difficulties associated with the creation of a truly African music form.

He began his career as a sax-player in an avant-garde jazz or 'juju' band (juju is a typically Nigerian jazz form). His political views made him something of a national hero, but he preferred to move to London, where he came into contact with and absorbed other musical influences. As a result, he grafted soul and ska orchestrations onto his Charlie Parker and Dizzy Gillespie-influenced jazz. A multi-talented musician and domineering, unpredictable character, Fela went home to Nigeria with the firm intention of denouncing the country's corrupt military régime. For many years, he was to write extremely critical lyrics. Recognized as one of the foremost stars of African rock in the early 1980s, he used his prestige as a musician to

further his political aims, which resulted in a a five-year prison sentence from which he was paroled after 18 months.

An elusive personality, Fela holds both nationalist and radical political views, and is a Muslim, but believes in the ancient gods of Africa.

An undeniable musical talent, the accomplished fusion of Western professionalism, absolute commitment to the Third World cause, and a blend of musical styles as fundamentally different as free jazz and African folks songs make Fela one of the foremost rock musicians in Africa today.

Fela Anipulapo Kuti (Barclay) and **Black Man's Cry** are typical of his forceful, up-tempo style.

Support

Fela was released from prison in 1986 after a worldwide protest campaign. He was serving a long sentence which could have resulted in his disappearance from the music scene. On his release, he immediately moved back into the African and European touring circuits and continued making incendiary remarks about the political situation in Nigeria.

'King' Fela Anipulapo Kuti

Aretha Franklin

1942–   R & B singer

'Lady Soul'

Possessing an incredible voice and sense of rhythm, she was easily the best black female soul singer to emerge from the late Sixties and early Seventies.

The gospel school

Aretha's father being one of the most famous Baptist preachers in the United States, she grew up surrounded by the best religious singers in the country: Mahalia Jackson and Clara Ward were her first teachers! However, it was the influence of Sam Cooke which encouraged her to use her voice for the more secular tones of R & B.

The Atlantic 'sound'

Aretha was signed to the Atlantic studio in 1966 and gradually emerged as the company's main female soul vocalist beside the big male stars such as Otis Redding, of whose 'Respect' she released a brilliant version. Her reprises of Sam Cooke's 'A Change Is Gonna Come' and 'Think' were her way as a musician of expressing her solidarity with the black civil rights movement. She appeared at religious and political rallies with Martin Luther

> **Cinema**
> Like many other black music legends, she appeared in John Landis's film *The Blues Brothers*. She played the role of a fast-food restaurant owner, and sang an extraordinarily dynamic and wry version of 'Think'.

King and, with her high quality live performances and charismatic, soulful voice, also gained a white following.

Freed from the influence of her gospel (Mahalia Jackson), soul (Ray Charles, Sam Cooke and Solomon Burke) and R & B mentors (Otis Redding and Sam and Dave), Aretha entered the most brilliant phase of her career, a period which lasted from 1967 to 1975 and is especially remarkable for her concert duet with Ray Charles in 1972 and her work with Stevie Wonder in 1973. However, soul was gradually losing ground to the rapidly expanding funk fashion and Aretha suddenly fell out of favour with black audiences. The 1985 album *Who's Zoomin' Who* included her first Top Ten singles for 13 years, and she has never surpassed the successes of her early career.

Aretha's Greatest Hits (Atlantic, 1971) is an excellent compilation, an absolute must.

Aretha Franklin

Marvin Gaye
1939–84   Soul music singer

Unrecognized forerunner

Adored by black Sixties' and Seventies' music fans, he has influenced all contemporary funk musicians.

The son of a minister, Marvin was introduced to gospel singing at the age of four, but he began his music career as a session drummer for Bo Diddley and Smokey Robinson and the Miracles. Formed in 1957, his band, the Marquees, was spotted by label-owner Berry Gordy. A few major hits made Marvin Gaye one of Detroit-based Tamla Motown's foremost artists. Between 1962 ('Can I Get A Witness' which was later covered by the Rolling Stones) and 1968 ('I Heard It Through the Grapevine', which was an international number one and was later added to Creedence Clearwater Revival's repertoire), he became popular with both rock and soul audiences, then with the 1971 single 'What's Goin' On?' (from the album of the same name), boosted flagging R & B sales. Released in 1982, *Sexual Healing* brought him a new generation of fans.

What's Goin' On? (Motown, 1971), **Let's Get It On** (Motown, 1973) and **Fifteen Greatest Hits** (Motown) are soul music monuments.

> **Quarrel**
> Marvin Gaye was killed by his own father, after an argument over a woman which has never been fully clarified.

Herbie Hancock
1940–   Jazz, jazz rock and electro-jazz singer and keyboards player

An experimental musician on the lookout for new styles

He was instrumental in defining several rock sub-genres.

Longstanding piano player with the Miles Davis line-up, and considered as a jazz dropout, during the 1960s he also played with such diverse artists as Ron Carter ('Jazz Rock') and Stan Getz, then began to experiment with emerging electronic techniques influenced by the new sounds being produced by the art and progressive rock groups. Hancock's sound went on to serve as an example to later funk bands, while he personally underwent another change in direction at the end of the 1970s, producing a series of critically acclaimed piano duets with Chick Corea.

One of the leading exponents of voice synthesizers, he influenced rap and had a number of hits including 'Lite Me Up' and especially 'Rock It' (1983) and 'Gimme the Night' (1980) with George Benson.

Maiden Voyage (Blue Note, 1964) was released during his jazz rock period.

Head Hunters (CBS, 1974) has a more electronic sound.

Sound System (CBS, 1983) is resolutely modern.

> **Reggae**
> Leaving no doubt as to his musical versatility, on *Secrets*, released in 1976, Hancock plays a mixture of jazz, blues and swing, and even includes a reggae version of his 1965 track 'Cantaloup Island'.

The Isley Brothers
Soul music band

Exceptionally long career

Launched by their hit 'Twist and Shout', their original popularity has never diminished. The Isley Brothers are still playing and recording together today.

After their gospel and doo-wop influenced early recordings, the three Isley Brothers embarked on a soul music career. By the end of the 1950s, their energy and the sheer quality of their vocal work had singled them out as the top R & B band in the country. 'Shout' (1959), then 'Twist and Shout' (1962), which was later immortalized by the Beatles, 'This Old Heart of Mine' (1965) and 'I Guess I Love You' all became R & B classics. Their close,

polished vocal harmony work influenced British pop singers.

They continued recording and performing live throughout the 1970s. Today, with a career that spans three decades, they are the oldest active soul band on the music scene.

Super Hits (Tamla Motown) is a compilation which gives a good idea of the quality of their work.

Little known
For dance music fans, we recommend the following three compilations: *Super Hits (1962–1968)*, *Timeless (1969–1972)* and *Forever Gold (1972–1977)*. Although it has a definite funk flavour, *Between the Sheets* (1983) is nevertheless representative of their style.

Michael Jackson
1958–   Soul, then electro-funk singer

The Peter Pan of show-business

Whatever the future may hold in store for him, Jackson was perhaps the biggest phenomenon to hit the contemporary music scene, equalling, and even surpassing, sales records attained by such greats as the Beatles, Presley and Ray Charles.

Child prodigy

Discovered by Berry Gordy and Smokey Robinson, the five Jackson brothers began their career in 1969, when Michael was 11.

The Jackson Five's father, failed musician but shrewd business manager Joe Jackson, gave up his job as a crane driver in Gary, Indiana, where he lived with his wife and seven children in the town's black quarter. As an amateur musician himself, he was quick to realize that his children, especially Michael, the youngest, had a possible (and lucrative) future in the music business. Father or not, he was to ruthlessly exploit Michael's extreme youth and mischievous personality. The Tamla Motown pundits, led by Berry Gordy, soon realized that they were on to a good thing, and encouraged the group to sing the soul music that was fashionable at the time.

In 1971, Michael, the child prodigy of soul music, began his solo career but continued to sing with the Jackson Five as the band's star attraction and money-spinner. By 1976, Motown had already sold 60 million Jackson Five albums. Joe Jackson decided not to renew his childrens' contract with Berry Gordy. He also launched Michael's movie career. Although *The Wiz* was a box-office failure, during filming Michael met the legendary composer-producer Quincy Jones, who was to direct much of his subsequent musical career. The union between teenage prodigy and brilliant musician resulted in the birth in 1980 of the Michael Jackson phenomenon.

Records

Off the Wall is the first product of the Jackson-Jones collaboration. The album was a clever blend of black funk and rock orchestrations and, at a time when the disco movement was gradually losing momentum and the charts were dominated by hard rock, sold over eight million copies within months of its release.

Two years later, after months of top secret recording sessions, *Thriller* took the music scene by storm. A trend-setting album, it provided Jackson with a whole series of singles which all became international hits: the music videos made for 'Billie Jean', 'Beat It' and 'Thriller' each had a Hollywood-scale budget and boosted album sales into the millions: one by one, the sales records held by Presley, Dylan, the Beatles and Fleetwood Mac were broken.

By this time, Michael Jackson had become so rich and powerful that he was able to outbid Paul McCartney when the rights to the Beatles' songs were put up for auction.

At the same time, Jackson's personality, which had always been highly individual (excessive pride, reclusive behaviour and a childish, obsessive love of Disney's cartoon characters) gradually underwent a profound change. Cosmetic surgery slowly changed his negroid features, he used

Michael Jackson

creams to lighten his skin, slept in an oxygen tent intended to delay the aging process, kept a flourishing menagerie (snakes, monkeys, etc) and abstained from any kind of sexual relationship, which did

Big sister
It was Motown star Diana Ross who managed to get the Jackson Five an audition. They were immediately given a contact.

Charity
Michael Jackson has taken part in several charity concerts, including Live Aid. He also co-wrote 'We Are the World' with Lionel Richie. Moreover, he has already contributed over a million dollars to an organization which takes care of black American underprivileged children.

Diana Ross?
The *Bad* album contains a track entitled 'Dirty Diana'. Could the bitter argument that caused a rift between Diana Ross and her discovery, Michael Jackson, also be at the root of this song, or was it just mere coincidence?

not prevent him from asking Elizabeth Taylor to marry him. Romantically linked with Brooke Shields (another child-star, but of the silver screen) he claims to be a virgin, despite having celebrated his 30th birthday in 1988.

In many respects, Michael Jackson is the victim of a serious identity crisis: he refuses to accept the colour of his skin, hence his attempts to lighten and change his features which distance him from the 'I'm Black and I'm Proud' attitude so dear to such artists as James Brown. He also refuses to accept his age and never wants to grow up. This syndrome has been further exacerbated by the fact that he has dropped from the number one spot: his album, *Bad*, was not nearly as successful as *Thriller*, and his world tour was overshadowed by a number of cancelled concerts due to low ticket sales. Michael

---

Copy

It is possible that Berry Gordy thought he could pull off another Stevie Wonder-style publicity scoop with Michael Jackson (before he became the adult star we know today, Wonder was known as 'Little Stevie Wonder'). Jackson has the advantage of superior mobility and, of course, his highly marketable strange behaviour.

The tour of the century

1.5 million fans at 49 concerts watched Jackson perform on a 28 metre-deep, 63 metre-wide stage flanked by four massive video screens with a further screen mounted above the stage for the benefit of those who were too far from the stage to see their idol properly.

Jackson's mental stability is obviously shaky. Victim of the star system, which at one time he thought he could control, record holder and multi-talented musician, sooner or later he is going to have to come to terms with the living legend he helped create.

The Jackson style

One thing is sure: Michael Jackson is a true musician: he composes, writes, arranges and performs. Evidence shows that, while he refined Michael Jackson's output, Quincy Jones in no way 'created' him. Like his mentor, show-business's Peter Pan is a perfectionist: not content with merely creating the new electro-funk genre, the album was also the first to be sold as an audio-visual package, completely overturning the accepted rules of the nascent music video industry. Often imitated, the short film *Thriller* has never been matched.

Michael Jackson's particular brand of music, a style he was the first to develop, is a blend of jazz and funk sophistication with the dynamic energy and verve of rock and American pop song. Original lyrics, which draw heavily on the black idiom but are also peppered with literary images, complete the picture.

Apart from his talents as a musician Jackson is also a dancer without equal: he has completely mastered the finer points of 'breakdancing', an extremely complex and taxing dance which emerged in the black areas of America's major cities. Every Jackson concert highlights the all-round talents of a performer to whom fame came too quickly . . .

Both **Thriller** (Epic, 1982) and **Bad** (CBS, 1987) are absolute musts.

The Best of Michael Jackson (Motown, 1975) covers his Jackson Five days.

Al Jarreau

c.1944–   Soul jazz singer

Music that is a cross between the two Americas

Internationally acclaimed today for his golden voice, he brought about a brilliant synthesis between two contradictory influences.

First and foremost a black musician, in the first years of his career, Jarreau confined himself to producing a kind of music that was too specific to have a wide appeal: attracted to bossa nova and clever jazz harmonies, he also touched on R & B melodies and arrangements, and even black rock.

It was not until later on in his career that he was recognized as one of the outstanding jazz-influenced singers on the

contemporary music scene, with his backing group of guitarists and keyboards players from totally different musical backgrounds (rock, jazz, funk and electronic, synthesized music).

Al Jarreau's concerts appeal to a wide variety of people and are musically extremely eclectic.

Jarreau (WEA, 1983) and **In London** (Warner, 1977), recorded live, are excellent.

Success
Usually a phenomenon more associated with the big rock stars, tickets for Al Jarreau's recent Paris concert sold out in a matter of days.

Mory Kanté

c. 1940–   Afro-rock singer and multi-talented musician

The first African rock musician to be recognized in Europe

Without making too many important concessions to white music, he popularized Mandingo country rock.

With his noble background and witch-doctor-artist father, Mory Kanté was first West Africa's foremost guitarist, then played the *balafon* for Salif Keita's band. During the 1960s, he specialized in traditional African stringed instruments, which he amplified to produce new sounds for rock. After a brief stay in the United States, he returned to Africa, signed to Barclay and moved to Paris. His Bercy show in 1985 with French singer and

guitarist Higelin was strikingly innovative (a colourful mixture of blonde backing singers, African dress, acoustic percussion section and synthesizers). With the release of *Yéké Yéké* in 1988, Mory Kanté entered the European charts.

Yéké Yéké (Barclay, 1988) is typical of contemporary Afro-rock.

Folk?
Mory Kanté plays three traditional instruments: the *balafon*, a kind of xylophone equipped with a sound box, held horizontally; the *kora*, a crude sort of guitar, and the *bolon* which is a *kora* with three bass strings.

Kassav'

French West Indian *zouk* band

Catchy creole calpyso rock

Kassav's fame has now spread to the United States.

Kassav' added synthesizers and other modern techniques to their basic calypso style, to create a sensual and catchy kind of music that gained a huge following first in their native West Indian islands, then in Africa and finally in North America. A well-balanced line up (Georges and Pierre-Édouard Decimus on bass and drums, Jacob Desvarieux on guitar and vocals and Jocelyne Bérouard on vocals), their

music is a smash hit in nightclubs, the charts and in concert.

Kassav' au Zénith (Sonodisc, 1986), **Love and Ka Dance** (Celluloid) and **Passport** (Polydor) are their best albums to date.

Both **The Compact Story of Kassav'** and **Best of Kassav'** (Carrère, 1989) are good CD compilations.

Zouk

A creole term (all of Kassav's tracks are sung in Creole), it describes a fast-moving dance in celebration of love and joy.

Salif Keita

1949–   Ivory Coast-born afro-rock singer

One of the creators of a genre

His aim was to synthesize traditional Peule, Bambara *and* Malinké *rhythms with Cuban and West Indian melodies.*

Struck by a serious handicap that made him the object of superstitious fear (he was albino) and put an end to a brilliant scholastic career, Salif Keita formed the Rail Band in 1970. Son of an ancient noble Mandingo family, he went on to earn his living by entertaining tourists in Abidjan's big hotels.

His numerous tours of the West African capitals brought him into close contact with Guinean dictator Sékou Touré, who was paradoxically one of the biggest supporters of true African music forms.

He became famous in 1978 with his song 'Mandjou'. After a spell in the United States, where he experienced genuinely professional recording techniques for the first time, he released 'Primpin' in 1981. Based in Paris since 1984, he is one of the foremost afro-rock musicians on the rock scene, and is internationally respected.

Ko-Yan (Island, 1989) gives a good idea of Salif Keita's style.

Drugs

The green and pink 'Séku pills', made fashionable by the dictator himself, were amphetamines which were sold in the capital's market. They were consumed legally by the population en masse!

Kid Creole and the Coconuts
American calypso-rock band

A blend of the Bronx and the West Indies

The Kid Creole line up, complete with white backing vocalists and a big band sound was particularly famous in the Eighties.

Kid Creole began his career in the 1960s, inevitably singing the soul music which was all the rage at the time, then virtually disappeared in the 1970s. It was not until 1980 that he reached a wider audience, mainly because of the original nature of the line up with its multi-racial, sexy image. Kid Creole constantly plays on his spicy reputation, adding a liberal sprinkling of double entendres to his lyrics. The single

'I'm a Wonderful Thing' taken from *Fresh Fruit in Foreign Places* (Sire, 1982) was a hit. The subsequent relese of *Tropical Gangsters* and a series of very successful tours in Britain and France spread the popularity of Caribbean rock USA-style.

Tropical Gangster (Sire, 1983) is a good buy.

Sexy
Much of Kid Creole's live success must be attributed to the Coconuts, his backing vocalists and dance troupe (largely inspired by Roxy Music album sleeves). Prince was also to make use of this sort of eye-catching gimmick.

Kool and the Gang
Pop funk band

Major influence on Michael Jackson and Prince

Robert 'Kool' Bell and his 'Gang' explored a new kind of black music.

Formed in 1969 by Robert Bell, the band were initially popular with American audiences who appreciated their brand of early funk ('Funky Stuff', 'Hollywood Swinging') mixed with a traditional black influence ('Jungle Boogie'). By the end of the 1970s, the Gang had moved into disco funk which prefigured the rap movement ('Oooh La La La, Let's Go Dancing'). In 1980, the international hit 'Celebration' propelled Kool and the Gang to the

forefront of the pop scene. Kool's skilfully crafted music, ideally suited for the dance floor, uses all the electronic means provided by modern technology. Deliberately aimed at the nightclubbing market, the Kool style has influenced the whole black music current, and is an amalgam of high technology, electronic rhythms and polished arrangments.

Twice as Kool (Polydor) and **Kool and the Gang Spin Their Top Hits** (De-lite, 1978) are excellent compilations.

Cinema
Sylvester Stallone used 'Summer Madness' as part of the soundtrack for *Rocky*.

216

Bob Marley

1945–81   Jamaican reggae singer and guitarist

Third World idol

He brought the plight of the Jamaican underprivileged to the attention of the whole world, and was the only reggae performer to become a superstar.

Crossover and synthesis

Son of a white British army captain and a black domestic servant, Bob Marley spent most of his life in the poverty-stricken slums of Kingston and Trenchtown. A law-abiding teenager despite difficult living conditions (he studied at a local metal-working school), it was at this stage in his life that Marley came into contact with the three major influences that were to shape the whole of his future career. From the impressive American 'Black Power' theories promoted by the Black Panthers, Marley drew his radical political views. Intrigued by Jamaican prophet Marcus Garvey's

Rasta religion, he eventually converted to the faith shared by so many of his fellow Jamaicans, becoming a vegetarian, growing 'dreadlocks' (the rope-like, solid strands of hair still popular in the Caribbean today, which symbolize a natural way of life) and using 'ganja' (a sort of Jamaican hashish which is believed to be an aid to enlightenment by Jah Rastafari, the god of the poor). The third major influence on the young Bob Marley was, of course, music. Like himself, the music he preferred was a mixture of white and black: he was equally fond of Fats Domino's black rock, Nat King Cole's 'whitened' jazz with its tropical rhythms, Presley and Ricky Nelson's rock and the black rock produced by unrecognized artists such as LaVern Baker and Larry Williams. He was also exposed to complicated jazz rhythms and melodies and, of course, the ever popular, powerful 'Memphis sound' of early soul music. He found the latter, with its use of horns to back up the rhythm section, and the emotive, gospel-style vocals particularly impressive. The final ingredient for this explosive musical cocktail was ska, reggae's ancestor, led by the great Jimmy Cliff.

Prophet, leader and musician

Thus, in his early twenties, Bob Marley was to base the philosophical raison d'être of his future art and public career on three elements: politics, religion and music.

The Wailers' (Bob Marley, Peter Tosh and Bunny Wailer had finally decided on this name after trying out a series of others) first track reflected this aspect of their music: 'Soul Rebel', their first truly original composition, not only showed that they were different from other bands in terms of sound, but it also brought them a certain amount of local fame. However, their earlier recordings were even more topical ('Rude Boy', 'Rule Them Rudie' and 'Rude Boy Get Bail' among others). Often naive, these early lyrics reflected the Wailers' childhood spent in Jamaican slums and their days as unemployed teenagers,

---

Reggae is not dead

Encouraged to keep the reggae flag flying by Rita Marley, Bob's widow, Ziggy Marley (and his band the Melody Makers) has continued his father's work; he has a clear voice, creates interesting arrangements and lyrics that reflect his father's thinking. Bob would not have been ashamed of Ziggy's *Bright Day*. Burning Spear (*Marcus Garvey*, Island), Steel Pulse (*Handsworth Revolution*, Island), Third World (*Prisoner in the Street*, Phonogram, UB40 (*The Singles Album*, AZ), Gregory Isaacs (*Cool Ruler*, Virgin) and Linton Kwesi Johnson (*Forces of Victory*, Phonogram) are all flourishing reggae bands or artists. Whether they take a reggae hard line, or are open to more commercial arrangements, in their own way all of these artists continue to relay the message of Jamaican rock.

---

continually in trouble for petty larceny and other, mainly inoffensive, illegal exploits. Having exhausted this vein, Marley went on to write more radical poetry, using simple Jamaican street language ('Catch a Fire' and 'Get Up, Stand Up' in 1973, and 'I Shot the Sheriff'). The theme of their most popular album, *Burning*, is the fire associated with revolution. *Uprising* later became the battle cry of rioters in Kingston, Brixton and Soweto in Jamaica, London and South Africa respectively. Marley's political views were tempered and moderated by his Rasta faith which, until his death, encouraged him to advocate peace and understanding between men, despite his incendiary, biblical-style remarks on the 'new Babylon', which took food from the mouths of the poor the world over.

Marley's music, which, at least at first, was conceived as the vehicle for his pro-African, Rasta message, audibly evolved and became more important in his eyes with the passing of the years. A simple ska band at the end of the 1960s, the Wailers gradually shrugged off the influence of Jimmy Cliff, afro-Cuban music and soul, and began to produce more autonomous reggae using electric and then electronic instruments alongside the traditional afro-Caribbean percussion section. The trademark of Marley's reggae soon became the jumpy off-beat strummed guitar chords. Always clearly audible, the bass plays an important role in defining the rhythm, while Marley's high-pitched vocals blend with unobtrusive electric guitar solos. Many later Jamaican (Toots and the Maytals), African (Alpha Blondy), multi-racial (UB40) and white (the Police) bands modelled themselves on the Marley sound.

Troubled life

Bob Marley's career indicates just how difficult it is for Third World artists to reach an international audience: it takes guts, perseverance, integrity, an original style and lots of luck to scale the ladder of fame.

For the original Wailers line-up, the most immediate and pressing problem was a technical one: in view of the lack of recording facilities, the only way for them to reach a sizeable audience was through the 'sound systems', a kind of crude, mobile discos which travelled through the poor areas on Saturday nights. Bob Marley and his Wailers were initially a vocal group with

an ill-defined style. Their first truly professional recording, 'Simmer Down', brought them fans from among the ghettos' youth. However, local celebrity was virtually all this record earned them, for the Wailers were paid a fixed fee, profits from the single's sales being pocketed by producer Coxsone Dodd. For obvious economic reasons, despite their popular success, the band were forced to split up.

Marley then moved to America, where he worked as a solderer until he received his draft papers for Vietnam. He returned to Jamaica, re-formed the Wailers and began touring in Britain after the release of the successful album *Catch a Fire* in 1973. By this time, the band had been together for five years without receiving a penny in royalties. The frustration of these artists, who heard their songs on the radio and knew that countless copies were being sold, is easy to imagine!

It was not until 1971 and their meeting with Chris Blackwell, a more honest and commercially au fait producer, that international fame came within their grasp. Helped by Eric Clapton, who recorded an extremely popular version of the Wailers' 'I Shot the Sheriff', Bob and the Wailers cut the unforgettable *Burning*, then *Babylon By Bus* and *Exodus*. 'No Woman, No Cry', 'Could You Be Loved' and 'Get Up, Stand Up' became all-time rock classics, influencing all songwriters, black and white, from Europe to the United States.

Faithful

Throughout almost his whole career, Bob Marley kept the same old Gibson Les Paul Junior guitar, for which, in his early days as a musician, he had saved up for months. More recent guitars did not interest him, with the exception of the American-made acoustic Ovation.

Lyrics

'Get up, stand up,
Stand up for your rights,
Get up, stand up,
Don't give up the fight'.
From one of the most famous songs produced by the Marley-Tosh partnership, this chorus indicates that reggae is Jamaican protest song.

Bob Marley

At the same time, Marley was increasingly involved in Jamaican political issues, even bringing about a reconciliation between two opposing political leaders. However, despite his neutral stance, he and his wife were shot and seriously wounded. Once he had recovered, he left Jamaica and went on a series of glorious world tours.

In 1980, it was revealed that he was being treated for lung cancer in Switzerland. Despite his desire to live and his courage in the face of adversity, the 'poor man's pope' died at his mother's house in Miami in 1981. His death plunged the whole of the Jamaican nation into mourning.

Legend (Island, 1984) is a good compilation, but Marley's best albums, all classics of the reggae genre, are musts: **Catch a Fire** (Island, 1972), **Burning** (Island, 1973), **Live** (Island, 1975), **Babylon By Bus** (Island, 1978) and **Uprising** (Island, 1980).

Exodus

The Rasta religion prophesizes the return of the tribes of Israel and the people of Jah to their homeland. Marley, like all the Rastafarian faithful, believed in this return of the black people to Africa, particularly to Ethiopia. Hailie Selassie was considered by Rastafarians to be Jah's representative on earth, and as such, immortal. The death of the Emperor, followed by that of Marley, threw Rasta believers into confusion: would the 'Exodus' ever happen?

The Platters

Doo-wop group

The most successful vocal harmony group of the 1950s

'Only You' was an international hit whose gospel-style choral work influenced rock music as a whole.

The onomatopoeic expression 'doo-wop' describes the baritone backing vocals used by vocal harmony groups at the start of the 1950s. It gave its name to an extremely commercial genre which, on the fringe of nascent white rock, popularized exceptionally high quality choral work.

At the same time as the R & B orientated line-ups, the Cadillacs and Frankie Lymon and the Teenagers, the more commercial Platters had their first hits in 1953, shortly after their meeting with prolific songwriter Buck Ram, who was to provide them with all their hits between 1955 and 1962. The recruitment of singer Zola Taylor, and the release of new songs ideally suited to the dance floor ('Only You', 'The Great Pretender', 'The Magic Touch', 'Twilight Time' and 'Smoke Gets In Your Eyes') put the Platters firmly at the head of a movement that was to influence many American (including the Beach Boys) and

British (the Beatles) vocal harmony groups.

Cover versions of white folk numbers (Merle Travis's 'Sixteen Tons') highlighted Herb Reed's extraordinary bass voice, while the combined talents of lead singer Tony Williams and female vocalist Zola Taylor largely contributed to the group's success.

Until the arrival of American surf and English pop on the music scene, the Platters cornered the market on slow numbers designed for nightclubs and dances. Constant changes in the line-up (both Tony Williams and Zola Taylor left) sped up the decline in the multi-millionaire band's popularity.

The best of the many Platters album and CD compilations are perhaps **Their Greatest Hits** and **Sixteen Greatest Hits** (Mercury).

Conquest

Almost all the Platters' big hits went platinum in the space of a year. At a time when record sales were perceptibly lower than they are today, this indicates that the group had also gained a white audience.

Vocal groups

During the 1950s, artists who had learnt the finer points of vocal harmony in church used their hard-earned skills to popularize the polished harmonies of gospel. The black vocal groups, which emerged from Tamla Motown with amazing regularity, developed a style which was exploited by American soul and British pop in the following decade.

The most famous black vocal harmony groups were the Supremes (with Diana Ross), Martha and the Vandellas, the Marvelettes, the Miracles (with Smokey Robinson), the Coasters, the Drifters (with Ben E King), the Isley Brothers, the Ink Spots, the Four Tops and the Temptations.

Prince

1958– Electro-funk singer and multi-talented musician

Provocative and elusive genius

At one point he presented himself as Michael Jackson's alter ego, but his contribution to funk goes far beyond a simple (albeit outrageous) image. Prince is a real creative spirit.

The Minneapolis kid

Son of a jazz band leader, and a professional musician from his early teens, Prince Roger Nelson can play 12 different instruments (he played all the instrumental parts for his first record *For You*) and behaves like a veritable tyrant, giving his all on stage and in the studio, and demanding that his musicians do the same.

A perfectionist and shrewd businessman, he is motivated by an unwavering flair for provocation on which at least part of his fame is based: small and slim (he is 5ft 1in tall), elegant and supple, his shows are either worked out down to the last detail or are totally improvised, the one constant being the backing bevy of beautiful women (Apollonia, then Vanity) and Sheila E, the drummer.

At the start of his career, he appeared on stage in a G-string, or performed strip-teases punctuated by suggestive gasps and pants. During his first concert in Paris, stripped virtually naked, he laid down on his guitar and simulated sexual intercourse. He has carried on this sexy image into even his most recent shows, inventing new erotic stage-acts, and adding further suggestive remarks and more explicit gestures. Initially dressed in black, then in mauve or purple, at the end of the 1970s, but especially at the start of the 1980s, Prince was seen as the dark side of funk, the light, acceptable side being represented by Michael Jackson. However, Prince's genuine talent soon emerged with 'Soft

and Wet' and 'I Wanna Be Your Lover', which laid down the basis for re-vamped, truly black funk.

Prince's electro-funk

Prince is quite definitely the inventor of this electronic dance music which has mingled R & B, jazz, disco and Sixties' and Seventies' funk. In 1983, his smash hit 'Little Red Corvette' launched his career and defined the sound of electro-funk: it was to be dry, catchy, fast and steamy. Electro-funk was Eighties' music.

The release of *1999* and then *Purple Rain* (both an album and a film) heralded a whole string of hits and sell-out tours. *Dirty Mind* was heaped with praise by the American liberal faction which was attempting to stand up to Reaganist puritanism. *Controversy* is quite frankly sensual. *Sign o' the Times* crowned him the leading songwriter in contemporary funk.

Prince's funk is stylistically raw and thematically seedy. In terms of the actual music, he removed all trace of his affiliation with Seventies' disco. He also broke with black commercial music traditions: he uses fewer horns, more synthesized sounds and prefers a forceful guitar sound. Prince's electro-funk has a much harder sound than that of Michael Jackson. Prince has no mentor, no Quincy Jones to help produce a polished, acceptable sound with wide public appeal. Prince only relies on Prince. He is absolute master of his career, and creates according to his own changing

Black Album
Nobody really knows for sure why Prince took it into his head to release a *Black Album* (like the Beatles' *White Album* 20 years earlier) on to the market. Distributors refused to stock it, as in their opinion, it would be impossible to sell. In a fit of anger, Prince had all the copies already pressed destroyed. The few dozen surviving albums immediately became much sought-after collections items.

tastes, releasing sexy ballads ('Purple Rain') or pulsating funk ('1999'). Whether laid-back or overtly sensual, Prince's funk is always original. With its jerky rhythms and reliance on electronic sound, it is instantly recognizable. Prince has also incorporated a whole range of guitar styles into his work: Hendrix-style solos blend with Tamla Motown and white rock rhythm patterns, and airy, Dire Straits-modelled fountains of notes contrast with bashed out hard rock and punk chords.

Prince, controversial songwriter, power-crazy maverick and professional par excellence, is the point at which 50 years of rock music meet.

To this, mention should be added of Prince's sexual image, which is as flashy as Hendrix or Marc Bolan's, as provocative as Jim Morrison's and as romantic as Baudelaire or Rimbaud's, poets he claims to know and admire. Prince's lyrics, through which runs a constant theme of sexual obsession, were an excellent antidote

to the puritanical mentality of the United States in the 1980s.

1999 (1982) and **Sign o' the Times** (1987) are his best albums, but a good idea of all his interesting excesses and developments can only be gained from the aptly named **Purple Rain** (1984), **Dirty Mind** (1980), **Controversy** (1981) and **LoveSexy** (1988).

Prince

> **Shrewd**
>
> An absolute one-off, Prince managed to get complete control of the production on his first record. He was therefore able to use his own instrumental talents, his songs and his arrangements without any interference from Warner. From one end to the other, the album is a one man show . . .

> **Censored**
>
> The sleeve for *LoveSexy* shows Prince totally nude in a position that is both erotic and pensive. *LoveSexy* was boycotted by most of the major record store chains.

Otis Redding

1941–67 R & B singer

James Brown's only real rival

He dominated the soul scene and won a white audience.

Otis Redding was born in the Deep South, at Dawson in Georgia. Son of a Baptist preacher, his early career developed along the same lines as most black singers: gospel at church on Sunday, where he learned the finer points of rhythm and his distinctive, emotive vocal style. Then, influenced by fellow Georgian Little Richard's rock'n'roll, he decided to become a professional musician.

It was really a stroke of luck that he recorded 'These Arms of Mine' during the recording session of another band (for whom he worked as chauffeur!) A slow number with histrionic lyrics, 'These Arms of Mine', was an instant hit. Otis Redding's career had begun.

The following year, 'Pain In My Heart' confirmed his reputation and was a transatlantic hit. In 1965, with the release of the famous 'Respect' he became an international star. 'I've Been Lovin' You Too Long' showed Otis Redding's extraordinary ability to express strong emotions in a sober, contained manner, while his cover versions of Sam Cooke's 'Shake' and the Rolling Stones' 'Satisfaction' took him closer to the rock world. With 'Try A Little Tenderness' he cut the most beautiful crescendo in the history of soul; on tour, he also proved himself to be an exceptionally talented showman. Shortly after his untimely death, 'Dock of the Bay' reached number one in the hit parades on both sides of the Atlantic.

The Otis Redding Story (Stax, 1968) is an excellent compilation.

The Dock of the Bay (CD Atlantic, 1987) contains this prolific recording artist's best 20 tracks.

> **Multi-racial**
> Otis Redding had the legendary Steve Cropper, a white musician with a penchant for R & B, as his guitarist in one of the first multi-racial line ups in the history of soul. Cropper also co-wrote the famous 'Dock of the Bay' with Redding.

Otis Redding

Diana Ross

1944– Soul Singer

The Sixties' Queen Of Pop

With female vocal group the Supremes she was responsible for the resurgence of black pop in the 1960s.

Raised in Detroit's Brewster-Douglass Housing projects, the Supremes began working together in the late 1950s as the Primettes, changing their name after signing to the Motown record label in 1961. Their early releases did not sell but in 1963 they were teamed with Motown's classic Holland-Dozier-Holland production and songwriting team, who immediately provided the group with their first Top 30 single, 'When the Lovelight Starts Shining Through His Eyes'. In July 1964 'Where Did Our Love Go' was the first in an incredible run of five American number one singles in a row.

Crossover

Carefully groomed by Motown founder Berry Gordy, the Supremes proved to be the label's most successful crossover act. It was while they were at their height (between late 1963 and early 1965) that Billboard suspended their R & B chart – for the first and only time – because black and white Americans were buying the same records.

Although founding member Florence Ballard had often served as the lead singer in the Supremes' early days, by 1965 Ross was firmly established as the group's leader. After Ballard left in 1967 they were billed as Diana Ross and the Supremes until, inevitably, Ross left to pursue a solo career in 1970.

Solo

Ross never recaptured the dynamism of the Supremes' heyday but the hits continued, notably 'Ain't No Mountain High Enough' (1970) and 'Touch Me In The Morning' (1973). She also remained one of Gordy's favourite performers and when Motown moved from Detroit to Los Angeles in 1971 it was at least partly because he wanted to launch Ross in a cinema career.

She played the role of Billie Holliday in the 1972 biopic *Lady Sings The Blues*, and while the film was critically panned, the soundtrack was a commercial success and Ross was nominated for an Oscar. She also starred alongside Michael Jackson in *The Wiz* (1978), a disastrous black remake of *The Wizard of Oz*.

Anthology (Motown) is a triple album compilation of the Supremes' finest work.

Schoolgirls

Diana Ross joined Florence Ballard and Mary Wilson in the Primettes when original member Betty Travis pulled out because her family felt it would interfere with her schoolwork. Uncharacteristically for a music business entrepreneur at the time, Berry Gordy initially refused to sign the group until after they had finished high school.

Sade
1959– British soul-jazz singer

Velvet voice and top model looks

Excellent in the studio, she never really proved herself live on stage, perhaps because of the cool, understated nature of her songs.

Of Nigerian-British parentage, Sade's music showed a variety of musical influences, ranging from both North and South American jazz arrangements to the most modern of rock sounds and cooler, low-key funk structures. With 'Smooth Operator' (1983), Sade became the darling of the hit parades on both sides of the Atlantic. The song also had a considerable impact on all the commercial rock produced in the mid-1980s.

Despite the release of a second, equally musically excellent album in 1985, Sade has virtually disappeared from the music scene, perhaps due to an unfortunate series of mediocre live performances in the late 1980s.

Diamond Life (Epic, 1984), **Stronger Than Pride** (CBS, 1988) and **Promise** (CBS, 1985) are all perfect examples of the cool sophistication and elegance of Sade's music.

Mistake
The sales figures for Sade's albums led her business managers to believe that they should have her play in massive concert halls. It was a failure every time, because her music is better adapted to smaller audiences. Imagine Tom Waits at Wembley . . .

Sam and Dave
R & B singers

The most influential duet in soul music

The quality of their arrangements stunned everybody. 'Hold On, I'm Comin'' is an absolutely unforgettable number.

The duet concept was not new to soul music (Rufus and Carla Thomas, and Otis Redding and Carla Thomas were already popular), principally because of the gospel choral tradition in which so many artists, including Samuel Moore and Dave Prater, had their musical roots. However, the verve of their songs and the melodic and rhythmic acrobatics they performed both in the studio and live on stage made Sam and Dave the most influential soul music duet of the 1960s.

Their recordings of 'Soul Man', 'You Got Me Hummin'' and 'Hold On, I'm Comin'' are feats of vocal ingenuity, their voices echoing each other against a solid background of the typical Stax house band sound.

The Best of Sam and Dave (Atlantic, 1969, re-released on CD in 1987) is a must.

Friendship
Sam and Dave got their contract with Stax through Otis Redding, before he had founded his own label and started producing his own stable of budding stars (such as Arthur Conley) who owe him their fame.

The Temptations
Soul music group

The Tamla Motown spearhead

Discovered by Berry Gordy, head of the Detroit-based company, the Temptations have twenty platinum discs to their name.

Although today they have been overshadowed by the massive popularity of James Brown, Aretha Franklin and Otis Redding, the magic Temptations duo, Eddie Kendricks and David Ruffin, was one of the first to explore the possibilities of black urban music that was both ideally suited to the dance floor and sophisticated in terms of the melody. The 'Motown sound' pervades all their biggest hits, from 'My Girl', which was later covered by Otis Redding, to 'Cloud Nine' and 'Just My Imagination', which the Rolling Stones later added to their repertoire. An album cut with Diana Ross and the Supremes in 1970 (*Together*) showed their ability to produce a more modern R & B sound. 'Papa Was a Rollin' Stone' gave the modified line up a number one hit in 1972, and showed that they could still influence white rock musicians.

All the Million Sellers (Tamla, 1982, CD: 1987) is an excellent compilation.

> **Composers**
> The Temptations owe their greatest hits to two extremely talented musicians, Smokey Robinson (who gave them 'My Girl' and 'The Way You Do the Things You Do') and Norman Whitfield (who wrote 'Ain't Too Proud to Beg', 'Just My Imagination' and 'Papa Was a Rollin' Stone').

Toots and the Maytals
Jamaican reggae band

He invented the term 'reggae'

Since their first recordings in 1962, Toots and his band have evolved from American soul to genuine reggae.

Their early career was influenced by the big soul singers (Otis Redding, James Brown, Solomon Burke and Sam Cooke), but by the end of the 1960s, their polished ska, which they called reggae ('Do the Reggay') and such hits as 'Funky Kingston', 'Pressure Drop' and '54-46' had made the band stars in Jamaica and with the British and American Caribbean immigrant communities. The Toots and the Maytals vocal trio was quite remarkable, for not only did they avoid falling into the trap of churning out dull reggae, but they also resisted the soul music influence. 'Monkey Man', 'Living in the Ghetto' and 'Rastaman' have become classic reggae anthems. With its versatile, hypnotic rhythms and topical, mystical lyrics, the Rasta cocktail popularized by Bob Marley and the Wailers is echoed strongly in the songs of Toots and the Maytals.

Toots in Memphis and **Funky Kingston** (Island, 1965) show the influence of soul music on the band's output.

Toots Live (Island-Mango, 1980) is a must.

> **Prison**
> Frederick 'Toots' Hibbert was imprisoned for several months for selling ganja. He was prisoner number 54 46, and used his experience as the basis for one of the best songs in the band's repertoire.

Peter Tosh
1944–87   Jamaican reggae singer and guitarist

The 'number one rebel', a perfect Rasta

Founder of the Wailers with Bob Marley, he left the band to pursue more radical goals.

He spent over 10 years playing with Bunny Wailer in the shadow of charismatic band leader, Bob Marley, backing him in concert and in the studio. However, Tosh and Wailer gradually lost patience with Marley's moderation and humanitarianism, preferring to become an active part of a more radical movement. Despite the success of 'Get Up, Stand Up', which he co-wrote, Peter broke away from Marley and threw himself into the campaign for the legalisation of ganja ('Legalize it') and a number of pacifist and pro-Third World causes ('No Nuclear War', 'Equal Rights' and 'Africa').

His pure, unadulterated reggae is still popular in Jamaica and with Rastafarians throughout the world.

Equal Rights (CBS, 1977), **No Nuclear War** (EMI, 1987) and **Mama Africa** (R S Records, 1983) are typical of his style.

> **Officially**
> 'I left the Wailers because of the conditions on tour. No food and no sleep. I lost 12 kilos in a few weeks. I'm not fat and I couldn't afford to go on like that.'

Ike and Tina Turner
1931–   and 1938–   R & B duet

The professional exploitation of sensuality

Ike Turner made full use of their look, and particularly his wife's sensual beauty, to attract a large following.

Initially a blues pianist, Ike Turner teamed up with a natural and physically attractive singer, fellow Southerner Annie Mae Bullock, to create a punchy R & B line-up that soon attracted the attention of some of the well-known professionals, including Phil Spector, who was to produce their first hit single 'River Deep, Mountain High'. The Turners then cut 'We Need an Understanding' and a series of cover versions taken from the white rock repertoire. They soon had an international audience and were a popular touring band. They played at the Altamont Festival and, after their separation, Tina Turner had a role in the film of the Who's rock opera *Tommy*.

Tina is still considered to be one of the most exciting live performers on the rock scene today. Her versions of Creedence Clearwater Revival's 'Proud Mary' and the Beatles' 'Come Together' even surpass the originals.

The Best of Ike and Tina Turner (United Artists, 1976) is excellent, but Tina's solo albums **Break Every Rule, Private Dancer** (Capitol) and especially **Live in Europe** (Capitol, 1988) should not be missed.

> **Return**
> Tina's second career, without Ike, included a major contribution to the film *Mad Max Beyond Thunderdome*. Not only did she sing the most important song on the soundtrack, but she also starred in the film.

228

Stevie Wonder

1951–   Soul and funk singer and instrumentalist

From child prodigy to all-round artist

In certain respects, his career prefigures that of another black music genius, Michael Jackson.

Blind from birth, 'Little' Stevie Wonder was first known as a harmonica player. Spotted by Smokey Robinson, he embarked on a brilliant career that began with panache: reaching number one in the charts with his fourth record, 'Fingertips', child prodigy Stevie Wonder, who was equally proficient on guitar, keyboards and drums, spent the next few years labelled a singer-harmonica player.

Throughout the 1960s he had a string of hits, playing either straight soul numbers or cover versions of white rock hits; steered towards commercial music by his Tamla Motown producers, Wonder was unwilling to become a second Ray Charles. Having broadened his knowledge of music theory (actual playing held no more secrets for him), he left Tamla in 1971 and embarked on an independent career.

All his accumulated practical and theoretical skills expressed themselves in a series of jazzy, funk-orientated hits, remarkable for their outstanding vocal work and his use of the first synthesizers. 'You Are the Sunshine of My Life' (1973) was followed by other chart topping numbers and the album *Songs in the Key of Life* (1976). 'Master Blaster' and then 'Ebony and Ivory' with Paul McCartney saw 20 years of painstaking efforts to bridge the gap between soul music and new electronic technology finally bear fruit.

Talking Book and **Inner Visions** (Tamla, 1972–3) are his first funk experiments.

Songs in the Key of Life and **Hotter than July** (Tamla, 1976, 1980) are both accomplished albums.

'Uncle Ray'
Ray Charles was the major influence on Stevie Wonder's early career. Stevie paid a tribute to his mentor with the excellent album *Tribute to Uncle Ray* (Tamla).

Stevie Wonder

The punk atmosphere, perfectly re-created in Alex Cox's film **Sid and Nancy***: the despair of filthy backstreets, dustbins, industrial areas with their walls covered in graffiti, leather jackets, boots and metal buckles. And yet, in the very depths of the abyss, love and tenderness . . .*

Rock on film

Rock and the movies: a longstanding liaison

In simplified terms, the birth of rock could be seen as the result of Richard Brooks's 1955 film, *The Blackboard Jungle*. The director, whose intention was to highlight the problems facing the education system in underprivileged, inner city areas, chose the title for obvious reasons. To illustrate the possible link between pre-delinquent teenagers and rock'n'roll (which, in actual fact, did not yet exist), Brooks, who had noticed that the younger generation living in poor areas had abandoned jazz in favour of a more up-tempo music, came upon the idea of using a single that had been released the year before behind the opening credits of his film. The single, 'Rock Around the Clock', had been recorded by a country and western band by the name of Bill Haley and the Comets. It is perhaps an exaggeration to state that the birth of rock'n'roll coincided with the release of the film; however, the record's sales figures are extremely eloquent and, without the impact of the film, rock'n'roll would certainly have taken much longer to catch on in an America that was in the tense throes of the Cold War.

Filmed rock is part of 20th-century culture. For a considerable length of time, it provided both the British and American film industries, which specialized in this type of work, with a large proportion of their income. Films starring Elvis Presley were huge money-spinners. So were the films starring the Beatles. Initially, these films were conceived as a way of promoting recording stars, but with the passing of time, rock began to take part in the definition of themes and in films that were not originally supposed to be musicals. Thus rock came to be used on the soundtracks of full-length films whose story-lines had nothing to do with music, which did not prevent the soundtracks later being sold as records. The circle was complete: in the tradition of all symbiotic relationships, rock and the cinema came to promote each other mutually.

The honeymoon was over when the films became hackneyed and mediocre and lost credibility in the eyes of the cinema-going public. The film industry responded to the public's lack of enthusiasm for rock musicals by developing documentaries which took the form of filmed concerts or biographies of bands, in a welcome move towards a realism totally ignored in Presley and Beatles films.

With all the biographies, filmed concerts, teen films, documentaries, musicals and mood films (and in more recent times, music video cassettes and videodiscs), rock has been, and still is, closely linked with the cinematographic (650 films in 35 years) and televised image (who knows just how many concerts are available on video cassette?). Rock's rapid growth and present status are as much due to the look of different bands as to their sound; an audio-visual art, rock continues to fascinate the film industry. Most of the big bands have tried to leave some sort of filmed record of their passage through the world (Prince, with *Purple Rain* and U2, with *Rattle and Hum* are among the most recent examples).

The film documentary

The film documentary category covers edited clips and biographies of artists and bands, filmed concerts and films on rock theory and history.

This is Elvis is certainly the film which gives the best idea of the joys and dramas which took the King from rags to riches, then to a kind of suicide. With the help of documents, interviews and some particularly moving scenes, we get a better understanding of Presley the man and his fruitless efforts to break out of the isolation imposed on him by the rock industry. *Jimi Hendrix* (1973), directed by J Boyd, J Head and G Weis, traces the meteoric rise of one of rock's greatest guitarists and also gives an excellent background to his talent, personality, loneliness and tragic death. The Alk and Findley film, *Janis* (1975), certainly influenced Mark Rydell's *The Rose* (1979). We learn a lot about Dylan's likes and dislikes, weaknesses and abilities as a singer-songwriter in D A Pennebaker's 1967 film, *Don't Look Back*. In its own way, Malcolm McLaren's crazy *The Great Rock'n'Roll Swindle* (1980) is a good documentary on the philosophy behind the music produced by the punk movement. Phil Joannou's film documentary on U2, *Rattle and Hum* (1988), follows the band on their American tour and shows them as human beings backstage, shy, tense and anxious before exploding into life as superstars on stage in front of massive capacity audiences.

Filmed concerts never replace the real thing, but they act as an adequate substitute for fans who want to avoid the crowds and stress of big rock events. Some 'historic' festivals have been filmed, and are definitely worth watching, if only for their educational value: Wadleigh's *Woodstock* (1970) is a well-edited film and gives a good idea of the massive scale of the festival, which brought together half a million young people in the ultimate celebration of rock and condemnation of war. Pennebaker's *Monterey Pop* (1967) and Lerner's *Festival* (1966) had set a precedent for this type of film. *Around the Beatles* (1964), produced by the BBC, and *The Beatles Live at the Washington Colosseum* (1964) give an insight into the 'Beatle-mania' (the screams of hysterical fans actually drowned out the band's music) that eventually pushed the Liverpool four into giving up live appearances for good. The Maysles and Zwerin film *Gimme Shelter* (1970) presents the violent flip-side of a concert which got out of hand and resulted in a fight during which one fan was stabbed to death. Adrien Maben's *Pink Floyd at Pompeii* (1971) is more calm and polished, and was particularly well filmed in view of the emphasis placed by the band on the visual aspect of the show that complimented their symphonic, sophisticated music. It would be impossible to leave the cinema having seen *The Last Waltz*, a filmed version of the Band's farewell concert, without feeling just a little bit demoralized. Brilliantly directed by Martin Scorsese, the overall tone of the film is oppressive, leaving the distinct impression that the concert also marked the end of rock itself. Luckily, over 10 years later, the ever-young Chuck Berry celebrated his sixtieth birthday in his home town: Taylor Hackford's *Hail! Hail! Rock'n'Roll!* not only records an extraordinary concert for posterity (Chuck, accompanied by Eric Clapton and Keith Richards, singing a duet with Etta James, etc), but it also gives a startling insight into the bitterness of an artist who, without racial segregation, could have become the king of rock'n'roll. In one unforgettable scene from the film, a visibly angry Chuck points to the steps of the building in which the concert is to take place and says 'Would you believe, sir, that my ancestors were sold here, here, like cattle? . . . like cattle!'

Fiction

Very often, the film industry has made use of the biographical novel device to overcome the definitive absence of a deceased artist or the practical difficulties involved in filming on location with well-known performers: Richard Lester's *A Hard Day's Night* and *Help!* (1964 and 1965) are both pleasant comedies which give at least a rough idea of what the life led by the Beatles might be like. *Bound For Glory* (1976) is Hal Ashby's adaptation of Woodie Guthrie's autobiography of the same name. Ashby also directed *Rolling Stones* in 1981. With the help of white guitarist Ry Cooder and the legendary black harmonica player Sonny Terry, Walter Hill's *Crossroads* (1986) is a perfect recreation of the rural blues mood.

However, the rock documentary is sometimes replaced by a fiction film which is just as intriguing, but for totally different reasons. In the case of the latter, the film's sole link with the rock world is its setting: the prime example is *The Blackboard Jungle*, which recreated the setting and used themes from nascent rock mythology. George Lucas was later to do the same in *American Graffiti* (1973). We have come a long way from *King Creole* (1958), starring Elvis Presley and directed by Hollywood old-timer Michael Curtiz. With his bad boy looks, the King was ideally suited to the black leather jacket image: *Jailhouse Rock* (1957) is as much about prison life as it is a musical film. The rock sequences are few, the emphasis being placed on the moral evolution of the character played by Elvis, under the direction of another experienced filmmaker, Richard Thorpe.

Dennis Hopper's *Easy Rider* (1968) and Arthur Penn's *Alice's Restaurant* (1969) are typical of late Sixties' rock counter-culture. These brilliantly-directed films, with their images of life in communes, soft drugs and motorbikes driving into the sunset, soon became cult movies. Despite its obvious fictitious roots, *The Harder They Come* has a distinct value as a documentary: with Jimmy Cliff 'playing' the part of a Rasta rebel, a squalid shanty-town setting and a background of reggae, in 1972, Perry Henzell revealed Jamaican music to the rest of the world. *Rude Boy* (1980) gives a fictionalized but everyday account of the Clash. Alex Cox's *Sid and Nancy* (1986) is an extraordinary biography of Sid Vicious and an excellent documentary on the punk movement.

Rock musicals

When Hollywood realized that classical musicals had had their day, the producers placed their bets on the rock phenomenon: younger than Fred Astaire, Presley was better suited to the new generation of movie-goers. Unfortunately, Elvis could only give good dramatic performances when he was well directed, and he was only rarely given the opportunity to work with good artistic directors. Most of the time, he was cast in lightweight, semi-autobiographical films, peppered with sentimental musical numbers; as rock was simply grafted onto typical Hollywood classic story-lines, it was rarely given the chance to shine. Other films were more original: *The Girl Can't Help It*, Frank Tashlin's pleasant light comedy starring Tom Ewell and Jane Mansfield gave the world its first, almost accidental, glimpse of the earliest rock musicians. It was, however, the first chance for performers such as Eddie Cochran, Gene Vincent, Little Richard and Julie London to appear on the silver screen; the performances of

Fats Domino and the Platters turned *The Girl Can't Help It* into a cult movie. George Denning's 1968 animated film, *Yellow Submarine*, used the Beatles' music for the soundtrack and was strongly marked by the expanding psychedelic movement. Featuring the Beatles in cartoon character form, *Yellow Submarine* scored a remarkable hit for the British film industry in a field that was almost totally dominated by the giant Disney corporation.

Other musicals were released during the 1970s, but most of the directors were moving into rock opera, the three main examples being Norman Jewison's *Jesus Christ Superstar* (1973), Ken Russell's *Tommy* (1975) and Milos Forman's *Hair* (1979). These three films demonstrate the fascination exerted by rock cinema over some of the big names in the film industry. They were not as successful as they might have been, for late Seventies' popular tastes ran more towards disco films: John Badham's *Saturday Night Fever* (1977) and Randal Kleiser's *Grease* (1978) are models of the musical genre. Not only do they have a plot and clever production, but the balance between drama and song and dance numbers shows undeniable savoir-faire. With its brutal images of modern society, Alan Parker's *The Wall* (1982) was perhaps the most striking musical of the decade. Adrian Lyne's *Flashdance* (1986) is more conventional, but also very good.

The Blackboard Jungle

233

Rock mood films

Since the end of the 1960s, rock has taken possession of film soundtracks. Many films, whose fictional plots have nothing to do with rock music, use it to suggest a particular mood or atmosphere. Since Mike Nichols's *The Graduate* (1967), the concept has been used systematically. Lyne's *9½ Weeks* (1985) brought Joe Cocker back to the forefront of the music scene. George Miller's *Mad Max Beyond Thunderdome* (1985) gave Tina Turner a chance at a second career. 'The Eye of the Tiger' became a hit thanks to Sylvester Stallone's *Rocky* (1982). Mark Knopfler wrote the music for Bill Forsyth's *Local Hero* (1983). The sound track for Scorsese's *Mean Streets* (1973) is almost entirely composed of Sixties' blues rock numbers. David Bowie loves acting: he played in *Merry Christmas Mr Lawrence* and also in *Absolute Beginners*. With Georgio Moroder he co-wrote the soundtrack for Paul Schrader's film *Cat People* (1983). Madonna had already acted in Susan Seidelman's 1985 film, *Desperately Seeking Susan*, before her record reached the top of the charts. Sting (former singer and bassist with the Police) has had bit parts in numerous films and has composed various soundtracks.

Towards a complete art

Today, bi-lateral exchanges between rock and cinema are the norm: many rock artists have some connection or other with the film industry, either through composing soundtracks or through actually performing; records are promoted by music videos, music TV stations and concerts on videodisc or video cassette. A veritable rock postcard industry has blossomed: the rock stars' carefully-created public images are now avaiable on photos taken of them in concert, posters and studio photographs.

Nonetheless, the fact is that rock images have become part of our daily life and our fantasies. The rock art is complete and multi-faceted: initially intended as music to be danced and listened to, rock now has a physical and intellectual effect on our society. Rock is the modern form of those ancient, trance-inducing rhythms whose beat still throbs in the heart of every man and woman.

The rock stars' nightmarish universe: the unbearable world through which the disorientated, distraught hero of **The Wall** *(played by Bob Geldof, future organizer of Live Aid for Ethiopia) drags himself is strewn with a mess of broken guitars, smashed records, an imploded TV set, bank notes, alcohol and marijuana. Distressing, creative, often inspired and occasionally pretentious, Alan Parker's film is one of the rock film industry's best productions.*

And now for a few more . . .

For practical reasons, the author has had to limit this anthology to 200 entries. To salve his conscience and to avoid upsetting too many artists, the author has included this appendix of 50 further groups which could (and perhaps should) have been presented in more detail in this book.

The Band (mainstream rock), *The Last Waltz* (Warner)

Bauhaus (new wave), *79–83* (Beggar's Banquet)

Pat Benatar (hard FM), *Crimes of Passion* (Chrysalis)

B52's (new wave), *The B52's* (Island)

Blood, Sweat and Tears (jazz rock), *Child Is the Father of the Man* (CBS)

The Boomtown Rats (new wave), *In the Long Grass* (Mercury)

Bronski Beat (new wave), *The Age of Consent* (Barclay)

Center (Soviet rock), *North-South* (Barclay)

Albert Collins (Chicago blues), *Ice Pickin'* (Sonet-Vogue)

Ry Cooder (country rock and blues), *Paradise and Lunch* (Warner)

Crazy Cavan (rockabilly), *Red Hot Rockabilly* (Charly)

Dead Kennedys (punk), *Plastic Surgery Disaster* (New rose/Musidisc)

Derek and the Dominos (pop rock and blues), *Layla* (Polydor)

Desmond Dekker (ska), *Black and Dekker* (Stiff)

Devo (new wave and cold wave), *Are We Not Men? We Are Devo* (Virgin)

Dexy's Midnight Runners (new wave), *Searching For the Young Soul Rebels* (Phonogram)

Dr Feelgood (pub rock), *Casebook* (Liberty)

Duran Duran (new wave), *Seven and the Ragged Tiger* (Pathé)

Echo and The Bunnymen (new wave), *Heaven up There* (WEA)

The Fabulous Thunderbirds (blues rock/R&B), *T'Bird Rhythm* (Chrysalis)

Frankie Goes to Hollywood (new wave), *Welcome to the Pleasuredome* (Phonogram)

Peter Gabriel (new wave), *Peter Gabriel Plays Live* (Virgin)

The J Geils Band (mainstream rock), *Bloodshot* (Atlantic)

Girlschool (heavy metal), *Hit and Run* (Bronze)

Emmylou Harris (country and western), *Profile: The Best of Emmylou Harris* (Warner)

Human League (new wave and cold wave), *Dare* (Virgin)

The Inmates (pub rock), *A Shot in the Dark* (WEA)

Luther Johnson (Chicago blues), *Luther's Blues* (Black and Blue)

Rickie Lee Jones (cool jazz blues), *Pirates* (Warner)

Joy Division (new wave and cold wave), *Substance, (Factory Records)*

Huey Lewis and The News (R&B), *Small World* (Chrysalis)

Magazine (new wave), *Real Life* (Virgin)

MC5 (hard rock), *Kicks Out the Jams* (Elektra-WEA)

Mott the Hoople (glam rock), *Mott* (CBS)

Ted Nugent (hard rock), *Nugent* (Atlantic)

Orchestral Manoeuvres in the Dark (new wave and cold wave), *OMD* (Virgin)

Public Image Limited (punk) *PIL* (Virgin)

The Ramones (punk), *Too Tough to Die* (Virgin)

The Smiths (new wave), *The World Won't Listen* (Warner)

The Sugarcubes (Icelandic rock), *Life's Too Good* (BMG)

Television (new wave), *Marquee Moon* (WEA)

Ten Years After (blues rock), *Shhh . . .* (Chrysalis)

Texas (blues rock), *Southside* (Phonogram)

Thin Lizzy (hard rock), *Renegade* (Phonogram)

Third World (reggae), *Prisoner in the Street* (Phonogram)

George Thorogood (blues rock), *Move it on Over* (Sonet)

38 Special (Southern rock), *Special Forces* (A and M)

Toto (FM rock), *Toto IV* (CBS)

Tony Joe White (swamp rock), *Best of* (Warner)

XTC (new wave), *Drums and Wires* (Virgin)

Index

Note: Performers are listed under their surname or second part of stage name eg Little Richard is indexed under Richard. Bands and groups are listed under the first word of their name eg Rolling Stones are indexed under Rolling, except where the first word is The, when they are indexed under the second word eg The Animals are indexed under Animals. When performers are linked to particular band or group a cross-reference to the band or group is added to their own entry.

Entries in **bold type** refer to articles headed with the name shown.